Planning and Implementing ASSESSMENT

RICHARD FREEMAN
·
ROGER LEWIS

KOGAN PAGE

YOURS TO HAVE AND TO HOLD

BUT NOT TO COPY

First published in 1998

Kogan Page Limited
120 Pentonville Road
London N1 9JN

© Richard Freeman and Roger Lewis, 1998

British Library Cataloguing in Publication Data

A CIP record for this book is available from the British Library.

ISBN 0 7494 2087 1

Typeset by Kogan Page
Printed and bound in Great Britain by Biddles Ltd, Guildford and King's Lynn

Contents

Acknowledgements

For material in Chapter 2: Extracts from Star Grade 3 from *The Rookie Trainer's Guide*. Permission granted by The Royal Life Saving Society UK (1997).

For Figure 5.2 in Chapter 5: Essay assessment profile from Brown, S, Rust, C, and Gibbs, G (1994) *Strategies for Diversifying Assessment in Higher Education*, Oxford Centre for Staff and Learning Development, p16. Permission granted by the Oxford Centre for Staff and Learning Development, Oxford Brookes University.

For Figure 5.3 in Chapter 5: Essay assessment sheet from Brown, S, Rust, C, and Gibbs, G (1994), *Strategies for Diversifying Assessment in Higher Education*, Oxford Centre for Staff and Learning Development pp41–2. Permission granted by the Oxford Centre for Staff and Learning Development, Oxford Brookes University.

For Chapter 6: Formative tutorial comment from Lewis, R (1981) *How to Tutor in an Open Learning Scheme* (self-study version), National Council for Educational Technology, London pp46–7. Permission granted by the British Educational Communications and Technology Agency (formerly the National Council for Educational Technology).

For Figure 7.2 in Chapter 7: Student involvement matrix from Mitchell, L, and Sturton, J (1993) *The Candidate's Role Project*, Research and Development Series Report No. 12, Employment Department's Methods Strategy Unit, Sheffield, p14. Crown copyright is reproduced with the permission of the Controller of Her Majesty's Stationery Office.

For Figure 12.1 in Chapter 12: How our group worked from Brown, G, with Bull, J, and Pendlebury, M (1997) *Assessing Student Learning in Higher Education*, Routledge, London, p177. Permission granted by Routledge.

For the mail order decision making example (page 170). Permission granted by the National Extension College.

For Tables 16.2 and 16.3 in Chapter 16: Exam specification table: step 2, question format. Permission granted by the Institute of Innkeepers.

For Figure 18.1 in Chapter 18: Presentation skills assessment form – an extract from the *Effective Learning Programme* (1997), University of Lincolnshire and Humberside. Permission granted by the University of Lincolnshire and Humberside.

For Figures 20.1 and Figure 20.2 in Chapter 20: Extracts from the *Reference Guide to the Planning and Production of an Independent Study* (1997), University of Lincolnshire and Humberside. Permission granted by the University of Lincolnshire and Humberside.

For Figure 25.1 in Chapter 25: Extracts from the *Effective Learning Programme* (1997), University of Lincolnshire and Humberside. Permission granted by the University of Lincolnshire and Humberside.

For Figure 25.2 in Chapter 25: Extract from undergraduate degree regulations (no date) from *Course Guide (Final Level) Bachelor (Hons) of Business Administration (BBA)*, University of Lincolnshire and Humberside. Permission granted by the University of Lincolnshire and Humberside.

For Figure 25.3 in Chapter 25: Information on an individual assignment from the *Student Guide to Employability and Career Development* (1997), University of Lincolnshire and Humberside. Permission granted by the University of Lincolnshire and Humberside.

For the example of class discussion of an assignment with 120 students in Chapter 27: Extract from Gibbs, G (1992) *Developing Teaching: Teaching More Students: 4 Assessing More Students*, Polytechnics and Colleges Funding Council, London, p17. Permission granted by the Oxford Centre for Staff and Learning Development, Oxford Brookes University.

Introduction

WHY HAS THIS BOOK BEEN WRITTEN?

Few topics are as important to teachers as assessment. (This is matched only by the importance of assessment to students.) Several good books on assessment exist (some of which are mentioned below), but we feel that there is a definite need for a book that is both authoritative (the information is based on research findings) and full of practical ideas. We cover both the principles of good assessment and the kinds of practice to which they should lead. We have tried to go beyond the fashions and fads of current assessment practice to the underlying realities.

WHO IS IT FOR?

This book is relevant across the various sectors of education and training – schools, colleges, universities, private and public training organizations. We hope that readers – wherever they work – will be able to use the ideas in the book as the underlying principles of good assessment practice apply whatever the age of the student or the subject they are studying.

The book is aimed at the professional teacher, tutor or trainer, particularly those who have a responsibility for one or more of the following:

- designing assessment
- operating assessment
- evaluating assessment.

The book will also be of use to those working in related roles, such as those within examination boards, and to educational managers and administrators.

Throughout we use the terms 'teacher', 'tutor', 'assessor', 'trainer' interchangeably; similarly, the terms 'student' and 'learner' are synonymous. If we intend a specific use, we make that clear at the relevant point.

HOW IS THE BOOK STRUCTURED?

The book is divided into six main parts.

Part One covers the underlying principles of assessment, such as its purposes, assessment criteria and the nature of good feedback. Included is a chapter on the proactive learner – stimulating students to make responsible decisions about assessment is a key principle for us.

Part Two explores the various methods of assessment open to teachers. At this point, the terminology we use is introduced. We follow Brown, *et al.* (1997) in distinguishing the three terms 'method', 'instrument' and 'source' of assessment, as follows:

- method – the means of assessing learning, for example essays, reports, practicals, performances, projects
- instrument – the framework used to implement the method, for example criteria, feedback sheets, marking schemes
- source – the person responsible for carrying out the assessment, for example the tutor.

These distinctions are useful as, in practice, there is much imprecision in the way assessment language is used. 'Peer assessment', for example, is not – as is often claimed – a 'method' of assessment, but, rather, a source that can be used with any method or instrument. Sound and helpful assessment requires the choice of appropriate combinations of source, instrument and method.

The main assessment methods are outlined, together with advice on when and how to use them. This prepares the way for Part Four, which explores each method in more detail, with examples.

Part Three covers three main sources of assessment: the students themselves (self-assessment), their peers and computers. The source is usually a person, though the computer is discussed as another source. Even here, however, the ultimate source is the human originator of whatever assessment the computer is carrying out.

Other sources are also possible, such as mentors, family and friends, and employers, and these are discussed at appropriate points (for example, the in-company mentor is relevant to work-based assessment, which is covered in Chapter 19).

Part Five discusses recording assessments and reporting results and Part Six explores a number of issues that frequently exercise the minds of teachers. These include how to prepare learners for assessment, ensuring fairness, preventing cheating, managing the workload, and how to make changes to assessment arrangements.

Each chapter ends with a list of key action points. These summarize the implications of the discussion for action, suggesting steps you might like to take.

We hope you find the book helpful and should be glad of any comments and suggestions. Please write to us care of the publisher.

Principles of assessment

Part One

Principles of assessment

Chapter I

The purposes of assessment

INTRODUCTION

Teachers, trainers or lecturers are inevitably involved in assessing learners. Indeed, this is probably the most important part of your work, although it may not occupy most of your time. This book will help you design and carry out assessment, taking account of the best current thinking and practice. We cover both the underlying principles (which are unchanging) and the best ways of achieving these. We begin by defining 'assessment' and looking at the purposes it serves to ensure that it meets the various, and sometimes conflicting, requirements of the main partners in the educational process – the students, teachers and society more generally.

The importance of assessment can scarcely be overemphasized. It is generally agreed to be the single most important influence on learning:

> If all other elements of the course point in one direction and the assessment arrangements in another, then the assessment arrangements are likely to have the greatest influence on the understood curriculum.
>
> Erwin and Knight, 1995, p181

Unfortunately, assessment often works against, rather than for, learning:

> Assessment can encourage passive, reproductive forms of learning while simultaneously hiding the inadequate understanding to which such forms of learning inevitably lead.

In some cases:

> courses tend neither to develop basic concepts well, nor use assessment tasks which allow staff *or students* to know whether concepts have been learned.
>
> Boud, 1995b, p39

Assessment myths

The design and practice of assessment can be hampered by a number of common myths, including that:

- assessment must always be a competitive process, with learners pitted against one another
- the excellence of the few requires the failure of the many
- fear of failure is the best form of motivation
- collaboration between learners is cheating
- assessment only happens at the end of a course
- assessment processes must be hidden from the learner
- anxiety and pain are necessary accompaniments to rigorous assessment
- assessment can be fully objective and scientific
- if students assess themselves, they are always overly generous.

The information you will find in this book dispels these myths. If you follow the practical advice, which is supported by research findings, you will be able to design effective assessment strategies that achieve their aims and promote learner success.

SOME DEFINITIONS

First, what is 'assessment', what is it to 'assess' someone? According to Brown, *et al.* (1997), the term comes from the Latin *'ad sedere'*, which means to sit down beside. Thus, they continue, assessment 'is primarily concerned with providing guidance and feedback to the learner'. We argue in the course of the book that this is indeed the main function of assessment, but the original use of this word was quite different. Looking it up in *The New Shorter Oxford English Dictionary* and *Chambers Dictionary* reveals that the sense of 'sit down beside' derives from the word's use by the legal profession, meaning to sit down beside judges in a court. Some five or six hundred years ago, an assessor was a person who advised a judge or magistrate on technical points (compare the word 'assize') and these technical points seem largely to have related to fines or taxes. Indeed, the word is still used in relation to income tax (a tax assessment) and various kinds of insurance (the assessment of loss). The main meanings of 'assess' (from earliest to latest use) have been to:

- fix the amount of a tax or fine
- impose a tax or fine on a person or community
- estimate the value of (property, income and so on) for taxation
- estimate the worth or extent of, judge or evaluate.

The last meaning is closest to the one we use in education – a meaning associated with the word only since the middle of the twentieth century. For the purposes of this book, the word 'assess' is used in this fourth sense – to judge the extent of students' learning.

Assessment as a sample of behaviour

Evidence of the extent of students' learning comes from their behaviour. We use the word 'behaviour' here in its broadest sense. This is because the students' behaviour may be specific to a course or more general; it may encompass a wide range of activities (oral, written and practical); what is assessed may be focused on a product (such as a report, a poem), on the process by which a product is created or on process alone; any combination of these. In contemporary parlance, these constitute the 'evidence' on which a judgement may be based.

You can assess only a sample of the behaviour – it is impracticable to do otherwise. With a mathematics course, for example, you cannot set questions on every possible combination of numbers. Equally, if someone is taking a driving test, you cannot see how they react to every conceivable motoring challenge.

Given this practical constraint, you have to think about two criteria of good assessment. First, you have to sample behaviour that is relevant (or 'repre-sentative') of the required performance. A student's writing ability is, for example, irrelevant to the assessment of a course designed to teach horse-riding. Second, your judgement has to be based on a sufficient sample. If you are teaching the four rules of arithmetic, you would have to include questions on addition, subtraction, multiplication and division, but also ensure that enough questions on these areas were asked for it to be possible to assume that the student could operate competently across the range.

When we assess, we make inferences about students' current and future performance. We draw conclusions about what they currently can and cannot do. Student A, for example, can add but not subtract up to three figures. This is also a prediction of future performance for, under normal circumstances, we assume Student A will continue to perform in this way.

Assessment – in current educational discussion in the United Kingdom – is distinct from 'evaluation' (in spite of the dictionary definition above). Assess-ment focuses on the learning of the students, evaluation on the way the various components of a course perform – such as, for example, the syllabus, resources and teacher. Assessment results are one source of information used for an evaluation. Assessment focuses on the performance of the students, evaluation on the performance of the provider and the provision. (In the USA the two terms are used differently.)

REASONS FOR ASSESSING: PURPOSES

Many different purposes underlie assessment. In practice, they overlap, but they can be grouped under five headings:

- to select
- to certificate
- to describe
- to aid learning
- to improve teaching.

To select

Assessment helps with selection – for example, when choosing students for a further course or for employment. This is an example of using assessment to predict – for instance, which students will benefit from further study or how individuals might perform in employment. This is seen most obviously in the old 11+ examination, and in the idea (increasingly discredited) that a certain level of performance at 'A' level predicts success at university. Selection can be independent of the learners' wishes. Someone failing the old 11+, for example, would have been very unlikely to have had their wish to go to a grammar school fulfilled. However, selection can help the learner make a choice, for example between options at a certain stage in their school career. In this case, it moves closer to the purpose of aiding learning.

Selection has historically been linked to the ranking of students and, thus, as the next chapter discusses, with 'norm-referenced assessment'. Assessment in this form has been a means of positioning students in order of merit or achievement. Then, those at the top of the list may be selected for further opportunities when these are (as is often the case) rationed.

To certificate

This somewhat ugly phrase relates to the function of confirming that a student has reached a particular standard. This may be in the form of a simple pass or fail (as with the driving test) or the same decision being phrased 'competent' or 'not yet competent', as is the case with national vocational qualifications. Assessment in these and similar circumstances certifies that a particular level of performance has been achieved. This can be linked to a licence to practise – for example, as a plumber or an airline pilot.

To describe

Sometimes the outcome of assessment is a bald statement – a certificate, grade, mark. Recently, there has been a move towards describing what a student has learned or can do in greater detail. For example, this can be done in the form of a 'profile' (see Chapter 23).

To aid learning

Assessment can help students learn. As mentioned earlier, we view this as being a particularly important purpose. Assessment can stimulate learning in many different ways. For example, by:

- prompting or otherwise motivating students
- giving students practice so they can see how well they are achieving learning outcomes
- following the practice with feedback to help students diagnose their strengths and areas that need to improve
- providing information that helps students plan what to do next
- helping students, and others concerned with their learning, to track progress.

To improve teaching

Earlier, we distinguished between 'assessment' and 'evaluation'. Assessment information can help you review the effectiveness of all your learning arrangements. If, for example, your students regularly find an assignment difficult, this might suggest that it is too demanding and you may need to change the learning methods, revise the learning outcomes or help the students gain some relevant technical skills, such as writing or setting up laboratory experiments. Assessment can help you see the impact of your teaching and make adjustments accordingly.

Erwin (1997) extends this point, saying that assessment results can also inform wider institutional decisions. For example:

- which units/modules a school or college continues to offer
- which staff to recruit.

Assessment results increasingly have resourcing implications, with, for instance, underperforming subjects perhaps being closed down. There is a growing need to demonstrate the effectiveness (and cost-effectiveness) of educational provision and a major way in which this can be addressed is by giving assessment results.

Conclusion

Discussion tends to polarize between assessment for selection and certification, and assessment for learning. Brown, *et al.* (1997) label these, respectively, the judgemental and developmental dimensions. The former is associated with public uses of assessment, such as certifying someone as competent to practise, the latter with more private and personal purposes. Developmental assessment necessarily describes – its outcome is a comment or a profile showing how performance matches particular criteria. Figure 1.1 summarizes all these dimensions (See, too, Rowntree, 1987.)

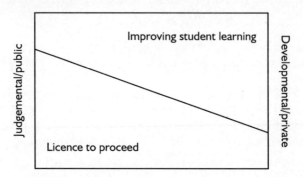

Figure 1.1 *The judgemental and developmental dimensions of assessment*

ASSESSMENT AND THE STAKEHOLDERS

Another way of looking at purposes is to consider what assessment can do, or is expected to do, for a number of different groups. These groups are the 'stakeholders', who each have a particular interest in assessment. The four main stakeholders are the:

- students
- teachers
- society
- educational institutions.

Stakeholders can be categorized in other ways, and the 'society' category can be further subdivided, but here we shall aim for simplicity.

Students

Students may be seeking an award or certificate, or a means of passing to some future desired experience, such as a further course or a job. Assessment can confirm and validate their performance and achievement.

Students also expect assessment to help them learn. By means of assessment feedback, they can recognize and build on their strengths and address their weaknesses. Receiving feedback should be both a motivating experience and an aid to future planning.

Teachers

Assessment can provide you with information on whether or not your students are learning (and what they are learning). It can validate (or otherwise) your efforts and professionalism. It can also indicate what you might need to change in the course. Thus, it can be a guide to future action.

Society

Society expects the maintenance of standards ('quality'), whether this is within an institution or across many of them. It is particularly concerned that qualified individuals really are capable of carrying out the claimed performance. However, in reality, exactly what this should comprise may be contested.

Educational institutions

Assessment enables institutions to create links with other stakeholders. For example, in schools, this is done by reporting results to parents and working in partnership with them to improve learning. Employers help to define the standards of performance required for national vocational qualifications (NVQs) and may also be involved in assessing students' work experience. Assessment can inform decisions on changes to be made to existing provision (an extension of assessment's usefulness to teachers discussed above) and what new courses or programmes to offer.

CONCLUSION

The different purposes of assessment overlap and are in tension with one another. Teachers and their institutions have to balance the purposes and expectations of the different stakeholders. Sometimes demands have to be resisted, or at least discussed. Students, for example, may ask how they compare with others in their group, but this may not be appropriate when assessment is criterion-referenced. The perceptions of 'society' may also need to be challenged. (See, too, the other assessment myths, instanced at the start of this chapter, that, as a professional, you may need to counter.)

It will always be possible to argue that some assessment purposes are met more fully than others. Teachers' needs for easily managed assessment arrangements may, for example, take priority over learners' needs for adequate information. Traditionally, assessment for the purposes of learning has been subordinated to assessment for selection.

This chapter has shown that we need to be clear about:

- why we assess
- what we assess
- how we assess it
- how and to whom we report results.

These are among the critical issues explored later in this book.

KEY ACTION POINTS

- Review the purposes your assessments seek to fulfil.
- Consider whether or not you are meeting the needs of the various stakeholders in ways that are relevant to your context.

Chapter 2

Norm- and criterion-referenced, and ipsative, or self-referenced, assessment

INTRODUCTION

We saw in the previous chapter that the two major purposes of assessment are to select or certify and to stimulate learning. These are linked to the two main types of assessment, which are norm- and criterion-referenced. In this chapter we look in detail at these and more briefly at a third, ipsative, or self-referenced assessment.

In this chapter we will discuss norm- (short for normative-) referenced assessment (NRA) and criterion-referenced assessment (CRA) as separate approaches to assessment. In practice, however, the distinction between NRA and CRA is not always clear-cut. Results from a criterion-referenced test could be used for student selection. To illustrate what we mean, take the case of running 100 metres in a set time. In strict CRA, once the athletes attain the set time, they cease to compete as they have achieved the criterion. If, however, all the athletes run the distance in the set time, it is possible to identify the fastest runner. In doing this, the CRA data is being used for an NRA purpose. As Lloyd-Jones, *et al.* (1992, p118), point out, the same test could be used for NRA or CRA as: 'It is the context in which tests are used and the purpose in administering them, and the nature of the follow up, which is [sic] different.'

Rowntree (1987, pp185–8) also discusses other ways in which NRA and CRA 'have more in common than is usually recognized'. He reminds us that the interpretation of assessment results is at least as important as the assessments themselves.

NORM-REFERENCED ASSESSMENT

NRA is used to establish a rank order of students in terms of their achievement. The performance of students (often called 'candidates' in a traditional examination) is assessed relative to others in the group, such as a class or year.

The purpose of this form of assessment is to differentiate between the students, comparing one with another. For the students, improvement means moving up the rank order at the expense of other students in the group. Whatever level is fixed as being the norm (except the lowest mark in the group) will always leave some students below this point. If the mean mark is used as the norm, typically half the students will be below this level – however well they perform. With a large body of students, performance on NRA often leads to the celebrated 'bell curve' of norm-referenced assessment results, shown in Figure 2.1. If the mean standard is, say, 50 in one year and 60 in another, a candidate scoring 50 in the first year is average, yet in the second year is well below average (see Figure 2.2).

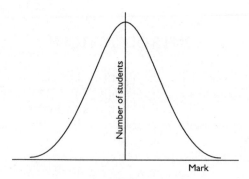

Figure 2.1 *A typical spread of marks from an NRA exam*

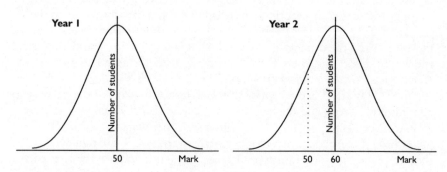

Figure 2.2 *NRA results for two different years*

NRA is often used for selection as only a certain proportion of candidates pass. A clear expression of this philosophy is that of Brereton (quoted in Rowntree, 1987, p54): 'the standard of an examination adjusts itself to the standard of those taking it'. He argues that the then School Certificate examinations should continue to give credit only to about half the candidates, however much students' ability and knowledge grow over the years.

NRA could also be said to have a cut-off point between competent and not competent performance. In NRA, though, this depends on the performance of students in a particular year. In contrast, in CRA the standard is declared in advance and students thus know what targets they have to achieve. In one sense, this is the only difference between NRA and CRA.

NRA when properly used

NRA exams make sense in one specific and important circumstance: selection. If a number of places has to be filled, then some form of selection that takes the best candidates to fill those places makes good sense. All that is needed is the additional precaution of checking that all the accepted candidates are above any minimum standard that is to be applied. This is NRA doing its job: it selects, but it selects to a variable standard depending on the cohort. In such circumstances, CRA would be unhelpful as, if the criteria were set at the minimum acceptable, the 'accepted' group might well exceed the number of places available, so NRA would still have to be resorted to for the final selection.

NRA when improperly used

The problem with NRA is that it is mostly used for purposes other than selection. It is used to imply that assessment is being made to a standard when no such standard has been defined. Students' results therefore depend on those of their colleagues, so they will be higher in a 'bad' year and lower in a 'good' year. While some students may be motivated by their success, those who 'fail' can scarcely be motivated – though some might argue that student motivation is not the purpose of NRA.

When used in this way, the results of NRA are usually uninformative as a global mark or grade is provided with no descriptive detail of what each particular candidate knows or can do. This can be a particular problem when syllabuses differ. A history graduate from university X, for example, may have quite different knowledge and skills to a history graduate from university Y.

Confusions between NRA and CRA

The public often reads into examining systems what it wishes to. Thus, when the UK GCSE and GCE 'A'-level exam results are published, press coverage claims that standards must be falling if more students pass or grades are higher. The assumption here is that these exams are norm-referenced. If fewer students pass or grades are lower, then poor teaching is blamed. The assumption in this case is that the very same exams are criterion-referenced! (They are, in fact, criterion-referenced, although there are enormous practical difficulties in defining a fixed standard over many years when syllabuses change.)

NRA and examinations

In most people's minds, traditional exams and NRA are the same thing. This results in all the deficiencies of traditional exams being attributed to NRA (particularly when the exams have been badly run). So, where traditional exams have, by and large, tested for the retention of factual information, underplaying the practical, the applied and the affective, these faults have been attributed to NRA. However, CRA could be used to test students in such a way, too.

A more accurate picture of the situation is that education has, for a long time, tended to neglect many important behaviours that are not easily amenable to assessment, such as the ability to retrieve information (rather than to just memorize it), diagnose and solve problems and work in teams. In tandem with this, education has also tended to favour norm-referenced exams. This can leave the impression that exams must be norm-referenced and NRA cannot be used when you want to test many behaviours.

In fact, NRA can be used to test anything that can be tested. All that happens in NRA is that the standard that is tested against comes from the group rather than from a more stable source.

CRITERION-REFERENCED ASSESSMENT

Criterion-referenced assessment measures students' performances against an explicit, previously determined standard. No attempt is made to compare students with one another, as with NRA – the only two relevant factors are the students' performances and the standard. In CRA, a 100 per cent success rate would not be a problem – if all candidates met the standard, then all would pass. Examples include the driving test and lifesaving awards. In both these cases, students' performances against a number of criteria are assessed at the conclusion of the exam as either a pass or a fail.

CRA is often used in circumstances that produce a results curve like that shown in Figure 2.3.

However, the curve in Figure 2.3 is not the only shape that can occur with CRA. If a test is set with, say, 50 questions, each with its own criteria for marking and with a pass mark of 60 per cent, then we have a CRA, but its results curve is likely to echo the shape of that shown in Figure 2.4. No, this is not a misprint, Figure 2.4 is exactly the same as Figure 2.1.

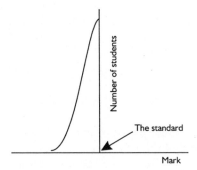

Figure 2.3 *Typical results from a CRA assessment used for 'does/does not meet the standard'*

We have made our point in this way in order to overcome a common misconception about CRA. Having clear criteria and a predetermined standard does not change that fact that people vary, as does their performance in tests.

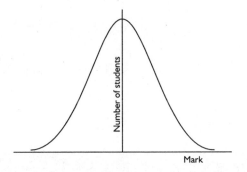

Figure 2.4 *The results curve from a CRA test with a large number of questions*

CRA requires human judgement to be exercised (as does NRA). The driving test instructor assesses the candidate against a list of criteria, but still has to make a personal interpretation of the evidence of the candidate's driving. The standards against which the candidate's performance are judged are themselves the product of judgement. They may be derived from past experience of what is needed to perform a task or learn a subject at a particular level (such as the maths skills someone needs to progress from 'O' to 'A' level) or set as part of a national curriculum framework that has resulted from discussion and debate among experts. Standards are often contested and they are not always easy to make explicit.

CRA when properly used

When properly used, CRA first establishes publicly stated standards, and then measures learners against these. Sometimes this results in a learner being said to have or not to have reached the standard. More usually, it results in a statement of the items of the test for which the standard has been reached. For example, the Rookie award Star Grade 3 of The Royal Life Saving Society (The Royal Life Saving Society UK 1997) includes the following standards:

- enter water using a straddle entry and a compact jump and explain when they are used
- scull head first or feet first for 10 metres
- swim 25 metres and, during the swim, surface dive head first and swim 2 metres under water fully submerged and recover an object from a depth of 1 metre.

A learner taking this test might fail to reach the overall standard, but achieve some of its constituent parts.

CRA when improperly used

It is hard to misuse CRA in the way that you can misuse NRA. It is, though, easy to implement CRA badly. Writing good criteria that do not trivialize what is being assessed is difficult. As written criteria look authoritative and then tend to be treated as the right criteria, if they have not been well conceived, clearly this causes all kinds of problems. CRA with poorly or inappropriately worded criteria is just plain bad assessment.

The benefits of CRA

The emphasis in CRA is on identifying what the student has achieved and has yet to achieve. It, thus, tends to be more informative than NRA, providing specific information on which the student and others can act.

CRA, it might be argued, is of greater utility than NRA in everyday life. If we want someone to install our central heating or fill our teeth, our chief concern is that they can carry out these tasks competently, rather than whether or not they are better than other operators or (as we shall see with ipsative assessment) they are getting better as measured against their own previous standards.

IPSATIVE ASSESSMENT

Rowntree (1987, p178) introduces a third basis for judgement: how well the student has performed compared with their own previous efforts. In the case of the 100-metre race, this would simply translate into assessing whether or not the student had improved on their time. This is a particularly appropriate form of assessment when students set their own learning objectives.

CONCLUSION

The various types of assessment can be used together. For example, a student who wishes to run a marathon may begin with ipsative assessment, setting themselves a target time in which to complete the race. Once this has been achieved, they may set a new personal best time, thereby striving to improve, measuring this against their own previous performance. They may then join a club and gain access to national criteria, setting out expected times for runners of their age. These could then form a kind of national standard. Note that the framework has now shifted from ipsative assessment to CRA. Later, our student may wish to compete with other runners in a 'normative group' – either all the runners in the race or all the runners within a certain age range. In the same race, others will be competing against an objective benchmark or target and some will simply wish to demonstrate to themselves that they are improving.

The choice of NRA, CRA or ipsative assessment has a succession of other impacts. NRA, for example, requires tests that discriminate between students, producing a scatter of marks to aid ranking. We have also seen how NRA is associated with a controlled and artificial assessment environment. CRA, on the other hand, requires clarity of standards and tests that assess these standards directly. The CRA assessment environment is often more naturalistic and students are given more information on their performance.

One practical conclusion to draw from this chapter is that all concerned need to be very clear about the basis on which any assessment judgement is made (norm, criterion or self). This is particularly important when it comes to reporting assessment results and deciding what action to take. Parents, for example, might misinterpret a low ranking as meaning that their child is 'slow' or incapable of improvement when, in fact, they need to look at the norm against which their child is being compared. Conversely, parents might interpret a 100 per cent result on a CRA test as showing that perfection has been achieved and no more effort is needed or that their child is the best in the class or a genius when all of these would be misinterpretations.

KEY ACTION POINTS

- Decide whether your assessment purpose needs NRA or CRA.
- Make sure that any statements you make about the results are consistent with the type of assessment you have used.

Chapter 3

Reliability and validity

'How can you possibly award prizes when everyone missed the target?' said Alice.
'Well,' said the Queen, 'Some missed by more than others and we have a fine
normal distribution of misses, which means we can forget about the target.'

Lewis Carroll, quoted in Rowntree, 1987, pp181–2

INTRODUCTION

We have seen that our society makes considerable demands of assessment. At
GCSE and 'A' level, efforts are made to ensure that standards are maintained
and the examining boards have many years' experience in assessment methods.
However, even they are not exempt from occasional criticism. Indeed, contro-
versy over assessment is a regular topic in the higher education press. Here are
some examples:

- a report from the Higher Education Quality Council's Division of Quality
  Audit found 'sometimes extreme' variations between university schools in
  the marking of scripts and allocation of degree classes (reported in the *The
  Times Higher Education Supplement*, 24 October, 1993)
- an analysis of Department for Education statistics showed 'continued
  marked differences between subjects, with physics departments, irrespective
  of sector, giving more than twice as many firsts and thirds than humanities
  departments' (Clive Church, 'Quandaries on the quality quest', *The Times
  Higher Education Supplement*, 16 July, 1993, pvii)
- the Higher Education Quality Council (HEQC) reported (1994) 'concern
  that students (within and across universities) may not be receiving fair and
  equal treatment in terms of the marking scales used to assess performance,
  the criteria used, or the methods used to record achievement' and that
  'methods used to monitor the effectiveness of assessment practices are,
  mostly, rudimentary'.

These reports call into question the reliability of some assessment.

In this chapter, we concentrate on how an understanding of reliability and the accompanying concept of validity can help us design sensible and appropriate assessments.

RELIABILITY

What is reliable assessment?

In Chapter 1, we defined assessment as the judgement of a sample of relevant student behaviour. This idea of a sample is important with regard to reliability. If an assessment is to be reliable, you need to cover all the learning outcomes (the sample must be broad) and for each outcome you must take a sufficiently large sample (the sample must be deep). An assessment is valuable only if the generalizations you wish to make about students' behaviour hold up, or are likely to, in other circumstances or on other occasions. However, this has to be managed within constraints. So, the challenge for the designer of assessment is that of ensuring sufficient breadth and depth – a matter of fine judgement. (See the second part of Chapter 8 for a further discussion of sampling.)

Reliability (or consistency) operates at two levels:

- that of the individual assessor
- that of a number of assessors.

A 'reliable' assessor makes the same decision on a particular assignment whenever they mark it. Thus, every time Assessor A is presented with an identical solution to a mathematical problem, they will give it the same mark. The same would be true of a reliable essay marker – essays showing a similar ability or level of approach will invariably score identical grades. In these two examples, the assessor and marker are consistent or 'reliable'.

When more than one assessor is concerned, reliability is achieved when, if presented with work of a similar standard, all assessors make the same judgement. When assessment is of practical performance (as in a driving test) or cognitive ability (as in a philosophy essay), 'reliable' assessors make the same judgements as one another.

Reliable assessment ensures accurate and consistent comparisons, whether between the performances of different pupils (in NRA) or between a student's performance and the criteria for success (in CRA).

Difficulties in ensuring reliability

Complete reliability, in either NRA or CRA, may well be unattainable. Nevertheless, as we shall see in the next section, there are steps we can take to make assessment more rather than less reliable.

Rowntree (1987) gives a number of instances of unreliable assessment. One of these is of a history professor who wrote a model answer paper. One of his colleagues got hold of it, thought it was a student's paper – and failed it! Others subsequently marked the same script and the marks ranged from 40 to 90. In another case, the opening of an 'A'-graded English essay was considered a 'good opening' by one examiner but struck through by a second examiner with the word 'Irrelevant' written in the margin. The first examiner's mark of 16 (an 'A' grade mark) was reduced by the second examiner to 7 (a 'fail' mark). This example prompts Rowntree to comment 'if the sophisticated cannot agree about what the question demands, it is hard on the candidate'.

Rowntree gives other examples, showing not only that there can be disagreement between markers, but also that an individual marker can give the same script significantly different grades on different occasions. Again, such findings should alert us to the need to observe good assessment practice, such as the formulation of clear criteria and discussion among markers to make similar judgements more likely.

Another variable that is difficult to control is the students themselves. Most discussions of reliability assume a constant student performance – that students will perform consistently whenever they undertakes an assessment. Unfortunately, this is not the case. Students (like their assessors) perform differently on different days depending, for example, on how they happen to be feeling. Some types of continuous assessment and assessment by portfolio are ways of overcoming this, allowing the student to submit their best attempts.

Generally, higher levels of reliability are easier to achieve when lower-level learning outcomes are being tested. However, as we shall see, it would be invalid to only ever test such outcomes, and you have to respond to the challenge of assessing higher-level outcomes as reliably as possible.

Ways of improving reliability

So, the ideal of 100 per cent reliability is illusory. You can, however, make assessment more rather than less reliable. A major way – one we shall return to again and again in this book – is to create, communicate and use clear criteria against which student performance is measured.

As we shall see in Chapter 5, good criteria are explicit, understood and agreed by all assessors and also by students. A small number of simple criteria usually lead to greater reliability than do complicated marking schemes, because they are more manageable and easier to hold in the mind when marking. They also clarify the nature of the task, thereby helping your students focus on exactly what is required. Creating and agreeing sound and usable criteria is, thus, the single most important way of improving reliability.

Another route to greater reliability is to increase the size of the sample of student behaviour. Let us suppose the assessment outcome is to grill a piece of meat. If we were to sample this student behaviour five times rather than once, we would have a more reliable basis for inferring competence. Similarly, the larger the number of questions on calculating a percentage, the more reliable the outcome – assuming, of course, the questions are sound.

Particularly in examination marking, assessors mark some sample scripts against the criteria or marking scheme, then come together to discuss the results. This can improve the markers' subsequent consistency of approach as it enhances reliability by increasing the consensus of how to interpret the criteria.

Another method commonly used to improve reliability is to adjust marks. If monitoring shows that an assessor is consistently more generous (or severe) than other assessors, their marks can be adjusted down (or up) proportionally. This process of adjustment is standard practice in examination marking. However, note the word 'consistently'. This method works only if the marker maintains the same bias throughout, and, unfortunately, the assessment literature shows that individuals can be erratic.

Assignments can also be 'double marked' – marked by two different assessors. However, double marking is time-consuming and best used sparingly, such as for a thesis or other major piece of assessment. For most assessment, other options are better, such as spending time establishing operable criteria.

Much of what has been said so far relates particularly to traditional forms of assessment. In newer forms, students are required to assemble a wide range of evidence of their competence or performance. In assessing such evidence, Simosko and Cook (1996) suggest the useful idea of triangulation as a route to greater reliability. For this, a number of different types and sources of evidence are taken together. These might include the candidate's own statements, evidence of performance gained directly by observing them and statements from third parties about the candidate. The more these perspectives coincide, the more confident you can be about the judgements that result.

VALIDITY

What is valid assessment?

Validity is important and, as we shall see, it has a number of facets. Essentially, though, it measures what it claims to measure and what it is important to measure.

As with reliability, there are regularly complaints about validity in the press. For example, employers say that students leave university unable to work in teams and use their initiative, which is a complaint about the validity of the way students are assessed. The employers' assumption is that a university degree should prepare students for work, but their experience is that the courses do not in fact succeed in doing this. If their assumption is correct, then the assessment would indeed have been invalid. Key learning outcomes – in this case, relating to preparation for employment – would have gone unassessed. This is not a new problem. In 1934, H G Wells said (quoted in Perraton, 1995) that an educational system was 'just missing the goal.... The only results we produced were examination results which merely looked like the real thing. In the true spirit of an age of individualistic competition, we were selling wooden nutmegs or umbrellas that wouldn't open, or brass sovereigns or a patent food without any nourishment in it'. Wells is drawing attention to one aspect of validity, which is 'construct validity' – the match between what assessment purports to measure and what it actually measures. The match here is low: instead of functioning umbrellas we have umbrellas that don't open.

Entwistle and Percy (1973) report a study in which lecturers were asked about the aims of higher education. There was a surprising agreement that it existed to promote what might be called higher order intellectual activity and outcomes, such as critical or creative thinking and conceptual understanding. However, when the accompanying assessment was scrutinized, this seemed to require merely the detailed and accurate reproduction of course content. Thus, there was a gap between the stated aims and the assessment as the assessment did not require performance appropriate to the stated aims and so it was likely to be invalid. Other studies (for example, Marton and Ramsden, 1988) point to a similar gap between stated aims and teaching methods.

The discussion so far points to a number of links in the assessment chain. Each needs to be valid, for example:

- the outcome must be defined and worth achieving ('valid' in the sense of worth while, sometimes called 'curriculum validity')
- the assessment must seem credible to students and other stakeholders (the technical term for this is 'face validity')
- the performance assessed must be an acceptable measure of the outcome ('valid' in the sense of being typical and indicative)
- the method used must be an appropriate way of assessing the performance (Chapter 10 explores this idea)
- the assessment must reflect the content and balance of the teaching and learning, not going beyond this – for example, it would not be valid to assess students by having them make an oral presentation if they had not had chances to use this method during the course ('content validity').

Predictive validity

Discussions of validity usually relate to students' past performance ('retrospective validity'). Predicting likely future performance ('predictive validity') is more problematical. One of the purposes of assessment is, as Chapter 1 showed, to select students for future opportunites, such as courses or careers. Such assessment needs to have predictive validity – that is, match conditions that apply in the future context. We will look at one example of this, which is assessment for the purpose of predicting the likely success of someone in the workplace.

Nuttall (no date, p6) claims that conventional 'paper and pencil' assessment tests have only:

> very modest predictive ability against criteria of occupational performance... the experience of organizations that allow open entry and self-selection is that much talent is wasted by relying on conventional selection devices.

Generally, and unsurprisingly, performance assessments have higher predictive validity than do paper and pencil tests – 'the more closely the sample of behaviour assessed resembles behaviour on the job... the stronger is the basis for validity' (Nuttall, no date, p6). And all this requires the relevant performance to be defined much more precisely than has been customary and for realistic assessment circumstances to be created – that is, ones that mimic those required by or that would exist at the time of the desired future performance.

Before leaving the subject of predictive validity, it is worth pointing out that retrospective validity is a prior necessity. If assessment of the student's current level of ability is invalid, then the basis for sound prediction is not available.

How to improve validity

A number of immediate guidelines on how to improve validity were given above, but, in addition, take note of the following:

- assess important rather than trivial outcomes, even if these are harder to assess
- create interesting assessment opportunities that motivate students to give of their best
- explain why you are assessing (and what you are assessing) so students are likely to find the experience credible and worth while
- use appropriate assessment methods – again, even if this means that there is a greater level of challenge in devising them
- assess what you have actually covered in the curriculum – if you have taught the causes of the French Revolution, do not ask questions about its main events instead.

The dominance of the selection purpose of assessment has meant that more attention has been paid to reliability than validity. Yet, in most circumstances, validity is the more important of the two. Rowntree (1987) speaks of occasions when assessment needs to be 'rich', for example in a group project, a presentation to a client or writing and then producing a play. In these instances, the student has to combine a number of skills or techniques, sometimes working interactively with other people. Such assessments are difficult to make, but you should not avoid making them for that reason. It is sometimes tempting to sacrifice validity for reliability, concentrating only on what we can most easily or consistently measure.

OTHER CRITERIA

Since the 1980s, increasing emphasis has been placed on competence-based assessment, particularly on assessment requiring a candidate to present a collection of evidence of their performance. Writing of this kind of assessment, Simosko and Cook (1996) begin by mentioning reliability and validity. The most important aspect of the latter is the relevance of the evidence to the standards of performance. Reliability is again thought of in terms of the consistency of the outcome – assessors should place similar values on pieces of evidence and make similar judgements when confronted with the same evidence.

They then go on to introduce two additional criteria:

- authenticity – the evidence should have been produced by, or apply to, the candidate
- currency – the evidence should be of performance that is sufficiently recent.

We can thus see how the changing purposes and nature of assessment require a broader and more complicated set of criteria. 'Currency', for example, has rarely been considered important in much assessment as, once qualified, an individual has, in the past, been considered to be qualified forever after. We can also see how assessment is becoming more of a partnership process. Traditionally the assessor (or assessing body) determined all aspects of assessment – what counted as evidence, where and when assessment took place and so on. Increasingly, these decisions are now shared. While the assessor makes the final decision, the candidate has much more chance (indeed, may be required) to participate in the assessment process (see Chapter 7).

One final criterion is simply that of utility. Assessment has to be affordable, convenient and flexible. This aspect can conflict with the other criteria listed above. You have to compromise. A good example of this is the driving test in the UK. Greater validity would be gained by including motorway driving and driving at night within the test, but this would make the cost of the test unacceptably high. Instead, the candidate merely has to answer questions on these aspects of driving. Thus, in this case, in the battle between validity and utility, the latter has come out on top.

CONCLUSION

Reliability and validity are complicated – validity being particularly so. Both are hard to attain, and they are not the only aspects of assessment you have to take into account. Some writers try to set out the degrees of reliability and validity of different assessment methods (see, for example, Lloyd-Jones, *et al.* 1992), but it is extremely difficult to generalize in this way. Much depends on the behaviour you are sampling, the size of the sample and on the context (where practicality becomes important). Assessment is not a science and requires human judgement and elements of artistry in, for example:

- choosing appropriate and practicable methods
- ensuring variety to maintain student interest
- integrating different methods within a coherent strategy.

KEY ACTION POINTS

- Reliability:
  - cover all learning outcomes
  - use a sufficient sample of student behaviour
  - use a manageable number of clear assessment criteria
  - ensure assessors (and students) understand the criteria
  - monitor assessors' marking and discuss the results with them
  - adjust marks/use double marking procedures where necessary
  - use triangulation (comparison of different sources of evidence or judgement).
- Validity:
  - cover all learning outcomes, not just those that are easy to assess
  - ensure the learning outcomes are worth achieving
  - ensure the performance you are assessing is relevant to the learning outcomes
  - use appropriate assessment methods.
- Consider also the criteria of authenticity and currency.
- Ensure your assessment arrangements are sufficiently affordable, convenient and flexible.

Chapter 4

Assessment modes and sources

INTRODUCTION

In this chapter, we explore a number of dimensions, or 'modes', of assessment:

- formal and informal
- formative and summative
- final and continuous
- assessment of product and process.

In each case, the mode can be seen as operating on a continuum with two extremes, but with most practice operating somewhere in between these.

We conclude the chapter by considering the various sources of assessment.

MODES OF ASSESSMENT

Formal and informal assessment

Tests
CLAIT.

Assessment is sometimes referred to in terms of its degree of formality. Formal assessment includes examinations, practical tests under controlled conditions, presentations and vivas. These are all structured events. They can be useful for ensuring that the work being assessed is, in fact, the student's own. The results of formal assessments are recorded and count as a pass, fail or credit.

Assessment can be 'informal' in a number of ways. It may take place casually without preplanning or it may be preplanned but not count for credit. The results of informal assessment may not always be recorded. According to Rowntree (1987), one of the benefits of informal assessment is that it is closer than the formal kind to the sort of assessment that operates for most of the time in everyday life. A danger, however, is that students may not have had the opportunity to prepare for the assessment or be aware that it is actually occurring. Students need to be clear about the status of all assessments.

Formative and summative assessment *But done*

Formative assessment

The main purpose of formative assessment is to provide information ('feedback') to students so they can improve their work. You need to time such assessment carefully, allowing time for the students to consider the feedback and take action as necessary. As we shall see in Chapter 6, formative feedback should also be given soon after the students complete a test or assignment. Formative assessment is provided during a course, rather than at the end. However, summative results can be formative if they are detailed enough to help students move on to a further goal.

Formative assessment is diagnostic as it seeks to uncover both strengths and weaknesses in students' work. The latter are particularly important as these require action. Formative assessment is thus mainly concerned to identify:

- what difficulties a student is having
- when the difficulties occur
- the reasons for the difficulties
- how the difficulties can be overcome.

Formative assessment also gives tutors information on which they may need to act. It shows you which students are having difficulties and it may suggest that you need to change some aspects of the learning environment. Skilled teachers know how to adjust what they are doing in the light of assessment results.

So, the main purpose of formative assessment is to provide feedback that the various participants can interpret and act on as necessary (see Chapter 6 for a fuller discussion of feedback).

Summative assessment

Summative assessment counts towards, or constitutes, a final grade or qualification. Note the phrase 'counts towards' – such assessment does not necessarily occur only at the end of a course. It is defined by its purpose rather than its timing. It leads to the making of a final judgement – for example, confirming that the student has achieved a particular standard or passed a particular part of a programme. The audience for summative assessment is often wider and more public than that for formative assessment, which is mainly for students and their tutors and so it is often brief and lacking in detail.

The distinction between formative and summative may not always be clear. Strictly speaking, formative assessment does not contribute to a student's marks or grades, yet in practice assessments are often both formative and summative. In the Open University, for example, most of a student's on-course assignments fulfil a dual purpose: the results count towards their final credit and they also provide an opportunity for the student to learn from feedback and take action before the next assignment or the examination. Linking assignments to a course credit is often necessary if students are to take them seriously and complete them.

Assessment is defined as formative or summative in reference to its primary purpose, not the particular source, method or instrument used. A checklist for changing a car tyre (an instrument), assessment from a peer (a source) or an essay (a method) could all thus be used for either formative or summative assessment.

Final and continuous assessment

As with the other modes, there are two poles: assessment taking place only at the end of a course and assessment occurring throughout. At first glance, this mode might seem to be the same as the previous one. However, as we have seen, summative assessment does not always occur at the end of a course and continuous assessment is not always formative.

Current thinking favours continuous assessment. This is because it generally enables you to take a wider sample of student behaviour, under a range of different conditions. It also helps you to take account of variability in students' performance. By means of continuous assessment you can also pace students, ensuring that they keep up with the work. For some students, though, continuous assessment can mean continuous stress and a failure to develop their own work rhythms and timetable. You can overcome these drawbacks by means of careful assessment design. For example, you can allow only a certain number of the most successful pieces of work to count towards the formal credit.

Continuous assessment works better on longer courses. Short modules or units may offer assessment only at the end, reducing the students' opportunities to learn from their first attempts or have a second chance to succeed. By the time they receive feedback, students may have moved on to another unrelated module. Assessment strategies have to catch up with these changes in curriculum structures.

Final assessment is often frowned upon as focusing stress at one particular point in the course and for creating artificial conditions in which the student has to perform. Some students do, though, find the process stimulating and it can give the tutor an opportunity to bring together a variety of skills previously assessed separately. Final assessment need not be in the form of a traditional exam; it can involve a presentation, a performance or the submission of a portfolio.

Assessment of product and process

Assessment usually focuses on an end product, such as an essay, a case study, a painting. Sometimes, however, there may be no product to assess or the process itself may be the object of assessment, such as the way an engineer establishes a client's needs or a doctor diagnoses a patient's problem. In other cases, the product may not tell us all we need to know. Gibbs (Brown *et al.* 1994) provides a vivid example from lab work. A student's report (the product) may seem excellent, yet the student 'may have taken three times as long as the rest, set fire to the bench, fiddled results, and be incapable of undertaking the procedure unsupervised'.

Assessing process also enables both you and the student to monitor the quality of learning and to take action as necessary, thus helping students develop more effective approaches to learning.

Brown *et al.* (1994) offer some useful suggestions on how you can extend the assessment of products so that they also offer means of assessment of the processes that have produced them. Table 4.1 is based on their work.

Table 4.1 *From assessments of products to assessments of products and processes*

Products	Products and processes
Lab report	Instant lab report, written at the time, marked before the student leaves the lab, quick feedback
Essay	Two-stage assignment: first, an outline for formative comment; annotated reading list; a viva on process – how the student tackled writing the essay
Project	Supervision meetings to explore the group's processes
Exam	Learning journal of how the student prepared for the exam
Work placement report	Journal discussing critical incidents during the placement
Team report	Observation of the team in action (not necessarily by the tutor); self-report (by individuals or the group); minutes of meetings

Implications for practice

This discussion of modes has established the following as being necessary for good practice:

34

- clarity of purpose (what is each assessment seeking to achieve?)
- clarity of expected student outcomes (what student behaviour are you looking for?)
- clarity and appropriateness of assessment methods, instruments and sources
- availability of guidance for students and tutors (for example, on criteria and procedures).

We have drawn attention to the strengths and weaknesses associated with the extremes of each mode. Too much reliance on formal assessment, for example, might make it difficult for students to apply their learning in the informal contexts usually found outside educational institutions. Equally, informal assessment needs some structure and shape or students may fail to prepare properly for it. Opportunities for formative assessment are important as this gives students the information they need in order to learn.

THE SOURCES OF ASSESSMENT

The 'source' of assessment is the person responsible for carrying it out. The main sources of assessment are:

- the students themselves
- their peers
- tutors and others within the learning environment
- those who operate outside the immediate learning environment.

The students

Chapter 7 outlines the various aspects of the students' role in assessment. Students need to identify the key assessment requirements of their courses and develop the capacity to assess themselves against these (see also Chapter 11). The current trend is to involve students more fully in assessment, for example via learning contracts and other negotiated arrangements.

Students' peers

Students are increasingly encouraged, or expected, to comment on one another's work. This is not just for reasons of cost-effectiveness – sometimes peer assessment is the most appropriate source. Informal peer assessment is also a useful next step from individual self-assessment before submitting work (revised as necessary) to a tutor. See also Chapter 12.

35

Tutors and others within the learning environment

We say 'tutors and others' because, at least in some parts of the education service, a range of people may become involved in assessment. As well as teachers and tutors, these may include staff working in libraries and resource centres and employers, as a result of various kinds of work experience.

Tutors' immediate responsibilities include:

- providing information on the course, including information on all assessments
- making explicit the criteria and standards used to judge students' work
- ensuring that students gain adequate feedback on their performance
- making sure that feedback is followed up
- responding to students' queries and any complaints
- managing the assessment process and associated recording procedures
- using feedback from assessment to improve the learning environment.

Tutors are also one of the major infuences in helping students play their role in assessment. Tutors may need to identify students' expectations and address these as necessary. If students have choices regarding their assessment (see Chapter 7), then tutors will usually need to give guidance and possibly negotiate and/or confirm assessment arrangements with the students. They thus act as consultants to help students present the best and most appropriate evidence of their performance. To do this, tutors need to be able to diagnose the students' capabilities and needs and give feedback.

In these circumstances, the tutors' role is that of adviser and consultant rather than anonymous and aloof assessor. This role now also includes working with partners outside the educational institution, such as parents and employers, and we look at this aspect next.

Those who operate outside the immediate learning environment

Formally appointed 'educators' are not the only people who can help students with assessment. Members of the family, friends, neighbours, mentors and others can play a variety of roles, including those of:

- asking the student questions about the assessments they are undertaking
- checking for areas within their competence (for example, a workplace mentor can check a report for technical accuracy)
- indicating parts of students' answers that seem unclear.

There is, increasingly, a shift towards involving a wider range of stakeholders in assessment. For example, in national vocational qualifications, employers make an important contribution, both in defining what should be assessed and in the actual assessment.

Orchestrating the roles

If possible, you and your students should incorporate as many sources of help as possible, using the strengths of each of them. Assessment then becomes a partnership, a collaboration between tutors, students and the other stakeholders. Our philosophy is that this collaboration should be driven by the learner (see Chapter 7). As well as being educationally desirable, the use of a number of sources may also lead to greater cost-effectiveness. The tutor is at the top of the ladder of assessment, but calling on others to contribute before the tutor makes a final judgement means you are making maximum use of that expensive resource. However, as mentioned earlier, this approach might conflict with students' (and some tutors') expectations, so addressing these has to be an important aspect of any strategy for effective assessment.

KEY ACTION POINTS

- Ensure clarity over the purposes of your assessment(s) – for example, formal and informal, formative and summative.
- Communicate your purposes to all concerned – students, other tutors, employers, parents and so on.
- Check that your assessment arrangements are fit for the purpose(s) you have established. For example, if the purpose is to provide formative assessment, you need to ensure that the feedback will be timely and informative.
- Choose appropriate assessment methods, instruments and sources.
- Use as wide a range of sources as appropriate and brief and otherwise support these sources.

Chapter 5

Assessment criteria

INTRODUCTION

A research study by Orsmond (1997) raises the issues this chapter will address. In the study, 200 students were asked the question, 'What makes a good essay?' The results showed that the views of tutors and students differed dramatically. This common problem can be at least partly solved by developing clear criteria and ensuring students use them to the full.

Explicit criteria help both tutors and students. They make the link between assessment and learning outcomes – they operationalize the outcomes. This helps students focus time, effort and resources on what is required. Explicit criteria make it possible for students to assess themselves and to involve others in this.

Explicit criteria also focus the efforts of the assessor, making effectiveness and efficiency more likely. They improve the likelihood of reliability – that is, of different tutors agreeing. They make it easier to assess large numbers of assignments and can also be used as a framework for giving students feedback.

As we shall emphasize, these benefits will be gained only if the criteria are manageable in number and distinct from each other.

This chapter begins by setting out the differing extents to which assessment criteria might be made explicit. We then suggest how to construct criteria and, in particular, involve students. However, even clear criteria alone may not be enough – students may need help in using them. One way to achieve this is by completing a feedback sheet to accompany marked work. We include a number of examples of such sheets.

This chapter is closely linked to Chapter 9, which contains examples of criteria linked to the different assessment methods.

DIFFERING DEGREES TO WHICH CRITERIA MIGHT BE MADE EXPLICIT

Criteria for assessment can be more or less explicit. At the lowest level, criteria are hidden, inaccessible both to tutors and students. In these circumstances both partners are operating 'blind'. Success or failure is a lottery, and as students go from tutor to tutor, each operating without guiding criteria, they are likely to pass through confusion to disillusion with the assessment process.

More commonly, criteria exist but are implicit, both for tutors and students, it being assumed that they both know and understand what the various assessments are seeking to test. The danger here is twofold. First, students may not in fact know what to do in order to succeed in their work. Second, different tutors may have different implicit criteria. A good example is the marking of written work. Here, tutors may differ in the emphasis they put on presentational aspects of students' work (spelling, punctuation, appearance, length). Because they are implicit, the criteria never surface for discussion and so the differences between tutors are never clarified.

The third level is when criteria are explicit to the tutor, but these are not revealed to the students. This, for example, would be the case in a traditional examination that is subsequently assessed by reference to a detailed marking scheme.

Brown, et al. (1997) identify two further levels:

- criteria are revealed to students, but without examples of what counts as evidence for fulfilling the criteria
- both the criteria and examples of evidence are provided to students.

A detailed marking scheme, available to students as well as tutors, could be seen as a further level.

The level of explicitness and accompanying detail can properly vary according to such factors as the:

- age and previous performance of the students
- curriculum area
- stage reached in a course
- purpose of the assessment
- task.

The position we take is that criteria are generally insufficiently explicit.

HOW TO SET CRITERIA

Where do the criteria actually come from? Chapter 8 explores this in detail in relation to topic lists, learning outcomes, question lists and performance statements. However, in addition, we would like to make the following suggestions.

Criteria may derive from a number of sources. There are, for example, generally agreed criteria against which a report can be judged (see Chapters 9 and 17). A particular subject area may apply these in a particular way and, within this, a particular tutor may wish to emphasize some criteria rather than others. In such circumstances, students need to be clear about which criteria are in operation and why they are being applied.

Tutors might ask 'What do I give/deduct marks for/ appreciate in the work of good students/criticize in the work of poor students?' Criteria should be easy to develop in the light of your answers to such questions.

Involving students in setting criteria

Students are more likely to understand and act on criteria if they have helped to formulate them. Student involvement can operate along a continuum. At one extreme, students make no contribution whatsoever to formulating the criteria, while, at the other, they are themselves wholly responsible for formulating them. What constitutes a sensible contribution usually falls between these two poles. Negotiation between tutor and students will often lead to a shared understanding of, and commitment to, criteria.

Another possible position is a core of non-negotiable criteria with additional criteria suggested by students and agreed with the assessor. As students gain more confidence, they might be expected to play a greater role in setting criteria. For example, at the final level of a degree course, students might be required to take a lead in proposing criteria for the assessment of a final project or dissertation. They may also be required to think about the adequacy of these in practice, in a reflective piece accompanying the assignment (see Chapter 20).

Group generation of criteria

A more elaborate way to generate (and, in this case, also prioritize) criteria is to use a structured group method, such as the nominal group technique. This makes an interesting exercise for tutor and students.

Figure 5.1 gives instructions for one possible sequence of events for this technique, which would take about two hours, assuming there were eight to ten participants (or a number of groups of this size, operating in parallel). The process may seem complicated and time-consuming, but it usually achieves clarity about criteria and their priority. Also, those taking part in the session gain a sense of ownership of the criteria, having taken part in constructing them. The method might be used for a major assessment task or to set general criteria for a unit or module as well as for a single assignment.

---

1. Explain the purpose of the session, which is the formulation of assessment criteria. (5 minutes)
2. Ask individuals to write a number of criteria for a particular assessment task. (Suggest three to five, an absolute maximum of seven items.) (10 minutes)
3. In plenary discussion, invite each person to contribute one item from their list. Put these on to a flip chart or acetate. All ideas should be accepted as being of equal worth, and individuals' own words should be used. Continue until all items have been recorded. (45 minutes)
4. Read out the list of points. Check that these make sense to everyone. Individuals can ask for an item to be clarified by its originator. At this point, duplicated items can be removed and any new ones added. (15 minutes)
5. Systematically merge, with the group, any identical or overlapping items (some editing will have already occured in the previous stage). (20 minutes)
6. Prioritize the criteria. One way to do this is to give each person five points to allocate across the items. They can use zero for criteria they think unimportant, or allot all their marks to one criterion. Then collect and total the scores and rank the criteria accordingly. (15 minutes)
7. At the end, double-check that the criteria are sufficiently clear. If necessary, seek further clarification – for example, by asking 'What does this criterion mean?' The responses should provide supplementary indicators. The resulting list of criteria can then be used for the forthcoming assessment task. (10 minutes)

Figure 5.1 *Example of a structured group method for generating and prioritizing assessment criteria*

Another group exercise you can do is ask students to work from their previous assessment experiences. You might use the following sequence:

- as individuals or in pairs, ask students to review their returned assignments
- ask them to make brief notes of what they gained or lost marks for
- from this list, ask them (still in individuals or pairs) to draw up a list of the criteria the tutor seemed to be using.

You could then put the students into larger groups (say groups of four or eight) to discuss their conclusions and produce a joint list. In a plenary discussion, you could confirm (or otherwise) their findings and discuss the implications of the criteria for future assignments.

GOING BEYOND CLEAR CRITERIA

Setting clear criteria and, if possible, involving students in this is an excellent start. However, you may need to do more. Stefani (1997) reports work showing that:

> correlations between student- and tutor-generated marks for individual criterion points were low. Discussions with students revealed very different ideas about the meaning of the criteria, despite verbal and written briefings and student assurances that they understood the terms.

The study thus suggested that 'there may be a mismatch between student and tutor interpretation of the language of assessment criteria'.

Such research highlights underlying problems that are often not brought to the surface. These may include underlying issues such as:

- differing expectations of the purposes of assessment (see Chapter 1)
- misinterpretation of tutor feedback on assignments (see Chapter 6).

Alternatively, the problems might relate specifically to assessment criteria, such as:

- differing perceptions by the main stakeholders of what the criteria mean
- a lack of understanding of criteria, even when these are made explicit
- an inability or unwillingness by students to use criteria, even when these are apparently understood.

So, students may need help in understanding and acting on criteria, even when these have been jointly constructed and are clear. Using a student feedback sheet can help ensure that this happens.

PRODUCING A STUDENT FEEDBACK SHEET

The information on a feedback sheet is twofold, consisting of:

- the criteria used to assess the assignment
- the extent to which the student has achieved them.

The degree of information given on each of these aspects can vary.

Information given on the criteria

The information can be global, the criteria simply being listed, without any elaboration. For a written assignment, such criteria could include, for example:

- structure and organization
- coherence of argument
- quality of argument
- style
- presentation
- sources.

These could each have further sets of criteria so that, for example, 'presentation' might include the criteria 'conforms to length', 'legible', 'attractive layout', 'appropriate use of illustration'. 'Style' could include 'spelling', 'punctuation', 'sentence structure', 'paragraphing'. Otherwise, space could be provided on the form for the tutor to write in criteria relevant to a particular assignment (see Chapter 9 for further examples of actual criteria.)

Similarly, the information given to students on their performance against the criteria can be simple or more elaborate. The tutor can simply tick one or more categories to show that the student has met the relevant criteria. For example, a tick beside 'style' but not beside 'presentation' would indicate that the style criteria had been met, but that those relating to presentation had not been met. Alternatively, the tutor might wish to indicate the extent to which a criterion had been met by ticking a letter grade or a box along a continuum, such as:

Presentation: A B C D E

Presentation: Excellent Good Capable of improvement A priority for improvement

Length acceptable ☐ ☐ ☐ ☐ ☐ Too short/too long

Erwin (1997) suggests that rating scales are more useful if they go beyond simple numbers, letters or words to include 'behavioural anchors or descriptors' for the relevant continuum (see Figure 5.3 for an example of such amplification).

Figure 5.2 is a feedback sheet used to accompany history essays. The criteria are listed and amplified in the left-hand column, under the informal heading 'Good points', and those the student has attained are ticked. The right-hand column shows an additional feature – a list of actions the student can take to improve their work. Again, the tutor ticks those that are relevant to the student.

Essay assessment profile

Name	Mark

GOOD POINTS	**SUGGESTIONS**

STRUCTURE/ARGUMENT

STRUCTURE/ARGUMENT

Introduction
Thesis/focus well defined

Introduction
Clearer focus needed ✓
Explain your approach

Argument
Well-stated ✓
Well supported by data/secondary
sources
Historically sound
Good synthesis skills
Critical use of material
Good understanding of question

Argument
Explain the direction of argument
Analyse more; describe less
Deeper analysis needed
Identify problems with interpretation
Rethink organisation
Stay in touch with question
Re-work/extend conclusion

Style presentation
Content
Well-chosen, relevant
Avoids trivial content
Differences between historians noted
Ideological positions explained ✓
Good selection of books used

Style presentation

Develop neater presentation
Improve your handwriting
Did you proof-read? ✓(Careless errors)
Get sentence structure right
Avoid bland quotes. Paraphrase!
Ensure meaning is clear. Be critical!

Technical
Sources acknowledged
References/bibliography correctly set
out

Subject specific skills
Content
Be ruthless with irrelevant material
Is all the detail strictly necessary?
Incorporate a range of interpretations
Use more sources – good ones! ✓
Demonstrate use of sources

Technical
Check your referencing format ✓
Use references!
Check layout of bibliography

Figure 5.2 *Example of an essay assessment profile feedback sheet*
Source: Brown, *et al.* (1994)

Feedback sheets also need to include standard information, such as the student's name, tutor's name, title of the assignment, course, date of submission, date of return.

The number of criteria should be contained – giving feedback on no more than seven main areas is a useful guideline – and the extent of feedback should be manageable for students. Too much information and the student will not be able to handle it, too little and they will not understand the basis on which the tutor is judging their work. You might supplement the feedback sheet with other information, such as a copy of a section in a course guide explaining criteria that apply throughout a course (see Figure 5.3). Students can refer to this for more information when they need it, and it cuts down the amount of detail that need appear on the feedback sheet.

You could elaborate the form to include the marks allocated (and gained) for each criterion or assessment component. This would show the relative importance allocated to the different aspects of performance. These might vary with each assignment. For example, you may decide at a particular stage in the course to mark style and presentation in great detail or to concentrate on these aspects in the case of an individual student (see Chapter 16 for a discussion of marking schemes). An example of a marking scheme can be found in Gibbs, *et al.* (1986).

Figure 5.3 shows several of the above features. It also includes space at the bottom to summarize the strengths of a student's work and specific areas for improvement.

You can find examples of criteria for a number of different assessment methods in Chapter 9. For further examples of feedback forms in different curriculum areas, see Gibbs (1992), Gibbs, *et al.* (1986), and Brown, *et al.* (1994).

KEY ACTION POINTS

- Decide how explicit the criteria in your course should be.
- Get tutors in your team to generate/share/standardize criteria.
- Involve students in setting criteria.
- Discuss criteria with students.
- Draw up a feedback sheet to accompany student assignments.

This sheet and the accompanying detailed criteria reveal a careful analysis of what is expected of the student. It has:

- a five point scale
- a box for the specific points the marker likes and one for points that need more work
- a strategy for using explicit criteria as a basis for detailed feedback. It directs students to a fuller set of comments, which clarify and explain the ratings given in each section of the assessment sheet. This full set of notes is given to students early in the course – perhaps in the course handbook – and is used for reference throughout the course.

The sheet below is attached to the students' work. The tutor marks the appropriate point the grading scale (from 'Excellent' to 'Needs much more work'). These refer the student to the detailed comments in the guidance notes. Examples of these are shown opposite.

Essay Assessment Sheet

Name		Marker	
Date in	Date back		Mark
Writer's Specific Requests For Feedback			
Marker's General View Of The Work			

Rating Scale	Excellent	Very good	Satisfactory	Needs some more work	Needs much more work
INTRODUCTION TO THE ESSAY					
Interpretation of title and introduction	......	......	......	......	......
DEVELOPMENT OF THE ESSAY					
Logical development	......	......	......	......	......
Insight and originality	......	......	......	......	......
Subject relevance	......	......	......	......	......
Use of sources	......	......	......	......	......
Use of evidence	......	......	......	......	......
Understanding of topic	......	......	......	......	......
Constructive critical analysis	......	......	......	......	......
CONCLUSION TO THE ESSAY	......	......	......	......	......
OTHER FEATURES					
Presentation of references	......	......	......	......	......
Legibility	......	......	......	......	......
Spelling	......	......	......	......	......
Grammar & Syntax	......	......	......	......	......
Style	......	......	......	......	......
Length	......	......	......	......	......
Overall presentation	......	......	......	......	......

SPECIFIC ASPECTS OF YOUR ESSAY ...... that the marker likes	SPECIFIC ASPECTS OF YOUR ESSAY ...... that need more work

Figure 5.3 *Example of an essay assessment feedback sheet*
Source: Brown, *et al.* (1994)

Figure 5.3 *cont.*

Below are examples of the detailed guidance notes students keep in their folders. Each expands on the headings in the essay assessment sheet, shown opposite.

What the ratings mean:

Notes
1   You will need to refer to those pages again. Please keep them safely.
2   Read through the criteria carefully before you start writing. They will be used during the marking of your written work, and will help us to give you detailed feedback on aspects of your work as quickly as possible.
3   There is a box on the Essay Assessment Sheet in which you can request feedback (in the form of very brief comments) on any specific aspects of your work that you may be interested in.
4   Please write your name, and the current date, on the Essay Assessment Sheet and attach it to your assignment before you hand it in.

INTRODUCTION TO THE ESSAY
'Interpretation of title and introduction'

Excellent/Very good	Introduction shows a sound grasp of the question and provides a clear outline of the scope of the essay
Satisfactory	Introduction rambles and scope of essay not defined.
Needs more/much more work	Launches straight in with no attempt to introduce and define the topic Questions may have been misunderstood.

DEVELOPMENT OF THE ESSAY
'Logical development'

Excellent/Very good	Develops a logical argument and materials ideas clearly.
Satisfactory	Could be better organised by sequencing some of the material more appropriately.
Needs more/much more work	Fails to develop a clear theme or line of argument.

'Use of sources'

Excellent/Very good	Critical and wide-range use of relevant literature
Satisfactory	Likely sources and materials covered.
Needs more/much more work	Little evidence of supportive reading. Inadequate preparation.

'Understanding of topic'

Excellent/Very good	Well argued. All main issues explored and evaluated and conclusion justified.
Satisfactory	Most main issues explored. Some analysis and critical evaluation.
Needs more/much more work	Work is descriptive, accepting and/or one-sided with little analysis or criticism.

CONCLUSION TO THE ESSAY

Excellent/Very good	Good concluding section which draws together the various important points made.
Satisfactory	Rather brief and formalised conclusion
Needs more/much more work	The essay abruptly and/or simply rephrases the introduction.

OTHER FEATURES
'Spelling'

Excellent/Very good	No problems
Satisfactory	A few spelling errors, including greater care required.
Needs more/much more work	Too many intrusive spelling errors, indicating a serious problem with spelling

Chapter 6

Feedback

INTRODUCTION

In this chapter we discuss feedback of a particular kind – that which stimulates learning and action. Students need information on which to act, and the motivation to use the information. The source of the feedback, and the form it takes, are both important influences on students' motivation.

Studies (Falchikov, 1995) show that these two conditions are not always met, such as when:

- teachers comment only on superficial errors
- written feedback is variable in extent and negative in tone
- students fail to read their tutor's feedback or, when they do, misunderstand it
- students read and understand the feedback but do not act on it.

This chapter has two main sections. The first describes the characteristics of good feedback, with suggestions on how to achieve it. The second part offers ideas on how students might be briefed to handle feedback. Giving good feedback can be time-consuming, but it is a vital part of the teacher's role – perhaps the most vital part. For ideas on how to carry out this task within a manageable timeframe, see Chapter 27.

WHAT IS GOOD FEEDBACK?

This section begins with points applying to all feedback. We then discuss four particularly important characteristics of good feedback on students' work, which are that it:

- is relevant
- is informative
- encourages self-assessment
- encourages dialogue.

For research underpinning these general points, see Brown *et al.* (1997).

General points

Good feedback generally focuses on behaviour or the outcome of behaviour rather than on the inherent characteristics of the person concerned. It leaves that person feeling positive and able to move forward.

The timing of feedback is important. It needs to be given as soon as possible after the event. The greater the delay, the less likely it is that the student will find it useful or be able or inclined to act on it.

Feedback also needs to be clear. Handwritten feedback should be legible. The language should be comprehensible to students.

You need to take care with style and tone as misunderstandings can easily arise. This particularly applies when feedback is written, as students will often not be able to respond immediately with any queries or problems. In these circumstances, you cannot check quickly and easily the impact of what you have written.

Feedback should also be accurate, so you should check it over carefully with this in mind.

Good feedback is relevant

Feedback needs to be relevant in two ways. First, it should be linked to the assessment criteria for the task. Students should be able to see how well they have met each criterion (and, particularly, be clear about criteria they have not met). Second, feedback needs to be relevant to the individual student, respecting the particular approach they took to the assessment task and other matters unique to the individual, such as their previous work and stage of development. In this connection, you need to recall previous feedback you have given, to avoid repetition and ensure variety. You may find it helpful to keep photocopies of previous assignments or brief summaries of comments previously made.

Good feedback is informative

We need to remember that the audience of feedback is students. Unlike conventional examination marking, your feedback is intended to prompt students to act and in order to do this it has to be sufficiently detailed. The word 'sufficiently' is important as too little information and too much information can be equally ineffective.

Information should be given on students' strengths. This is encouraging and good for motivation; it also helps students plan ahead – they may not need to put any more work into those things they are already good at. You should also indicate priority areas for improvement or development and suggest how students might tackle these. Much feedback tends to take strengths for granted and merely shows errors, but good feedback goes further than this.

Suggestions for improvement need to be sensitively handled. They should be perceived by students to be attainable, within their grasp, as research shows that students are most motivated when they feel they can achieve results with reasonable effort. You should thus aim to help students move ahead one or two steps.

It is generally best to give students an overview of their work, complemented and exemplified by detailed examples, such as in the margins of an essay.

Here are two examples of tutors' feedback (Lewis, 1981). They are written in an informal style and tone and attempt to move the students forward in their courses.

(a) I see you describe sociology as a science. As we go through more of the material, it won't be long before you'll discover that sociologists are by no means agreed about this! Some sociologists think sociology is a science, some think it ought to be as scientific as possible, others think that not only can it not be scientific but it shouldn't want to be. You'll deal with all these arguments later in detail. You could also read Chapter 2 in the set text.

(b) Results can be written in a number of ways, but a good way is to do a table such as this.

Area	Number of spots tested	Number of these which were cold spots
Back of hand	20	15
Etc	–	–
Etc	–	–

Another way of showing results for this experiment is to do a diagram of each area tested, as that shows clearly the distribution of spots. You need to do the same number of tests (eg 20) each time so you can compare areas.

Good feedback encourages self-assessment

 We emphasize throughout this book the importance of the students being proactive in assessment. One part of this is their willingness to assess their own work critically and to internalize criteria and standards. You can support this by, for example:

- asking students to send, with their assignments, their own assessments of them (see Chapter 11)
- asking questions and inviting students to respond (possibly in writing). *start following of loan*

Good feedback encourages dialogue

The point we have just made suggests that good feedback is a two-way process. This is indeed the case, and you should try to stimulate a response and a continuing dialogue – whether this be on the topics that formed the basis of the assignment or aspects of students' performance or the feedback itself.

You should also try to find out how helpful students find the feedback, and how it might be improved in future. Every so often, you could ask students, individually or in a group, to:

- find one or two examples of feedback comments they found helpful
- explain how they helped
- find one or two examples of feedback comments they found unhelpful
- explain why these were unhelpful
- say what they would welcome feedback on in future.

This kind of exercise serves two useful purposes. First, it alerts students to the importance of considering and using feedback. Second, it gives you the information you need to reflect on your practice.

Getting a response from students is not always easy, however. You will probably need to make a concerted effort to stimulate them, and maintain this effort until they understand that a response from them really is required and will be taken seriously. One idea is to allocate marks for the quality of students' responses to the feedback they receive, from whatever source. Evidence for this could be the difference between an earlier (formative) version of the assessment and the final version, such as the rough draft of an essay and the amended version. Here you would look for evidence that the final version has changed as a result of comments made earlier. Alternatively, you could ask students to comment on what they found helpful/unhelpful in the feedback they received earlier and what changes they have made in the light of it. Students could thus submit self-reflective notes with the revised version of the assignment. The feedback on which they are commenting need not have been from the tutor they are handing in the assignment to – it could, for example, have come from their peers. In this case, students would need to summarize the feedback and show what use they made of it. Here are some examples of this:

I've included the information about x in tabular form to make it easier to read.
I've analysed the Treaty of Y because before it was only mentioned.
I've put all the references into the Harvard style.
My mum said it would look better if I did a contents page using the photograph as a shadowy background.

You could hold back a proportion of the mark until after students have received their assignment with accompanying feedback. They could then gain the final proportion of their mark by submitting an analysis of the feedback together with their plans for acting on it. These notes could accompany the next assignment and you could then assess how adequately the students' responses have been acted on in that assignment.

These activities serve not only to foster dialogue; they are equally effective at stimulating students' own self-assessment skills (see Chapter 11). See also the discussion of feedback sheets in Chapter 5.

BRIEFING STUDENTS ON FEEDBACK

Tutors wishing to help students benefit from feedback will need to address the topic explicitly and revisit it several times during each course. You may need to explain the purposes behind feedback and give advice and practice in how to use it. The following is a list of points that could be incorporated into briefing notes given to students. They could, for example, be turned into a handout to which the tutor refers at appropriate points in the course.

Be prepared for feedback! It is given to help you learn. Receiving feedback is sometimes uncomfortable, especially when it is drawing your attention to improvements you need to make, but remember that its purpose is to help you.

Consider all the feedback carefully; don't jump in with an immediate response. Try not to be too sensitive. If the feedback is written, it is possible to misinterpret the tone of comments. If you are unhappy with the feedback – for example, if you disagree or need more information – then discuss this with your tutor.

Tutors are wasting their time if the feedback they give is unhelpful. However, you have a responsibility, too. Say what kind of feedback you find useful. This will help your tutor focus their feedback on areas that are priorities for you. It might also mean that you are more likely to act on the feedback, which is the real point of it all!

Respond to the feedback. This could be a simple 'thank you' or asking for clarification or taking issue with the tutor – though this should be done positively and with reference to specific points.

Ask others for feedback – don't rely entirely on your tutor. It often helps to involve other students in assessment, asking them to comment on your work and acting as necessary on what they say. You can improve an assignment in this way before submitting it to your tutor.

Remember that you should become the best critic of your work. Developing your own insight as an assessor will mean that you can continue to learn whatever your age or purpose.

KEY ACTION POINTS

- Check that your feedback:
  - is positive
  - looks forward
  - is prompt
  - is clear
  - is accurate
  - is relevant (to the assessment criteria and to the individual student)
  - is informative (it gives an overview and more detailed points; strengths as well as suggestions for improvement)
  - encourages self-assessment
  - encourages dialogue (including a response on the usefulness of your feedback).
- Draw up a plan to stimulate students to respond to feedback and use it.

Chapter 7

The proactive learner

INTRODUCTION

The contribution the learner makes to assessment is not usually fully considered in books on assessment. The assumption appears to be that students are passive or, at best, reactive rather than proactive. This is even true in newer forms of assessment, which would seem to require the learner to play a more active role. Mitchell and Sturton (1993), writing about competence-based assessment, say 'the input which candidates can make to decisions and action' is 'barely mentioned at present in the "official" literature'. Brown, Rust and Gibbs (1994) quote research from Australia: 'recent graduates rated the ability to assess their own performance among the most important skills used in their jobs, *but one that their degree courses had almost totally ignored*' (our emphasis). Experience in schools is variable, though, increasingly, many syllabuses require evidence of self-management by students, particularly in newer programmes, such as GNVQs.

Mitchell and Sturton (1993) focus on the proactive role of the student in assessment. They distinguish this from 'reactive' assessment, in which students act on instructions from someone else. In this chapter, we make extensive reference to this work (see the References and further reading section at the end of the book).

The term 'proactive' has only been used in the sense in which we are using in the late twentieth century. A proactive person is, according to *The New Shorter Oxford English Dictionary* (1993), someone who creates or controls a situation 'by taking the initiative or anticipating events', someone who tends to make things happen. (The prefix 'pro-' is from the Greek meaning 'before, earlier than, in front of'.) This definition links easily to the idea of exercising choice over the various aspects of the assessment process. We begin by looking at the benefits of developing learners who participate more fully in assessment.

BENEFITS OF INCREASING LEARNERS' PROACTIVITY

Learning benefits

There are strong educational arguments for increasing students' involvement in assessment. Research suggests that students (of whatever age) are more confident and motivated if they feel that their actions can affect the extent to which they succeed (see Entwistle, 1996). Greater participation in assessment is likely to raise students' feelings of self-worth. This, in turn, might stimulate students to perform at the highest levels of which they are capable. Alverno College (one of the leading American colleges in promoting learner autonomy) refers to this as 'expansive' assessment (quoted in Mitchell and Sturton, 1993).

Benefits in employment

Employers frequently state that they are looking for employees who capable of using their initiative and working independently. Such attributes are considered, in many sectors, necessary for business success – especially in smaller, entrepreneurial companies. They are developed by people exercising choice. Hence, students who have been proactive about their assessment might carry over these skills and improve the effectiveness of the organizations within which they later work (see Mitchell and Sturton, 1993).

Benefits in terms of resources

It is also possible that greater student participation in, and responsibility for, assessment might reduce the workload of other assessors. We have to be tentative because this is a complicated topic on which little data seems to exist. Savings in tutors' time might be offset by the support students need to carry out their proactive role – at least in the short term. Alverno College found that teachers spent their time differently, rather than spending less time. Even if costs stay the same, however, considerable value might be added in the form of greater learner participation, enhanced learning and increased productivity. This would then amount to greater cost-effectiveness. (Refer to Mitchell and Sturton, 1993, pp47–50, for a discussion of this topic in relation to competence-based assessment.)

AREAS OF ASSESSMENT IN WHICH STUDENTS CAN BE PROACTIVE

You can give students choice in many aspects of assessment. These are set out below under the stages in the process when they occur:

- **planning** including initial assessment, diagnosis, making assessment arrangements (the what, when, how, who, where?)
- **collecting evidence/undertaking assignments** including generating, recording, storing and reviewing evidence of performance
- **summative assessment** including preparation for and participation in the final judgement.

In the following list, we have tried to keep the language as generic as possible, to cover a variety of assessment situations across curricula, student ages and contexts. The 'evidence' of 'performance' could be collected during the completion of course assignments or assembled in a portfolio (as in competence-based assessment). (For an elaborated list, specific to competence-based assessment, see Mitchell and Sturton, 1993, pp12–13.) Not all items will apply in any particular case; you will need to adapt the list to suit your own context.

Planning

Students would be interested in:

- reviewing their existing performance (before the start of a learning process) – that is, an initial assessment
- setting learning outcomes
- drawing up a plan for the assessment – what will be assessed, when, how, who will be involved, where and so on
- deciding what evidence of performance will be considered
- confirming what kind of feedback will be given, when and where and by whom
- choosing assessment tasks
- setting assessment tasks
- choosing the contexts in which assessment will take place
- choosing/setting assessment criteria (see Chapters 5 and 9)
- clarifying any weightings between components or criteria.

Collecting evidence/undertaking assignments

Students would be proactive in:

- producing/collecting/recording the evidence
- completing assignments
- carrying out self- and peer assessment of assignments
- organizing and storing evidence
- reviewing feedback on performance and planning accordingly.

Summative assessment

Here, proactive aspects would consist of:

- commenting on their own work
- commenting on peers' work
- suggesting a grade for their own performance
- suggesting a grade for a peer's performance
- negotiating assessment results.

At the end of the summative assessment stage, a student may return to the planning stage to complete the cycle again. This would occur, for example, when beginning a further course.

Overall proactivity

At each stage, different types of student involvement may apply. Mitchell and Sturton (1993) list four types:

- having access to information about assessment (for example, the criteria against which they will be assessed, where, when and how assessments will take place)
- making decisions about the process of assessment (for example, concerning the timing, place, who will be involved, the assessment methods to be used)
- taking action (for example, in collecting and organizing evidence, completing assignments and recording decisions)
- judging evidence (whether in a formative or a summative sense).

The most immediate place to look for learner proactivity is in the assessment method used and, within that, the task set. Some assessment tasks require greater proactivity than others. Multiple choice tests demand a different level of participation from students than do self-designed projects – though both kinds of assessment can make vital contributions to learning. Assessment by portfolio requires more learner decision making (and over a longer term) than would be the case for assessment by a three-hour examination. Similarly, some sources and instruments of assessment may be better at encouraging proactivity than others. For example, self- and peer assessment using feedback sheets and rating scales have particular potential. Part Three of this book looks at assessment sources in more detail, and various assessment methods and accompanying instruments are considered in Parts Two, Four and Five.

DEGREES OF PARTICIPATION

In the previous section, we set out the aspects of the assessment process students may be encouraged to participate in. With each aspect, students may be more or less proactive – that is, participation is a relative concept. For each aspect, it is thus possible to draw a continuum, with no choice/participation at one extreme, and total choice/participation at the other.

Figure 7.1 shows, as an example, the formulation of assessment criteria. The four points on the scale show:

- criteria set externally that cannot be changed
- fixed, core criteria with the possibility of negotiating additional criteria
- student-proposed criteria that have to be agreed by the tutor
- student-set criteria.

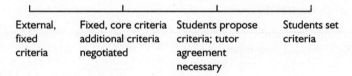

Figure 7.1 *Student participation in assessment criteria*

How many staging points you include along the way, and the way you label them, is arbitrary. The value of this process is that it helps you to review all (or selected) aspects of your assessment practice and modify them as necessary. It is your responsibility (or that of the tutorial team) to decide over which aspects students need to become more proactive and by how much. (As the next section points out, you might choose to exercise this responsibility by involving students in the decisions.)

Mitchell and Sturton (1993) set out the type and degree of student involvement (see Figure 7.2).

We have already discussed the types of involvement (the vertical axis in Figure 7.2) earlier in this chapter. Note that 'reactive' means that students act on instructions from someone else. As usual, most situations fit at some point along the spectrum rather than at one or the other end. For example, learners usually have at least some information and rarely, if ever, make the final judgement of competence unilaterally. Also, the extent of involvement in one area affects the involvement in another, so that, for example, a student with no information would be badly positioned to make decisions about process or action.

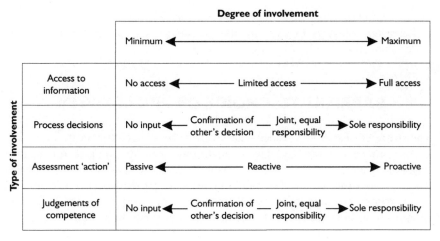

Figure 7.2 *Student involvement matrix*

SUPPORTING STUDENTS

The previous section seems to suggest that tutors themselves can make all the decisions about how, and over which aspects, students should be proactive. This rather misses the point of involving students as, ironically, they need to participate in the process of determining how proactive they should be! Students may resist this for a variety of reasons, including a lack of confidence and a disinclination for the hard work and responsibility that such participation brings. Therefore, you may thus need to explain the rationale for greater involvement and the benefits students might expect from it. The process is best seen as a gradual one. Students need the support of midway positions along the continuum as they gradually acquire greater confidence in how to manage their own learning and its assessment.

Mitchell and Sturton (1993) suggest that students may be supported in accepting increased responsibility for assessment by providing:

- peer support groups for exchanging ideas and drawing up plans
- time, resources and encouragement in the college/workplace
- good, clear information on assessment criteria and on how to prepare for assessment
- a clear definition of roles and responsibilities

- discussion of the roles of students and teachers, breaking down traditional perceptions
- flexibility in the scheduling of assessment.

For other suggestions, see Mitchell and Sturton (1993).

Learning contracts or agreements are often used to agree work to be undertaken and the roles of student, tutor and anyone else involved.

BARRIERS TO CHOICE OR PROACTIVITY

The attitudes of staff and students are likely to be a major barrier to increased learner proactivity. We have given suggestions for responding to this in the previous section, but here we will look at Mitchell and Sturton's (1993) discussion of other factors that can limit students' participation. Their discussion is specific to competence-based assessment, but the points they make can be applied beyond this method. The barriers they mention include:

- practical/logistical/environmental factors – for example, when students are isolated, unsupported or lack access to the necessary equipment or experience
- factors relating to the nature and ability of students – for example, when they lack confidence or cannot interpret criteria or complete an assignment
- moral/political/ethical factors – for example, when those responsible for assessment feel it inappropriate to involve students in it.

Mitchell and Sturton (1993) make the interesting point that 'the more complex the context and the assessment process, the more the candidate should play an active role'. (See this source for additional difficulties students might encounter in competence-based assessment – for example, in identifying and collecting evidence and linking it to standards.)

KEY ACTION POINTS

- Consider the benefits of greater proactivity to your students (and yourself).
- Decide which stages and aspects of assessment it is possible for learners to exercise more choice about and the extent to which they can do so.
- Identify what support your students may need in exercising choice.
- Analyse the barriers you might meet in increasing student choice and how you will remove or minimize these.

Chapter 8

Describing the learning

INTRODUCTION

Before you can write an assessment, you need some method for describing the range of learning to be assessed. When it comes to planning assessments, some ways of expressing learning are more useful than others. Equally, some of the most useful methods, in one sense, are also the most cumbersome to use. You therefore need to find an approach that offers you the level of detail that you need – neither so shallow that they lead you to plan assessments that are invalid, nor so detailed that you become overwhelmed.

In this chapter, we look at four common methods of describing learning, reviewing each in terms of its usefulness in assessment planning:

- topic lists
- learning outcomes
- question lists
- performance criteria.

No one method is likely to meet all your needs all of the time, but this chapter should help you decide which ones you wish to explore further.

After introducing the four methods, we look at how you can derive performance criteria in each case. Finally, we look at how you can review the balance of the learning in a course – is there too much knowledge, too much application and so on.

The first step in planning assessment is the identification of what is to be assessed – that is, the learning sought from the course or that part of the course. In some cases, the learning is defined by an external syllabus, but often this needs to be interpreted in order to create usable teaching objectives and assessment items. In this chapter, we shall discuss how to choose items and set performance criteria, largely in relation to teacher-controlled content. If you do not have full control of your content, then you need to adapt what we suggest to those aspects of content and assessment that you can control.

Table 8.1 *Four ways of defining a piece of learning*

Method	Definition of the learning
A topic list	Use of spreadsheets for cash flow
Learning outcomes	Given appropriate data, the student should be able to create a cash flow spreadsheet
A question list	1. Using the given data [not shown here], create a cash flow spreadsheet. Lock your headings, labels and formulae. Enter the data, displaying it to the appropriate number of decimal places. Give your spreadsheet a suitable title. Save and print your spreadsheet. 2. Explain what the cash balance row means. 3. Give two examples of who might use the cash flow. 4. Give two examples of what the cash flow might be used for.
Performance criteria	Performance criteria: • enters appropriate title • sets up suitable column headings and row labels • creates appropriate formulae • copies formulae using replication commands • locks headings, labels and formulae • enters data without errors • sets numerical display to appropriate number of decimal places • verifies that the spreadsheet is correct • saves and prints the spreadsheet. Range statement Any cash flow data for a 12-month period. Evidence The student should also: • explain what the cash balance row means • give two examples of who might use the cash flow • give two examples of what the cash flow might be used for.

The content of a course can be described in various ways, for example as a topic list (most syllabi are in this form), a set of learning outcomes, a set of questions or a set of performance criteria. To a certain extent, all these approaches are equivalent to each other, but each has its strengths and weaknesses. As an illustration of four possible ways of defining content, we shall discuss creating cash flow spreadsheets. The four approaches are summarized in Table 8.1.

These methods are now discussed in more detail.

A TOPIC LIST

Perhaps the oldest and best-known method is simply a topic list. In the case of our spreadsheet example, this just produces the one topic – 'Use of spreadsheets for cash flow'.

Of the four approaches, this is by far the easiest to write down. However, as a guide as to what to teach or what to assess, it does not say much. Ten teachers are likely to interpret this in as many different ways. As an approach to deciding what to assess, the topic list is too vague for us to wish to pursue it further in this book. If you are unfortunate enough to have been handed a topic list and asked to teach it, then we suggest that you first convert it into one of the remaining three formats.

LEARNING OUTCOMES

Defining courses by means of learning outcomes (or objectives) has become increasingly popular in recent years. In this book, we shall stick to the term 'learning outcomes' rather than 'learning objectives'. This is simply because it seems to be the preferred term among teachers, rather than because we inherently prefer one term to the other. Some authors, though, maintain that there is real distinction between the terms (such as Brown *et al.*, 1997).

Inspection of the example in Table 8.1 helps to explain the popularity of learning outcomes. The outcome 'Given appropriate data, the student should be able to create a cash flow spreadsheet' is more precise and informative than the topic description 'Use of spreadsheets for cash flow'. Ten teachers' interpretations of this outcome are likely to be closer than would be the case with the topic description. Moreover, as this book is about assessment, it is worth noting that the statement 'Given appropriate data, the student should be able to create a cash flow spreadsheet' is, in itself, a description of an assessment item. In other words, the learning outcomes approach goes a long way towards specifying what needs to be assessed and how it might be assessed.

A QUESTION LIST

The third example in Table 8.1 sets out a series of questions for students to answer. Here we have simply taken the learning outcome and written questions that would test it. Theoretically, the learning outcome and the question are equivalent. However, there is a major practical difference between the two, which we can explain solely by appealing to our personal experience.

When training teachers to write courses or prepare assessment tests, it is our experience that the questions they write are more precise and better matched to their assessment intentions than are their learning outcomes. Asking 'How would you establish whether or not a student can do this?' helps focus teachers' minds. We do not believe that this is a criticism of the teachers' capacities to write learning outcomes. Rather, it reflects the fact that, for all their apparent precision, learning outcomes are less precise than real assessment items.

Despite this, learning outcomes have their place. For example, their brevity (compared to questions) makes them useful when summarizing the content of a course.

PERFORMANCE CRITERIA

We have put performance criteria last because we think that their strengths and weaknesses are best considered against those of the other three methods above.

A glance at Table 8.1 shows the major difficulty of this approach: it is verbose. Indeed, we have written this example specially to spare you from the even longer examples that are in daily use. So, does this verbosity offer any benefits?

There are two clear benefits of this approach over the others. First, the performance criteria method leads to more precise statements than is the case with any of the other approaches. Second, because the performance criteria describe what students should do, they also define the nature of the assessment. Performance criteria merge content and assessment into one statement, ensuring complete congruence between them. Finally, as performance criteria are effectively marking criteria, and as the criteria are so explicit, variations between different markers should be minimal.

WHEN THE FOUR METHODS ARE USED

We have discussed the four methods as if every teacher could choose from all the methods. In practice, some subjects are inherently less describable in learning outcome and performance criteria terms. For example, it is very difficult to produce performance criteria for the creative arts.

This illustrates the need to choose from the possible methods on the basis of what works for you and your subject. No one approach is best for all occasions.

LEARNING DEFINITIONS COMPARED

Now that we have set out four possible methods of defining learning, we can consider their relative helpfulness in the context of planning assessments. The point that we are trying to arrive at is a set of questions that provides a valid and reliable assessment of a course or section of a course. In Table 8.2, we have taken the same examples that we used in Table 8.1 and attempted to predict how helpful the four approaches are likely to be in producing valid and reliable assessments.

Table 8.2 *Comparison of learning description approaches when planning assessment*

Method	Will produce valid assessment?	Will produce reliable assessment?
A topic list	Unlikely to be valid as different teachers will interpret the list in different ways. The different ways cannot all validly represent the original intention behind the topic	The variations that will result from the different interpretations that can be put on the topic automatically mean that the assessments will not be reliable
Learning outcomes	Likely to be moderately valid as their clarity limits the interpretations that teachers will make	Learning outcomes do not say much about the marking criteria, so different markers are likely to produce varying results. This will affect reliability
A question list	Yes, if the questions accurately reflect the skills and knowledge required	As worded, the questions give fairly strong marking guidance, so they should deliver fairly reliable assessments
Performance criteria	Yes, if the criteria accurately reflect the skills and knowledge required	The very explicit marking criteria should deliver reliable assessments

You will see that the first two approaches (a topic list and learning outcomes) are not particularly helpful when it comes to developing assessment. That this is the case for the topic approach should not be surprising. That it is the case for learning outcomes, however, may seem unexpected. Our experience of creating assessment items from learning outcomes leads us to believe that any given outcome is capable of many interpretations. Learning outcomes are rarely as precise as they appear.

Not surprisingly, when either a question list or performance criteria are used to define learning, they both prove to be better prospects for planning assessment. This is because the two approaches effectively use assessment to define learning. In other words, in answer to the intractable problem 'How do we get from learning to assessment?', both methods turn this round and ask 'How do we get to learning *from* assessment?' The latter journey is decidedly easier than the former.

The four methods are not necessarily mutually exclusive – you could use a mix of them in any one course. For example, you might use both learning outcomes and a set of questions to define the content. If you do mix the methods, though, you then have the additional task of ensuring that they do not contradict each other. If your outcomes describe one set of learning and your questions another set, both you and the learners will be confused.

WRITING OUTCOMES AND PERFORMANCE CRITERIA

Performance criteria are essential to well-designed assessment. In some cases, you may also want to write learning objectives or learning outcomes. We will now discuss how outcomes should be written.

Of the four methods in Table 8.1, one – listing topics – has no particular conventions and one – writing questions – is dealt with at length later in this book. The other two – learning outcomes and performance criteria – have conventional formats, which we now discuss.

Writing outcomes

Mager (1962) describes a learning outcome (although he uses the term 'instructional objective') as having three parts, as illustrated in Table 8.3.

Applying this to the spreadsheet example, we could formulate an outcome as being:

> Given the data, the student should be able to create a cash flow spreadsheet with appropriate formulae and without any data entry errors.

Table 8.3 *Parts of a learning outcome*

Task	What the person has to do
Condition	The conditions under which they should be able to do it
Criterion	The standard to which they should be able to do it

This outcome demonstrates Mager's three parts. The condition is 'given the data', the task is 'create a cash flow spreadsheet' and the criterion is 'with appropriate formulae and without any data entry errors'. Often, the condition is not stated because it is sufficiently obvious. Also, the criterion may not be stated. Its absence implies an understood criterion, such as 'correctly' or 'without any mistakes'. Thus, our outcome above could be written as follows:

The student should be able to create a cash flow spreadsheet.

In the context of this book, Mager's more detailed format is perhaps to be preferred as it reminds us of just what our test must do. However, the shortened form is quite adequate for many purposes.

The most important point about a learning outcome is that it must contain an active verb, which is a verb that tells us what the student will do. Mager's suggestions of dos and don'ts include the terms given in Table 8.4. In the context of assessment, these lists have a special importance as the verbs in the 'suitable' column begin to suggest the form that the assessment might take. Clarity about what is to be taught or learnt aids clarity about what needs to be assessed and how it might be assessed.

Table 8.4 *Verbs to use and avoid in formulating learning outcomes (based on Mager, 1962, p11)*

Suitable verbs	Verbs to avoid
Calculate	Appreciate
Compare	Know
Construct	Understand
Draw	
Describe	
Identify	
List	
Solve	

Writing performance criteria

Performance criteria (which are a form of marking criteria) specify in detail how a particular item is to be assessed. If (which is highly desirable) the criteria are given to the students as part of the assessment task, then they also make explicit what performance is required. An example of such detailed criteria is shown in Table 8.5. Here we are drawing on the strengths of the question and performance criteria approaches. The question approach helps us to write a clear question (column 1 in the table), while the performance criteria approach helps us to be precise about how it will be marked (column 2 in the table).

As with any well-written criteria, they remind the students of what is accepted practice in the topic area. Some teachers might feel that this is being too helpful. The alternative – to write vague questions where the task is hard to discern – is hardly attractive as poor performance in response to such questions may just reflect the ambiguity of the question rather than the ability of the student. It thus leads to invalid assessment.

Table 8.5 *Detailed criteria for an assessment question*

Task	Criteria
1. Using the given data [not shown here] create a cash flow spreadsheet. Lock your headings, labels and formulae. Enter the data, displaying it to the appropriate number of decimal places. Give your spreadsheet a suitable title. Save and print your spreadsheet.	• column headings clear • row labels clear • monthly income formulae correct • monthly expenditure formulae correct • monthly balance formulae correct • cumulative balance formulae correct • opening balance correct • monthly data entered correctly • money cells set to two decimal places • appropriate title • spreadsheet saved • spreadsheet printed
2. Explain what the cash balance row means	implications of the cash balance row explained
3. Give two examples of who might use the cash flow	examples are realistic users of cash flow
4. Give two examples of what the cash flow might be used for	examples are realistic applications of cash flow

In our example in Table 8.5 we were able to suggest some quite precise marking criteria. At the higher levels in Bloom's taxonomy, the criteria are necessarily more generalized, but still useful and important. An example of this can be seen in Figures 5.2 and 5.3 in Chapter 5, which set out the more generalized criteria that might be used for an essay question.

DECIDING THE BALANCE OF THE CONTENT

The content of the assessment of a course needs to reflect the content of the course itself. Ideally, this will have been planned to provide a considered balance of the different types of learning in the course. For example, the course might have been planned to give 25 per cent to knowledge, 25 per cent to comprehension and 50 per cent to application. Where this balance has not been specified, it is useful to do so before planning the assessment. Without this, there is a danger that the content will be biased in a way that you had not intended. For example, you might have too many low-level items.

One way to check the balance is to jot down the proposed test contents using the headings of Bloom's taxonomy of educational objectives (Bloom, 1956). (The summary version of this taxonomy appears in Appendix A at the end of this chapter.) We use Bloom because it is a well-developed and well-known taxonomy. However, you can use any taxonomy that you feel comfortable with; the purpose is simply to reveal the balance in your thinking.

Table 8.6 is an example of our use of Bloom, showing our initial thoughts on a possible test on cash flow spreadsheets. We have identified the main items of knowledge, comprehension and application and have decided that this task does not involve the three higher-level skills.

Now comes the question of balance. This may have been specified in the course outline, but we will illustrate the process here as part of test planning.

Table 8.6 *Using the taxonomy to show the spread of learning outcomes*

Level	Possible test items	Default weight
Knowledge	Words: cash flow	20%
	Methods: structure of a cash flow	20%
Comprehension	Data: put into appropriate cells in spreadsheet	20%
	Interpret: meaning of cash flow display in spreadsheet	20%
Application	Create: column headings, row labels, formulae	20%

We have five possible test items. If we say that each is just as important as the others, then each would get a weighting of 20 per cent. That would give us 40 per cent for knowledge (there are two items), 40 per cent for comprehension (another two items) and 20 per cent for application (one item). Yet, creating the spreadsheet is the most important thing in this topic. So, we turn the table round, as in Table 8.7, and say 'What weight do we wish to give to knowledge, to comprehension, to application?' Answering this, we have chosen 50 per cent for application, as this is the dominant skill, 30 per cent for comprehension and 20 per cent for knowledge.

Table 8.7 *Using the taxonomy to weight learning outcomes*

Level	Possible items	Revised weight
Knowledge	Words: cash flow	10%
	Methods: structure of a cash flow	10%
Comprehension	Data: put into appropriate cells in spreadsheet	15%
	Interpret: meaning of cash flow display in spreadsheet	15%
Application	Create: column headings, row labels, formulae	50%

The actual weights to use in any circumstance depend on the judgement of those who have an interest in the test outcome as they know best what the learning is for. For example, if the learning is in preparation for a particular type of work, then the priorities in that work might determine the priorities for the assessment. However, tests with a low application weighting raise questions as to why the material is being taught in the first place. If it has little application, what is its purpose? In this sense 'application' occurs in all subjects – even those that seem to be applied very rarely. For example, you can apply the ideas of philosophy by using them when writing a critical essay.

Sampling

So far, we have assumed that all that is to be learnt will be tested. In practice, there is not enough time to test everything so the assessment has to cover a sample of the course content. This section discusses the principles of sampling course content.

The distribution of the content of a hypothetical short course is shown in column 2 of Table 8.8. Assuming that there are too many items to test in the time available, the assessment must sample from this content. One approach is to take a uniform sample across all the content. For example, there might be time to test half the items, so the assessment would be based on 50 per cent of the knowledge items, 50 per cent of the comprehension items and so on. The resulting sample is shown in column 3 of Table 8.8. This sample illustrates a potential problem with uniform sampling, which is that the resulting test may have only one test item for certain levels. As you have seen in Chapter 3, the fewer the number of items, the lower the reliability of a test. So, in the case of the test illustrated Table 8.8, the reliability of the items on application and analysis might be dubious. This leads to an alternative to uniform sampling – weighted sampling.

Table 8.8 *A 50 per cent uniform sample from the short course*

Level	Course content (no. of items)	Assessment (based on a 50% sample)
Knowledge	10	5
Comprehension	8	4
Application	4	2
Analysis	2	1
Synthesis		
Evaluation		
Total items	24	12

Weighted sampling

The second approach to sampling is that of weighting – that is, to sample more heavily from some areas than from others. There is no set rule as to how to weight. All that matters is that the weighting ensures that the items you consider most important are strengthened in the test. In our example, we might consider that the higher-level outcomes of application and analysis are so important that they should all be tested. Perhaps a minimum of half the comprehension and one-third of the knowledge might be tested. The resulting test is shown in the last column of Table 8.9. The test has a similar number of items to Table 8.8, but it gives more weight to the higher-level outcomes.

Table 8.9 *A weighted sample from the short course*

Level	Course content (no. of items)	Assessment sample (proportion taken)	Assessment sample (no. of items)
Knowledge	10	One-third	3
Comprehension	8	Half	4
Application	4	All	4
Analysis	2	All	2
Synthesis			
Evaluation			
Total items	24		13

SUMMARY

We have looked at four methods of describing learning and discussed how helpful they are when planning assessment. We have also looked at how to write questions in each of these formats and how to consider the balance between topics in your assessment.

Now that you know what you want to assess, you can move on to consider what assessment methods are at your disposal. This we do in the next chapter.

KEY ACTION POINTS

- Choose a method (or combination of methods) to describe the learning that is sufficiently precise for your needs. You might use a topic list (rarely precise enough), learning outcomes, a question list or performance criteria.
- Write outcomes to include task, conditions and criteria. If the conditions or criteria are obvious, they can be omitted.
- Use the format of Table 8.5 to write performance criteria.
- Check the balance of any test across the levels of Bloom's taxonomy (or across the levels of a taxonomy of your choice).
- When there is too much to test, sample the contents.
- Use sampling to achieve the balance that you desire within your taxonomy.

APPENDIX: BLOOM'S TAXONOMY OF EDUCATIONAL OBJECTIVES – COGNITIVE DOMAIN

The following list shows the headings of the summary version of Bloom's taxonomy. For an explanation of what each heading comprises, see pages 201–7 of Bloom (1956).

1.00 Knowledge

1.10 Knowledge of specifics
1.11 Knowledge of terminology
1.12 Knowledge of specific facts
1.20 Knowledge of ways and means [methods] of dealing with specifics
1.21 Knowledge of conventions
1.22 Knowledge of trends and sequences
1.23 Knowledge of classifications and categories
1.24 Knowledge of criteria

1.25 Knowledge of methodologies
1.30 Knowledge of universals and abstractions in a field
1.31 Knowledge of principles and generalizations
1.32 Knowledge of theories and structures

2.00 Comprehension

2.10 Translation
2.20 Interpretation
2.30 Extrapolation

3.00 Application

4.00 Analysis

4.10 Analysis of elements
4.20 Analysis of relationships
4.30 Analysis of organizational principles

5.00 Synthesis

5.10 Production of a unique communication
5.20 Production of a plan, or proposed set of operations
5.30 Derivation of a set of abstract relations

6.00 Evaluation

6.10 Judgements in terms of internal evidence
6.20 Judgements in terms of external criteria

PART TWO

The methods toolbox

Chapter 9

Methods and their characteristics

INTRODUCTION

In this chapter, we give a brief overview of the main assessment methods in regular use. As far as possible, we confine our discussion to the main uses of each method. In Chapter 10, we discuss how to choose which method to use when. Chapters 14–21 go into more detail on how to design assessment items for some of these methods.

Our discussion starts with four types of written objective question. In addition to briefly describing each type, we discuss for which learning outcomes they can be used (Chapter 14 expands much further on the design of such questions). We then describe short-answer questions, which you will meet again, described in more detail, in Chapter 15.

The next section covers long-answer methods – plans, reports, essays and dissertations. The format of such methods is too well established to need much discussion, so we concentrate our approach on the uses of long-answer questions and on their marking criteria (Chapter 17 explores other aspects of extended written work).

There are then two more specialized sections. The first discusses assessing artefacts – that is, things that learners have made. This presents special problems (and opportunities) as the thing to be assessed has all the complexities of the real world rather than the simplified nature of a test item.

The second part of this section looks at assessing performances such as presentations (these are pursued in more depth in Chapters 18 and 19).

This chapter contains many examples of questions – some worded well, others not. Where we consider that you will need to know the right answer, then we have given it. In some cases, however – such as when we illustrate poorly worded questions – little purpose would be served by attempting an answer.

Finally, we discuss what we have chosen to call 'quasi' assessment methods. These are methods that other authors describe as 'summative' assessment methods, but which are not assessment methods *per se*. For example, we discuss projects and placements. These are clearly not assessment methods as you can go on a placement without any assessment. However, you can assess what was learnt on a placement – hence 'quasi' assessment methods. (Work placement is discussed in more detail in Chapter 19.)

WRITTEN OBJECTIVE QUESTIONS

The word 'objective' in the term 'objective questions' refers to the method of marking the questions. That is, objective questions can be marked without any judgement being made on the part of the marker. The marking is an entirely mechanical process and so can be done by computer. In no sense does the term 'objective tests' imply that such tests are any more objective in their assessment of learners than any other possible tests. Nor does the term imply that the teacher's choice of what to test is any less subjective than for any other assessment method.

Multiple-choice questions

Multiple-choice questions have a format similar to the one below. Usually there is just one correct answer – in this case, B. (We have followed the convention of indicating the correct answer by an asterisk. Naturally, this does not appear in the learner's version of the question.)

What were the dates of the Second World War?
A   1940–1945
B*   1939–1945
C   1938–1946
D   1938–1944

The design of questions of this kind is discussed in detail in Chapter 14, but here we wish to mention some of their uses.

The importance of multiple-choice questions lies in:

• the large number of questions that a student can complete in a given time
• the fact that the questions can be machine-marked.

Many forms of assessment are time-consuming for the learners, so limiting the amount that can be tested. As we saw in Chapter 3, the smaller the number of questions, the lower the reliability of a test becomes. The large number of questions in a multiple-choice test is a useful indicator of likely reliability for the topic areas covered by the questions.

Apart from the difficulty of writing good questions (see Chapter 14), multiple-choice questions are often rejected on the grounds that they test only the knowledge level covered by Bloom's taxonomy. With ingenuity, though, they can be used to test a very wide range of outcomes. Examples of questions that test knowledge, comprehension, application and analysis are given in Chapter 14.

True/false

The true/false question takes the following format.

> Moderate alcohol consumption can reduce the risk of heart attacks.
>
> True* ☐   False ☐

Such questions are truncated multiple-choice questions, offering just two options – a statement and its opposite. All the points about multiple-choice questions made above also apply to true/false ones, including their capacity to test quite high-level learning. For example, in Chapter 14, we give the following example of a multiple-choice question to test analysis:

> The following measurements were taken in a circuit containing one resistor. Each set of results was taken twice. (1) V = 20, I = 2; (2) V = 30, I = 1.5; (3) V = 40, I = 1.33. Which of the following is the most likely explanation?
>
> A   The results are just what Ohm's Law predicts.
> B   There is a poor connection in the circuit.
> C* The resistor is changing value as the current changes.
> D   The high voltages are affecting the meter.

This question can easily be rewritten in true/false format as follows:

> The following measurements were taken in a circuit containing one resistor. Each set of results was taken twice. (1) V = 20, I = 2; (2) V = 30, I = 1.5; (3) V = 40, I = 1.33. The likely explanation is that there is a poor connection in the circuit.
>
> True ☐   False* ☐

This exercise illustrates two things. First, you can write true/false questions that require a deep understanding of a topic. Second, where you can think of further distractors, the multiple-choice question is to be preferred as the greater number of distractors, the lower the chance of simply guessing the correct answer. (The design of true/false questions is discussed further in Chapter 14.)

Matching

Matching questions have the following format (we have indicated the correct answers in column 1, but this would normally be left blank).

List 1, below, gives a number of woodworking tasks. For each item in list 1, choose the best type of saw from List 2. Put the letter matching the saw type in the answer spaces for List 1. Each item in List 2 may be used once, more than once or not at all.

Answer	List 1	List 2
E	1. Cutting timber with the grain	A Coping saw
B	2. Cutting timber across the grain	B Cross-cut saw
D	3. All-round sawing	C Dovetail saw
F	4. Cutting joints	D Panel saw
C	5. Cutting fine joints	E Rip saw
		F Tenon saw

This is generally the most efficient format whenever you wish to test the ability to classify, or to know or identify relationships between two lists of items. (In assessment, 'efficient' refers to minimizing the time learners need to demonstrate what they know and the time that teachers need to mark the assessment.)

Fill in the blank

The fill-in-the-blank question presents one or more sentences with a number of missing words that learners have either to supply or select from a jumbled list. A typical question (with no words supplied) is as follows.

The process of neutralizing an object's magnetism is called _____.

This example is a test of recall, the word 'degaussing' being required. However, fill-in-the-blank questions can also be used to test higher levels of learning. For example, the application question on Ohm's law in Chapter 14 could be written as:

A current of 4 amps flows through a circuit with a resistance of 20Ω produces a voltage across the circuit of ____ volts.

Perhaps the biggest advantage of fill-in-the-blank questions is that they are relatively easy to write as they use 'natural' sentences rather than carefully crafted multiple-choice statements. However, they are difficult to machine mark when you allow learners a free choice of words – the marking routine must take account of permissible variations in spelling anyway. This problem can be avoided if the computer presents a jumbled list of words for learners to drag into the blanks.

WRITTEN SHORT-ANSWER METHODS

Lists, short answers, diagrams and tables

There are many different forms of short-answer question, including fill-in-the-blank (discussed above), producing a list, one-sentence answers, completing a table and completing a diagram. They can be used to test quite a wide range of learning, as the following examples show. (The way we have matched question types to learning levels is arbitrary. We could have used any of the four types at any of the four levels.)

To test knowledge (using a list):

List three methods of preserving food.

To test comprehension (using a paragraph):

Why should a Forsythia bush be pruned immediately after flowering?

To test application (using a table):

A company manufactures diaries, which it sells to UK stationery wholesalers. It is considering options for changing its product strategy. In each box of the table, below, give one example of a development that the company might make.

	Existing markets	New markets
Existing products		
New products		

To test analysis (using a diagram):

> A cup of tea, including milk, tea and sugar, can be made in various ways according to the order in which you add the items to the empty cup. Complete the diagram below to show all the possible orders for making a cup of tea.

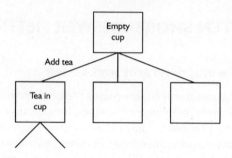

(Tea making example based on Kahney, 1986.)

Essay outlines

This final form of short-answer assessment is unusual because it is an offshoot of one of the lengthiest forms – the essay. Essays test the ability to formulate and present a coherent argument, making appropriate use of evidence from cited sources. The essay is well suited to testing at the higher levels of analysis, synthesis and evaluation. However, essays have two major drawbacks: they take a long time to write and a long time to mark. As a consequence, teachers have to severely limit the number of essays that they set, which can lead to higher-level skills being underassessed. One way to assess these skills more frequently, yet without an excessive workload for learners or teachers, is to use essay outlines.

At first sight, an essay outline might seem a poor substitute for an essay. However, most poor essays are poor because they are not coherent – the argument does not follow a logical order and evidence is used badly or not even presented. These are all faults in the planning of essays, indicating that students need more practice in planning essays rather than in writing them. The essay outline is an effective means of enhancing these skills.

Typical criteria for an essay outline are:

- logical order
- key points made
- counter arguments considered
- sensible, sustainable conclusions.

You can see from this list that the criteria highlight those aspects of essay construction that can be assessed from an outline. Compare these with the fuller criteria for a completed essay shown in Figures 5.2 and 5.3 of Chapter 5.

Essay outlines are valuable from two points of view. First, they can be used to help students learn the subskills of essay writing, such as putting points in a logical order. Developing such skills is more difficult when faced with the task of writing a full essay. Second, essay outlines are an efficient way of providing assessment as they reveal a lot about a student's capacity to think and analyse, yet they do not take a long time to mark. By setting essay outlines, teachers can provide formative assessment more frequently than would otherwise be possible, which is always to the benefit of students.

WRITTEN LONG-ANSWER METHODS

In this section, we discuss four long-answer methods:

- plans
- reports
- essays
- dissertations.

These methods move us into difficult territory for assessment as each demands considerable competence (on the part of students) in the method, irrespective of the subject being assessed. For example, the methods all (to varying degrees) require the following abilities:

- having a sense of audience and purpose
- choosing the argument to be presented (and the boundaries of that argument)
- ordering the argument
- selecting evidence
- presenting an argument logically
- avoiding problems such as unstated premises or *non sequiturs*.

In other words, unless learners have mastered all these skills, long-answer methods will fail to reveal what they have and have not learnt about subject. Nor should we ignore the demands that these methods make on students' general writing skills – they need to be able to write a sentence or a paragraph that says what they mean unambiguously and so it has a readable flow. (Where these are the very skills that you wish to assess, long-answer methods then become valid.)

Long-answer methods, then, fail to provide valid assessments when learners do not possess the skills that are intrinsic to the methods. This leads us to suggest a two-step rule for deciding whether or not to use one of these methods. Simply answer the following two questions.

- Could your assessment goals be met using some other method that does not present major additional (or irrelevant) challenges to the student? If yes, use that method in preference to a long-written answer.
- Do the learners possess the skills intrinsic to your chosen long-answer form? If yes, use a long-answer method. If no, look for some other assessment method.

We now discuss the five methods in a little more detail. We have treated them in what we suspect is their increasing order of intrinsic skill. In each case, we have focused on the likely criteria for assessing the method as doing this brings out the key features of each.

Plans

A 'plan' here means a prose document setting out how some objective will be achieved. It does not mean maps and drawings, although such items may form part of the plan.

At present, plans are not widely used for assessment, but we believe that they have considerable potential. After all, writing plans is an essential part of a very wide range of jobs. They offer an opportunity to analyse, synthesize and evaluate – high-level skills that other test methods tend to discount.

Plans can be used to assess the skill in writing plans, but are not of much use elsewhere. Learners should only be asked to write a plan when it is the skills of planning that need to be tested. For example, writing a plan for an audit would not be a valid way to assess auditing skills. Equally, writing a computer program would not be a valid way to assess planning the installation of a new computer system. This need to focus on planning skills when using a plan for assessment is highlighted by the typical criteria that are used when assessing plans.

In Table 9.1, we have set out a wide range of criteria that might be set for writing a marketing plan. Many other plans would need similar criteria. In particular cases, some of these criteria might be dropped and others introduced. In every case, the weighting of marks between the different criteria will need to be decided.

Table 9.1 also illustrates a more general point about criteria that applies to some of the other lists of general criteria in this chapter. We mentioned in Chapter 5 that lists of criteria should be kept to five to seven items. However, where a list of criteria is more like a checklist of particular aspects (for example, 'summary included?'), the list can be legitimately longer. That is because, in the checklist format, you only need apply a few criteria to any one part of the item being assessed.

Table 9.1   *General criteria for marking a plan*

Criteria	Meets no requirements	Meets few requirements	Meets some requirements	Meets most requirements	Meets all requirements
Background	None stated	Vague points	Some points	Most points	Fully adequate
Purpose of the plan	None stated	Vague	Some points	Almost complete	Complete
Assumptions	None stated	Vague assumptions	Some assumptions	Most assumptions	Full assumptions
Rationale	None stated	Vague	Some points	Almost complete	Complete
Steps in the plan	None stated	Few stated	Some stated	Most stated	All stated
Resources needed	None stated	Few identified	Some identified	Most identified	All identified
Schedule	None stated	Few dates	Some dates clear	Most dates clear	All dates clear
Responsibilities	None stated	Few shown	Some shown	Most shown	All shown
Possible problems	Not identified	Few identified	Some identified	Most identified	All identified
Contingencies	None suggested	Few suggested	Some suggested	Most suggested	All suggested
Summary	None	Vague	Some points	Almost complete	Complete
Appendices – presence	None	Few	Some	Most	All
Appendices – quality	Of no value	Vague points	Some points	Most points	Fully adequate
Language – grammar, spelling, syntax	Can barely be understood	Many deficiencies	Some deficiencies	A few deficiencies	Near faultless
Layout	Chaotic	Presents many difficulties	Presents some difficulties	Mostly clear	Very clear
Illustrations – presence	None	Few	Some	Most	All
Illustrations – quality	Can barely be understood	Present many difficulties	Present some difficulties	Mostly clear	Very clear
References/ sources	None	A few	Reasonable coverage	Mostly present	Fully documented

Five-point scales

Table 9.1 follows a common format for criteria, using a five-point scale. Such scales are normally broad enough to mark the full range of learners' work, whereas fewer bands can result in each having too wide a span.

The difficult part of using such scales is deciding on the descriptors for each criterion at each level. Given that we shall use these scales several times, we shall explain how they can be constructed for any given case. We shall do this by referring to the plans case above, but the method can be used for any five-point scale.

One way to create your own descriptors is to take three pieces of work – one very poor, one middling and one excellent – and use these to guide what you write in the boxes. For example, look at how the excellent plan treats 'Purpose of the plan' and use that to fill the box for highest performance level. Then use the worst plan to get a descriptor for the lowest level of performance. The middling plan will provide the descriptor for the middle level. That leaves the two intermediate levels, which can be completed by interpolating between the boxes on each side of them. (Chapter 5 gives suggestions on how to construct and use feedback forms, incorporating various types of rating scale.)

Reports

Reports can be used in two entirely different ways. First, they can be used to assess learners' ability to write reports – for example, a report on the accessibility of the leisure facilities in a city. In this case, it is report-writing skills that are being assessed, so no other assessment method will do. General report-writing criteria, such as those shown in Table 9.2, should therefore be used. In particular cases, some of these criteria might be dropped and others might be introduced. In every case, the weighting of marks between the different criteria will need to be decided.

Second, reports can be used to assess the quality of something that the learner has done. For example, reports can be used to assess a piece of fieldwork or a work placement. In this case, the ability to write reports is not central to the assessment, so the criteria should reflect the experience being assessed, not the report itself. Here task-specific criteria should be developed in place of general report-writing criteria.

Essays

We discussed essays and their characteristics in Chapter 5 and have nothing further to add here.

Table 9.2 *General criteria for marking reports*

Criteria	Meets no requirements	Meets few requirements	Meets some requirements	Meets most requirements	Meets all requirements
Background	None stated	Vague points	Some points	Most points	Fully adequate
Purpose of the report	None stated	Vague	Some points	Almost complete	Complete
Assumptions	None stated	Vague assumptions	Some assumptions	Most assumptions	Full assumptions
Rationale	None stated	Vague	Some points	Almost complete	Complete
Method used	None stated	Vague	Moderately clear	Mostly described	Clearly described
Organization of the report	Chaotic	Difficult to follow	Moderately clear	Clear	Very clear
Summary	None	Vague	Some points	Almost complete	Complete
Conclusions/ recommendations	None	Difficult to identify	Moderately clear	Clear	Very clear
Appendices – presence	None	Few	Some	Most	All
Appendices – quality	Of no value	Vague points	Some points	Most points	Fully adequate
Language – grammar, spelling, syntax	Can barely be understood	Many deficiencies	Some deficiencies	A few deficiencies	Fluent and accurate
Layout	Chaotic	Presents many difficulties	Presents some difficulties	Mostly clear	Very clear
Illustrations – presence	None	Few	Some	Most	All
Illustrations – quality	Can barely be understood	Present many difficulties	Present some difficulties	Mostly clear	Very clear
References/ sources	None	A few	Reasonable coverage	Mostly present	Fully documented

Dissertations

Dissertations have much in common with essays, but they tend to be used at the most advanced stages of learning a subject. This is reflected in the criteria that are used to assess them – there is more emphasis on theory, critical analysis and the deep understanding of a subject than is the case with other forms.

Simpler dissertations might use the essay criteria (see Chapter 5) but, in general, dissertations have their own criteria, such as those shown in Table 9.3.

As with the other forms of long-answer assessment, thought has to be given to what the dissertation is testing. Its primary purpose is to test learners' understanding of the fundamentals of a subject and its methods. The dissertation therefore explores the use of a subject's methods and is written within the conventions of the subject. It operates in the terrain where the content of the subject and the skills of the assessment method (the dissertation) become inextricably merged. In other words, the dissertation is used to assess aspects of a subject that could not be assessed by any of the other methods discussed.

Another form of assessment that is closely linked to dissertations is the independent study. This is discussed in Chapter 20.

Table 9.3 *General criteria for marking dissertations*

Criteria	*Meets no requirements*	*Meets few requirements*	*Meets some requirements*	*Meets most requirements*	*Meets all requirements*
Relevance to the topic	None stated	Vague points	Some points	Most points	Fully adequate
Understanding of topic	Not understood	Poorly understood	Reasonable understanding	Well understood	Fully understood
Theory – clarity and relevance	None stated	Poorly developed	Adequate, but partial	Good command of theory	Excellent command of theory
Length as percentage of requirement	More than 40% over or under	More than 30% over or under	More than 20% over or under	More than 10% over or under	Within 10%
Referencing – frequency	None	Few items referenced	Some items referenced	Most items referenced	All items referenced
Referencing – correctness	None accurate	Few accurate	Some accurate	Most accurate	All accurate
Plagiarism	Extensive	Quite a lot	Some	Little	None
Reading round the subject	None	Little	Some	A good deal	Substantial
Critical analysis	None	Little	Some	A good deal	Substantial
Evaluation and conclusions	Shows no understanding	Shows little understanding	Shows some understanding	Shows good understanding	Shows deep understanding
Presentation	Chaotic	Presents many difficulties	Presents some difficulties	Mostly clear	Very clear
Language – grammar, spelling, syntax	Can barely be understood	Many deficiencies	Some deficiencies	A few deficiencies	Fluent and accurate

ARTEFACT METHODS

All the methods that we have discussed so far require learners to do something beyond their study in order that they can be assessed. They answer some multiple-choice questions, prepare a report or write an essay. All these are the special devices that education uses in order to assess learners. There is, though, one group of assessment methods (if that term can justifiably be used) that does not use an additional assessment device – the assessment of artefacts.

By 'artefact' we mean something that the learner has created, not necessarily for assessment, and which has a life beyond the assessment. For example, the learner might type a letter, write a poem, create a database, carve a sculpture or change the wheel of a car. Much work-based assessment uses artefacts, but the differences implied by the term 'work-based' are unimportant. For example, there is more in common between assessing creating a database at work and at college than there is between creating a database at college and role-playing interviewing at college. The current strong interest in work-based assessment perhaps obscures how much it has in common with the assessment of artefacts in any context.

Artefacts may be capable of quite precise specification with clear criteria (changing a tyre, for example) or be both hard to specify and can only be assessed according to the most subjective of criteria (creating a statue, for example). What they all have in common, though, is that the marking criteria refer to what can be seen once the artefact exists – the emphasis is on product, not process. Does it work? Does it look right? Does it inspire?

So far in our discussion of methods we have either been able to describe a precise format for an assessment task (such as the format for a multiple-choice question) or to give precise, if general, criteria (such as those for marking a report). We can do neither for artefacts in general. They can be used in a wide variety of ways, each requiring its own criteria. Artefact-based assessments have very high validity (provided you are sure it is all the learner's own work) in that you assess the real thing and not an educational proxy for it. To make the point in an extreme form, asking learners to write an essay on how they would direct a play has little validity, but asking them to direct a play and then assessing that provides irrefutable evidence that they do or do not possess the skills needed for directing.

In general, the marking criteria for an artefact will be a combination of general criteria that apply to most artefacts of that type and specific ones that relate to the particular artefact that has been created. The greater the proportion of specific criteria, the more you need to negotiate these with the learner or other stakeholder.

Table 9.4 illustrates the use of general and specific criteria for assessing artefacts. For example, one typed letter (Task 1) has much in common with another, so most of the criteria for such a task will be general ones. A few local conventions might result in some specific criteria. By way of contrast, databases vary greatly depending on the data they are to hold and the queries that they will be used to answer. So, databases may have more specific criteria as in Task 2. In Task 3, the general criteria apply to all poems, while the specific apply to poems of particular formats.

Table 9.4 *Examples of general and specific criteria for artefacts*

Task	Typical general criteria	Typical specific criteria
1. Type a letter	Accurately spelt Follows standard layout conventions Uses correct modes of address and salutation	Follows company conventions
2. Create a database	Record structure appropriate to the data Data entered correctly Data validation applied where appropriate	Specific fields required Specific queries that the database must be able to answer Specific report formats that are required
3. Write a poem	Forms a satisfying pattern Communicates convincingly The form chosen matches the experience	Follows conventions of ... (sonnet, ballad, etc.) Includes particular feature(s) (metaphor, alliteration, etc.)

PERFORMANCE METHODS

Performance methods are closely allied to artefacts as, once again, they do not require a separate assessment device – you assess the presentation itself. Examples of performance methods include making a presentation, acting, dancing, singing and playing a musical instrument. (However, presentations are only performance methods when what is being assessed is the skill of presenting. If the presentation is merely a device to present some other piece of work, then it comes under quasi methods and is discussed later.) Most of these methods are highly specialized, so we will only discuss presentations as they are widely used.

Presentations

Presentations have become a popular method of assessing. In part, this reflects the importance of presentation skills in the workplace today. Almost anyone in a skilled job will find themselves presenting material, if only to close colleagues. In part, though, the popularity of assessment by means of presentations is because it offers variety and, if the option of group presentations is chosen, eases the assessment load for the teacher.

When presentations are used to assess presentation skills, the method has high validity and it is not difficult to develop suitable assessment criteria, such as those given in Table 9.5. In practice, some of these criteria are difficult to apply as there is an inevitable degree of subjectivity. For example, a presentation that one person found clear and interesting might have been obscure and dull to another. Here, assessment by a group can help because, if a majority of the audience found the presentation clear, the odd person who found it obscure can be discounted (some of these points are discussed in more detail in Chapters 18 and 26).

Problems begin to arise when presentations are used to assess another piece of work – for example, when learners present the results of their survey of people living on the street in their local city. The issues are exactly the same as those we discussed above in relation to using reports to assess other work. What happens if the learner's presentation skills are poor? Will the lack of these skills obscure what has been achieved prior to the presentation? The same cautions that we expressed over report writing apply here – using a presentation to assess some other piece of work may be far from valid. Generally, the method will only be valid if the learner has confident and excellent presentation skills. Also, if a presentation is used to assess some other piece of work, it is essential that none of the criteria refers to presentation skills. Criteria such as those in Table 9.5 only apply when the skill of presenting is being tested.

A presentation is sometimes use to assess both achievement in a subject and presentation skills. In such cases, two sets of criteria are required. One set will be the general criteria (adjusted as needed), such as those in Table 9.5. The other set will be derived from the subject material itself. When using two very different sets of criteria, you need to consider the balance between them. What proportion of the marks will be for presentation and what proportion for the subject? Is there a need to pass on each set individually or only on the aggregate score? Often, double assessments of this kind are of dubious validity as subject performance can interfere with the presentation performance, and vice versa.

As usual, the list of criteria in Table 9.5 needs to be selected from and modified to suit a particular presentation.

QUASI ASSESSMENT METHODS

In this final section, we come to a collection of activities that, although often talked of as assessment methods, are not quite. We explain our reservations about each of the methods that we discuss below.

Table 9.5 *General criteria for a presentation*

Criteria	Meets no requirements	Meets few requirements	Meets some requirements	Meets most requirements	Meets all requirements
Appearance of presenter	Totally lacking in confidence	Not at all confident	Fairly confident	Confident	Confident, professional
Introduction of self	Did not introduce self	Poor introduction, such as apologetic	Acceptable introduction	Good introduction	Confident, reassuring introduction
Introduction of presentation	None given	Vague introduction	Some overview and purpose	Good overview and purpose	Excellent overview and purpose
Content of presentation	Boring; impossible to follow	Difficult to follow	Can be followed with little difficulty	Clear	Excellently clear
Logic, order of presentation	No apparent logic to order	Order just discernible	Ordered, but some flaws in ordering	Order logical	Perfect order
Summary	None	Vague reference to what had said	Summary of some points	Summary of most points	Summary of all relevant points
Eye contact	None	Some contact	Maintained fairly regularly	Generally maintained	Maintained whenever feasible
Audibility	Inaudible	Very difficult to hear	Some parts difficult to hear	Mostly easy to hear	All easy to hear
Enthusiasm of presenter	None	Little	Some	A lot	Very enthusiastic
Handling of questions during presentation	Ignored questions	Made a small attempt to handle	Made a reasonable attempt to handle	Mostly handled	Handled all
Handling of questions after presentation	Could not respond	Responded in a perfunctory manner	Responded satisfactorily	Responded well	Responded excellently
Handouts – quality and relevance	None or unusable	Very poor	Adequate	Good	Excellent: a substantial addition to the presentation
Use of visual aids	None used or used very badly	Poorly used	Adequately used	Well used	Excellently used
Use of other aids	None used or used very badly	Poorly used	Adequately used	Well used	Excellently used

Projects and placements

Both projects and placements are sometimes described as assessment methods. We would argue that they are better defined as 'learning methods'. You learn by doing a project; you learn by going on a placement.

Rightly, of course, what is learnt by means of projects and placements needs to be assessed, but how? Almost certainly by using one of the assessment methods we have discussed above. For example, a project to develop a more effective egg carton might be assessed by means of a report and examples of the carton (which are artefacts). In other words, the assessment method is not 'by project' but 'by report and artefact' (see Chapters 19 and 20 for a fuller discussion of placements and projects).

Diaries, journals and logs

Diaries, journals and logs are sometimes used for summative assessment and so are sometimes referred to as assessment methods. This tends to obscure their primary purpose, which is usually to collect data, promote reflection and aid formative assessment. As soon as they are used for summative assessment, learners may feel inhibited about what they write or be tempted to write what they think their teachers wish to see.

When diaries, journals and logs are used for summative assessment, the assessment can take one of two forms:

- direct assessment of the diary, log or journal
- indirect assessment of something that the learner has written using data from the diary, log or journal.

There are four things that we might wish to establish from a diary (see Table 9.6), which can be found by asking the following questions.

- Is the learner able to keep records in diary format?
- What does the diary tell us about what the learner learnt?
- What processes did the learner use?
- How has keeping the diary affected the learner?

Each of these needs its own criteria, as set out in column 2 of Table 9.6. Whatever approach is taken, the usual issue arises: what are to be the criteria? The first question above asks 'Can the learner keep a record?' To assess this, it will be necessary to inspect the record – perhaps at regular intervals in order to be certain that it was not written long after the events. This inspection will have a considerable influence on what the learner chooses to write.

The second criterion refers to the use of the record to find out what the learner has learnt. What we have said about validity (Chapter 3) would suggest that using a record for this purpose is dubious. For example, learners may record (and present convincing evidence) that they have learnt how to plan diets for diabetics or how to ask for directions in German. In these cases, more valid assessment methods would involve seeing the diet plans and conversing with the learner in German.

The third criterion refers to what the learner experienced. Being aware of how one learns (and how one does not learn) is generally seen as a key meta skill for learners (see, for example, Mezirow, *et al.*, 1990, and Schön, 1991). The extent to which this should be left to formative assessment or should be summatively assessed is less clear.

The fourth criterion concerns the impact on the learner of keeping the record. This can be an important criterion where learners are preparing for work in a profession where keeping personal records is the norm (such as in nursing).

It is doubtful that the impact on the learner could be assessed by direct inspection of the diary, so you might have to search for other supporting evidence. This sort of evidence is best found by challenging learners to demonstrate that they have learnt as a result of keeping the diary. This can be done within a negotiated assessment system. However, a limitation of this method is that students may become adept at faking a response that they know to be appropriate or expected. In other words, they may not have had the experience to which they are laying claim. The assessor should perhaps seek supporting evidence, say by giving them a viva or holding a group discussion. (Some of the practical aspects of using diaries in assessment are discussed in Chapter 22.)

Table 9.6 *Criteria for assessing diaries, logs and journals*

Item being measured	Criteria needed	Comments
Can the learner keep such a record?	Process criteria about keeping a diary, log or journal	A valid method of assessing the capacity to keep a record
What does the record show that the learner learnt?	Criteria that relate to the learning referred to in the diary	Of dubious validity. There are almost certainly more valid methods of assessing what has been learnt
How did the learner learn?	Criteria that relate to the processes the learner underwent	Valuable in both formative and summative assessment
How has keeping the record affected the learner?	Criteria that relate to what has been learnt by means of the acts referred to in the diary, log or journal	A valid method of assessing the impact of recordkeeping on the learner – provided the learner has been honest

Case studies

Case studies are particularly problematical as they are a fairly ill-defined genre. We can dismiss the easy bit, first, though. The raw material for the case study is not a factor in the assessment. Rather, the assessment is concerned with what the learners are asked to do with the case study. This leads us to ask, what is the purpose of a case study? It may be one or more of the sorts of things mentioned in the second column of Table 9.7. This illustrates the fact that case studies can be used for a wide range of purposes, so a wide range of criteria and question types might be needed. For example, the 'comprehension' aspects might use multiple-choice or short-answer formats. 'Application' might ask for a report. 'Analysis' might use a short- or long-answer format.

Generally, though, case studies do not have a particular set of criteria associated with them, nor a particular range of question formats. The case study is a loose and adaptable genre that needs careful control if it is to test what you want it to test.

Table 9.7 *Potential types of case study learning*

Level	Purpose
Comprehension	Can the learners understand what is happening in a situation with real-life complexity?
Application	Can the learners take the ideas of the case study and apply them elsewhere, such as to their own work?
Analysis	Can the learners analyse a complicated situation in order to understand what is happening – say, identify relationships, causes and effects
Synthesis	Can the learners make sense of apparently conflicting or unrelated ideas? (This sort of analysis might be more relevant when more than one case is being studied)
Evaluation	Can the learners identify what value they attach (and why) to the experience of the case study?

Portfolios when used for assessment

Portfolios *per se* are not necessarily an assessment method: a portfolio is just a collection of examples of the learner's work. The collection might be a jumble or a selection of a learner's best pieces of work or a selection made on some other basis. Moreover, a portfolio may include the learner's reflections on the portfolio or some other documents that summarize and present the portfolio for the assessor.

Two things enable a portfolio to be used for summative assessment:

- the assessment criteria for the portfolio
- guidelines on what should be in the portfolio.

The order here is deliberate. If a portfolio is to be used for assessment, then the criteria should be clear before the learner begins to put the portfolio together as they govern what to include in it.

As portfolios are not an assessment method, but a device for collecting items that might be assessed, they have no intrinsic assessment criteria. The criteria in any given case will depend on what type of items are in the portfolio and for what they are being assessed. For example, a portfolio might well contain a report or some artefacts. In such cases, what we have said about reports and artefacts would be relevant in developing criteria. (Further discussion of the practicalities of using portfolios can be found in Chapter 24.)

Presenting the assessment in different ways

Our final group of quasi assessment methods deals with methods of presenting what is to be assessed. The two methods that we have chosen to discuss as examples of a wider range are videos and exhibitions. (Exhibitions and posters are discussed in more detail in Chapter 19.) In each case, of course, we are discussing the use of these methods other than to assess the skill of video making or the skill of exhibition mounting. If these skills were to be assessed, then the video and the exhibition would become artefacts and should be assessed as such.

Videos

Learners sometimes submit something for assessment on a video. Except where the skills of video making are being assessed, the video will just be a recording device to show something else and similar points to those made about diaries will apply. For example, if the video showed a presentation, then the criteria would be those for a presentation as, say, in Table 9.5.

Exhibitions

Exhibitions are another presentation method (unless the skill of exhibition mounting is being assessed). The criteria to apply will depend on the work that the exhibition records and what you intend to assess. For example, you could assess the exhibits *per se* or a brochure or leaflet that describes the exhibition, and so on.

The method is particularly suitable when group work is to be assessed by other groups as it avoids the necessity of preparing additional copies of what is to be assessed.

KEY ACTION POINTS

- Use multiple-choice questions when you need to sample a wide range of students' performances. They are easiest to set at the first three levels of Bloom's hierarchy, although can be set at the higher levels.
- Use true/false questions when you cannot find enough distractors to create multiple-choice questions.
- Use matching questions to test classification and relationships.
- Use fill-in-the-blank when you do not have enough time to develop other objective question formats.
- Make full use of the very wide range of short-answer question types.
- Use long-answer methods only when unavoidable.
- Use artefact methods when possible – they have high validity.
- Use performance methods when you wish to assess performance skills. If you wish to assess anything else, be careful that the learners' difficulties with presentation do not obscure what you wish to assess.
- Use quasi assessment methods with care – generally, they are better suited to learning than to assessment.

Chapter 10

Choosing methods

INTRODUCTION

In the last chapter, we reviewed a range of assessment methods and briefly looked at the main characteristics of each. In designing an assessment, the next question that arises is how to choose which method to use for any given outcome. In this chapter, we discuss how that choice might be made. In our previous discussion we classified certain methods as quasi methods. In debating whether or not to omit quasi methods from this chapter, we decided that they were best left in, even though, from some points of view, such methods are nearer to being learning methods than assessment methods.

Our aim is to provide guidance that will help you select a suitable method. This does not mean that other methods cannot be made to work in a given instance, only that other methods might be difficult to use.

The approach we have followed in this chapter is in two parts. First, we introduce a four-step method for identifying which methods are appropriate for a given assessment. Then we look in detail at the methods that are suitable for each of the six levels of Bloom's hierarchy. At the end of the chapter, our guidance is summarized in Table 10.3.

AN ALGORITHM FOR CHOOSING A METHOD

There are many factors that affect which assessment method you might use. For example, the method must be valid. It must also be suited to the assessment source. If, for example, you want students to mark their own work, then an essay might not be your best choice; if you plan to machine mark, that rules out using a project. You also need to take account of where the assessment is to be undertaken. Some methods are more suited to the workplace than others, for example.

Given the wide range of factors that affect choice, we have devised an algorithm that takes account of the main ones and ensures a systematic choice of method. The algorithm is illustrated in Figure 10.1. It starts by assuming that you will decide what it is you wish to assess and for what purpose. As you have seen in Chapter 9, these have a strong impact on the choice of method. A method that you might use for summative tutor assessment of presentation skills might be very different from the method chosen for formative self-assessment of French vocabulary.

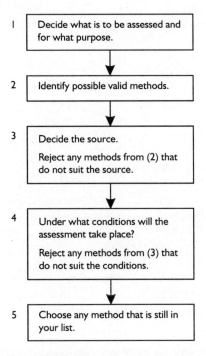

Figure 10.1 *Methods choice algorithm*

We shall illustrate how the algorithm can be used by considering the formative tutor assessment of writing a short business letter using an appropriate layout, appropriate methods of opening and closing the letter and including a clearly and politely phrased message. The test is to be deliverable to 40 students at a time in a classroom and should be suitable for use with subsequent cohorts of students. Here the item to be assessed is business letter writing and the purpose is formative – that is, the assessment method chosen must be one that aids further learning. We know that the circumstances are 'in a classroom and to 40 students'. After following this example through, you should then try to apply it to a situation in your own professional area.

Step 1: identify valid methods

Writing business letters involves application, so we first consider methods appropriate to application. These are as follows (we say more about this list later in the chapter):

- short-answer question
- fill-in-the-blank question
- problem/calculation
- create/do something
- long-answer question (such as a report or, possibly, an essay)
- project
- case study.

Problem/calculation is not valid for letter writing as calculations are not involved, so we can drop it from the list of potential methods. Similarly, the last three methods in the list do not offer much prospect of validity for letter writing, so we can drop these as well. The remaining methods all offer some prospect of validity. If we used a short-answer format, we could ask learners questions such as 'Write down how you would start the letter to....' While this does not test the creation of a letter as a whole, it is quite a good method of identifying specific learning problems and offering feedback on them. Similarly, although the second method does not ask the learners to write a whole letter, by completing partially completed letters, problems can be identified. Finally, the fourth method would, in this case, involve writing a whole letter and is therefore a valid method.

So, in this first step, we have illustrated how consideration of what is to be assessed eliminates certain methods. In this case, at the end of step 1, we are left with the first, second and fourth methods methods to choose from.

Step 2: who is going to assess?

We know that a tutor will assess the work and that we still have a choice of three methods. All of these could be marked by a tutor, while some could be marked by another source, such as a learner using a self-marking scheme. However, if a is tutor available, it might be preferable to make use of the richness of the method that best employs the expensive time of this skilled source (the fourth method).

So, by considering who is going to assess (in this case), we begin to feel that the fourth method might be a better choice than either the first or second methods.

Stage 3: under what conditions will the assessment take place?

The test has to be suitable to use in a classroom with 40 students. All the three remaining methods (the first, second and fourth) can be used in a classroom as they are paper and pencil methods. However, marking 40 letters is a huge workload, so we might begin to think of the benefits of short-answer and fill-in-the-blank formats. These would take the tutor far less time to mark. (There might even be the prospect of machine marking, but we do not know this for sure.)

So, at the end of stage 3, the first, second and fourth methods are all still feasible, although the fourth method might involve too great a volume of marking for it to be practicable.

Stage 4: choose between the remaining methods

We are now left with short-answer questions, fill-in-the-blank and create/do something as possible assessment methods. With no further information on the possibility of machine marking, we can now rank the three remaining methods, given the circumstances that we have had to consider. Our conclusion in this instance is to opt for the short-answer test. We summarize our reasoning for this in Table 10.1.

Table 10.1 *Ranking choices for the letter writing test*

Rank	Method	Reason
1.	Short-answer question	Easy to mark, even with 40 students Involves writing, so has enough validity for our purpose
2.	Fill-in-the-blank question	Easy to mark, even with 40 students But cannot involve writing sentences so it is not as valid as the short-answer format
3.	Write a letter	Takes too long to mark in this instance, so, despite its high validity, we rank it last

If you feel that we have not reached a perfect decision with our letter-writing assessment, we would agree with you. Circumstances often constrain us to use an assessment system that is 'good enough', but not perfect. However, because we used a systematic approach to reach our conclusion, we can feel reasonably confident that we have made the best possible compromise.

Having established an algorithm for choosing between methods, we will now discuss the second stage in more detail – that is, what is the validity of each of the methods that are available?

VALIDITY AND LEARNING OUTCOMES

As you saw in Chapter 3, an assessment will only be valid if the method is correctly matched to the level of outcome and the nature of the learning to be assessed. You can't use a true/false question to test speaking a foreign language; nor can you use an essay to assess presentation skills. So, the first thing to consider is which methods can be used to test a given level in Bloom's hierarchy. Generally, this step will identify several possible methods. You can then use the steps shown in Figure 10.1 to make your final choice.

Methods for assessing knowledge

The term knowledge is used to mean many things from simple facts such as names (grass, noun, oxygen) to understanding complicated theories and methods. However, in this book, we use the term in its restricted sense of being able to recall (without necessarily understanding) facts (Bloom, 1956). Understanding of those facts is classified as comprehension. (If your types of teaching have little place for this type of knowledge, then you can treat all knowledge as comprehension – see below.)

In this restricted sense, knowledge refers to what are the accepted facts in a particular knowledge domain. For example, all the following are knowledge items:

- definitions, such as the definition of mass
- names of things, such as cup, London, tennis racquet
- specific facts, such as Dickens wrote *A Christmas Carol*
- conventions, such as that an arrow means 'in this direction', that a red light means 'stop'
- classifications, such as Fiat, Rover and Citroën are manufacturers of cars.

Knowledge items can be tested by asking the learner to recognize (R) the fact or to give (G) the fact. For example, the first question below tests whether or not learners can recognize the name Lord Nelson as being the correct answer, while the second question requires the learner to give the name. The latter task is the more difficult, but which one you choose depends on the learning outcome you wish to test. If the outcome uses words such as 'give', 'list' and 'state', then the assessment item should require the learner to give the answer. If the outcome uses words like 'recognize' then the assessment item can merely require recognition.

The admiral in charge of the British fleet at the Battle of Trafalgar was:
A   Lord Fisher
B*   Lord Nelson

C   The Duke of Wellington
D   Earl Jellicoe

The admiral in charge of the British fleet at the Battle of Trafalgar was _____.

In giving these examples we have already used two of the question formats that are best suited to assessing knowledge. The full range is:

- multiple-choice question (with one or more correct answers) (R)
- true/false (R)
- matching (R)
- fill-in-the-blank question (G, but heavily cued)
- short-answer question (G).

Three of these methods involve recognition of the correct answer, while two require learners to give the answer. However, fill-in-the-blank questions tend to be heavily cued and so hover between recognizing and giving the correct answer.

Once the range of possible methods has been identified (as in the list above), you have to decide which method to use for a particular purpose. If you want students to give the answer, then you are restricted to just two methods: fill-in-the-blank and short-answer questions. Generally, though, whether students give or just recall the answer is not critical, so you can choose between the five methods. The choice can be reached by using the principles set out in Figure 10.2. While there is only one efficient way to test matching (use a

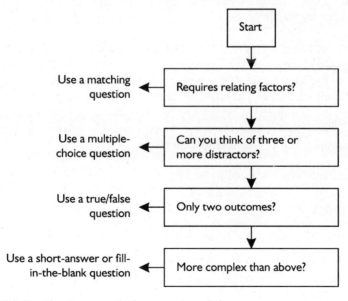

Figure 10.2 *Choosing a method to assess knowledge*

matching question) four methods are available for other types of knowledge. Generally, the multiple-choice question is superior to the other methods because it:

- is easy to mark
- powerfully distinguishes between those who know something and those who do not.

Where it is not possible to write a multiple-choice question, then a true/false question is often an alternative. Short-answer and fill-in-the-blank questions are the most difficult to mark and so are perhaps best used where feedback is more important than grading (for example, in self- and formative assessment).

Methods for assessing comprehension

Comprehension involves being able to explain something. This may be carried out in various ways, including:

- offering a verbal explanation, such as explaining why the sun is lower in the sky in winter than in summer
- using the knowledge in a way that demonstrates understanding, such as correctly classifying ten geranium plants into varieties
- recognizing a correct explanation, such as, when given a black and white photograph with poor contrast, choosing which of three explanations accounts for the problem.

With one addition, all that we have said about testing knowledge also applies to testing comprehension. In particular, the methods listed earlier and the algorithm for selecting methods shown in Figure 10.2 are equally applicable to testing comprehension. The wording of the questions changes, of course. For example, the first question below tests the recognition of a definition and so is a knowledge test. The second question – assuming that learners have not seen these examples before – tests comprehension.

An uncount noun is one which refers to:

A* things like qualities and feelings
B   things you can't count
C   nouns that are unimportant
D   words you can't put 'a' or 'an' in front of

Which of the following are uncount nouns?

A   music
B   information
C   notice

D   opera
E*   happiness
F   infinity

The one addition is that, in principle, you can use essay questions to test comprehension. In practice, though, this is an inefficient method, both for students and teachers. Wherever an essay is used to test comprehension, it will be possible to devise much shorter and more effective questions in some other format.

Methods for assessing application

Application questions use a situation or present a problem to be solved. Examples of situations used in application are:

- case studies (real or fictional)
- role plays, such as a role play where students have to practise the use of open and closed questions
- a piece of equipment, such as a car engine that has to be tuned correctly.

The other form of application – problems to be solved – comes in forms such as:

- data to be manipulated, for example, data for a mathematical problem
- data that has to be translated into some other format, such as translating into a foreign language or making a bar chart from raw data.

In each case, the principles and methods to be applied must have been taught to the learners, but the situation or problem must be novel to them. (If it was not novel, then students could answer the questions from memory, thereby turning a test of application into a test of knowledge.) For example, a student who answers the following question correctly, never having seen the answer before, is showing the ability to apply certain rules of French grammar, such as the rules for forming possessives.

Translate the following into French:
My husband is an engineer.

On the other hand, a student who had been taught that the French for 'My husband is an engineer' is 'Mon mari est ingénieur' would not have to apply any grammatical rules to answer the question. Such students could just recall the answer. So, in everything that we say about testing application, we always assume that the problem or situation is novel to the students.

The choice of which question type to use in a particular application depends on whether you are testing recognition of a correct application or the capacity to carry out the application. For example, the following question tests for recognition that an application (the method of laying out a word processed letter) has been correctly done.

Look at the three word processed letters in the figure [not shown here]. Which of these is correctly laid out?
A
B
C

On the other hand, if you want to find out if students can carry out an application, then you need a different type of question, such as:

The word processed letter in the figure [not shown here] has three mistakes in its layout. Correct these and print out a copy of your work.

Where you only wish to check recognition of a correct application, then multiple-choice, true/false and matching question methods are appropriate. They are particularly appropriate for paper-based problem solving, as in maths, languages and the sciences. The following three examples, using the various methods, all test application.

The graph $y = x^2 + 2x - 8$ crosses the x-axis at:
A $y = -8$
B $x = -2$ and $x = 4$
C $x = 2$ and $x = -8$
D* $x = 2$ and $x = -4$

An electric fire with a rating of 1000 watts at 250 volts consumes a current of 25 amps.
True ☐   False ☐

Match the correct form of di plus the definite article from List 2 to go in front of the nouns in List 1.

List 1	List 2
signori	del
scuola	dello
corso	della
stato	dell'
arbri	dei
archivo	degli
	delle

When writing such questions, you need to be careful that you are not accidentally testing knowledge of how to apply instead of the process of application. For example, superficially, the following question looks like an application test, but it really only asks for knowledge of first aid, rather than the use of such knowledge in new circumstances.

The first step in helping an injured person is:
A   Carry out the ABC check
B* Ensure your safety and that of others
C   Call an ambulance
D   Ask the injured person if they want any help.

Often we need to test the result of application without showing students what the possible answers are. When this is the case, the methods listed in Table 10.2 are all applicable. All application questions like those shown follow the same basic principles:

- students are presented with a problem or scenario
- they apply some method to solve the problem
- they record the results of its application.

(You may wish them to record and perhaps analyse the process they used to solve the problem. If that is the case then, for that aspect of the question, you would need to use the methods discussed under Methods for assessing analysis, below.)

The second column of Table 10.2 gives some examples of how the methods can be used to test application. In order to concentrate on the principles of choosing a question type, the questions in the table are in outline form only. Real questions would need more detail and more explicit criteria.

The first type of question – the short-answer format – is easy to mark and well suited to situations where a short statement can provide a good indication of whether or not a student has applied a method correctly. In our example, students have to apply the guidelines for recognizing cell abnormalities. If they can correctly classify cells as normal or abnormal, that in itself is a good indication of being able to use the method. In the case of the example question, though, the question also asks for a description of the abnormalities, thus providing a check on the students' reasoning.

The fill-in-the-blank question presents a description of a real-life situation that a car mechanic might have to tackle. While the assessment method does not permit the learner to demonstrate application (that is, to find the fault and fix the car), it is possible to use this method to establish that the mechanic understands and can interpret the symptoms correctly.

Table 10.2 *Some methods for testing application*

Question types	Examples
1. Short-answer question	Examine the cell tissue slides 1–3 provided [not shown here]. For each slide, briefly describe any abnormalities in the tissue.
2. Fill-in-the-blank question	In the panel [not shown here] are the symptoms that were observed in a malfunctioning car engine. Complete the following sentence to show your diagnosis of the problem: The symptom of _____ is an indication that the _____ _____ or the _____ may be faulty.
3. Problem/calculation	A raffle has first, second and third prizes of £750, £500 and £250. The organizers have sold 4000 tickets at £1 each, of which you have bought 10. How much can you expect to win?
4. Create/do something	Type a letter of complaint about some mouldy bread that you bought at a supermarket. Create a database to store the following data [not shown here]. Change the near-side rear wheel of the workshop car.
5. Long-answer question (such as a report or, possibly, an essay)	You are to survey the views of ten of your fellow students on the content, teaching and organization of the last module they studied, using the questionnaire provided [not shown here]. Write a report describing how you carried out the survey, what you found out and what conclusions you have drawn. Your report should mention any limitations of your survey methods.
6. Project	Design and carry out a project to investigate the access and mobility problems of handicapped people who live in their own homes.
7. Case study	While on your work placement, carry out a study of the market research methods that the company uses.

The third format – problems and calculations – is one of the most clear-cut question types. It is generally fairly obvious when to use it. Thus, we only need to add that, if the student has previously seen the identical problem and its solution, then it ceases to be a test of application and, instead, becomes a test of knowledge.

The fourth category is a very wide one – getting the student to make something using a well-defined method. For example, students might type letters, create databases, change the wheel of a car, make a chemical using a known method or give a presentation. The essential point here is that, while you might wish to observe the process of creation, what really matters is the final product. A well-presented letter is more important than how the letter was typed. An excellent and interesting presentation is more important than how the student planned it. So, these tests of application focus on the finished work.

The three remaining methods (long-answer questions, projects and case studies) all share a common weakness, which is that they are difficult to constrain in terms of time and focus. They also share a common strength – that they are capable of engaging the learner's interest to a very high degree, especially if 'real' audiences are involved, which helps them to perform better. Deciding when the balance of their strengths outweighs their weaknesses is difficult.

Methods for assessing analysis

Analysis involves looking at a whole and identifying its parts and the relationships between them. Testing for analysis may focus on one or more of these aspects. When the focus is on identifying the parts, students are tested for their ability to do such things as identify:

- assumptions
- facts
- hypotheses
- motives and reasons
- conclusions.

When the focus is on the relationships, students will be asked to identify aspects such as:

- cause-and-effect relationships
- fallacies
- oppositions and tensions
- the author's viewpoint or philosophical position.

One interesting aspect of assessing analysis is that, whereas this is a high-level skill, brief answers are often quite sufficient to reveal students' powers of analysis. A long, rambling article and the task 'What two assumptions is the author making here?' might be a powerful test of analysis. Good students can provide an excellent answer in 20 words. Poor ones might use 200 words to reveal their complete failure to find the author's assumptions.

We make this point because, so often, the assumption is that something as important as analysis demands some meaty form of assessment, such as writing an essay. True, essays are well suited to testing certain types of analysis, but, often, short, crisp questions will do the job just as well, if not better. By 'if not better' we have in mind that, for many students, writing essays is so taxing that they lose sight of what they are communicating. Shorter questions can help students to appreciate and reflect on their own powers of analysis.

There is a rich choice of testing methods for analysis, but they divide into two key groups, as follows. First, methods to use when you wish the learner to identify elements or relationships that you regard as being the correct answers:

- multiple-choice questions (one or more correct answers)
- true/false questions
- matching
- short-answer questions
- fill-in-the-blank questions.

Second, those methods used when you wish learners to produce original analyses where you are unable to predict the answers:

- short-answer questions
- long-answer questions (essay)
- report
- project
- case study
- logs, diaries
- video.

Those methods included in the first group are suited to situations where there are correct answers that you expect students to find. For example, 'What conclusion does... reach in her article?' The methods that appear in the second group are more suited to situations where the answers are less clear-cut and where students may need to explain their reasoning as well as state their conclusions. We shall discuss testing methods where the answers are predictable first.

Before we do that, here is an example of a multiple-choice question to test the ability to distinguish a major cause of something from other subsidiary causes.

In the article [not shown here] the author states that the main reason for the company going into receivership was:

A   The strike
B   Poor management
C   The fire at the factory
D* Changes in the market.

In this next question, students have to identify the hypotheses in a situation.

When people argue that longer prison sentences would reduce crime, what two hypotheses are they making?

And, in the final example of analysis questions suited to situations with predictable answers, questions can be asked about the methods used in creating an argument.

In the advertisement [not shown here] for ice-cream, what technique is the advertising using to persuade you to buy this particular product?

When we move on to the other methods mentioned in the list above – those suited to questions where the answers are less predictable – the questions tend to invite longer, more discursive answers. Only the short-answer format is similar to the methods for predictable answers. Generally, the marking schemes for the longer methods will give considerable weight to students' justifications of their answers.

The key methods here are the long-answer questions (essay), report, project and case study. Their strength lies in their potential for depth and sustained argument. Their weakness lies in the difficulty of setting clear questions and criteria.

Also mentioned are logs, diaries and video. We have done so with some reservations as these methods are more suited to collecting data for later analysis than for analysis *per se*. If you do use these methods to test analysis, your students may need considerable help in separating what is raw data from what is analysis.

Methods for assessing synthesis

Synthesis involves creating something. The four main products of synthesis are (Bloom, 1956):

- unique communications, such as a letter or an essay
- plans
- abstract relations
- hypotheses.

In general, most assessment of synthesis concentrates on the first two items in this list. As both are about producing fairly major peices of work, an assessment method must be chosen from among those that involve the production of something complete. In some cases, the method is fairly obvious. For example, the ability to compose music (which is an act of synthesis) can only be demonstrated by writing a piece of music. Similarly, the ability to write poetry is best tested by writing poetry. Producing plans is a specific form of synthesis and can only be tested by either writing a plan or writing an outline for a plan.

The final types of synthesis – creating abstract relationships and formulating hypotheses – are best tested by means of short-answer questions.

Some of the various methods that can be used to assess synthesis are, for unique communications:

- essay outline
- essay
- compose music
- write poetry
- report
- project
- case study
- logs, diaries
- video

for producing plans:

- outline of the plan
- written plan

for creating abstract relationships and formulating hypotheses:

- short-answer questions.

Methods for assessing evaluation

Essentially, there are four parts to evaluating:

- choosing criteria
- collecting evidence
- assessing the evidence against the criteria
- drawing conclusions.

The assessment of evaluation, like that of analysis, can often be carried out using short but taxing questions. Although evaluation is the highest skill in Bloom's hierarchy, it does not require the longest answers (which generally occur in synthesis). The ability to recognize appropriate criteria, evidence or conclusions can be tested using any form of objective test or short-answer question. For example, the ability to recognize suitable criteria can be tested objectively:

> When evaluating a course, the most important criterion would be:
> A   the standard attained by the students
> B   students' satisfaction with the course
> C   the proportion of students who get jobs
> D*   the added-value performance of the students.

The ability to identify criteria being used can be tested using a short-answer question:

> In the discussion on the videotape [not shown here] what three criteria did the team use to choose the new member of staff?
> 1.
> 2.
> 3.

Both of these examples could have been written in other formats. For example, we could have written the first as a short-answer question and the second as a multiple-choice one.

When it comes to carrying out an evaluation, including all the four steps identified above, only the long-answer formats are suitable. The same cautions about the use of these that were discussed under assessing analysis apply to assessing evaluation. Also, the same limitations apply to the use of logs, diaries and videos.

SUMMARY

We have discussed how you can choose a test method that matches the learning outcome you wish to test. In some cases, the choice is fairly obvious (for example, using a plan to test writing a plan). In other cases, the choice is wide (as it is for testing synthesis). In others, it is all too easy to choose a method that tests something you had not intended to test (for example, writing a comprehension question that, in practice, will only test knowledge). So, the decision about which method to choose needs to be made with some care. Our general approach to this is summarized in Table 10.3. This is not intended to be comprehensive, but sets out the commonest methods for assessing each level of learning.

KEY ACTION POINTS

- Use the four-step method (or an equivalent) to identify your options for an assessment method for any given circumstance.
- Make sure that your chosen method is valid for the learning outcome you wish to assess.
- Use Table 10.3 to check that you have not overlooked any possibilities.

Table 10.3 *Summary of choosing methods*

Category	*Suitable assessment methods*
Knowledge	Multiple-choice questions (one or more correct answers) (R) True/false (R) Matching (R) Fill-in-the-blank questions (G, but heavily cued) Short-answer questions (G)
Comprehension	Multiple-choice questions (one or more correct answers) (R) True/false (R) Matching (R) Fill-in-the-blank questions (G, but heavily cued) Short-answer questions (G) Long-answer question (essay) (G, but rarely efficient)
Application	Where recognition of how to apply is sufficient: Multiple-choice questions (one or more correct answers) (R) True/false (R) Matching (R) (Not often appropriate) Where actual application of method is required: Short-answer questions (G) Fill-in-the-blank questions (G, but heavily cued) Create/do something (say, type a letter, create a database, change a car wheel) (G) Long-answer questions (G) Project (G) Case study (G)

Analysis	When you wish the learner to identify elements/relationships you regard as being the correct answers: Multiple-choice questions (one or more correct answers) (R) True/false (R) Matching (R) (Not often appropriate) Short-answer questions (G) Fill-in-the-blank questions (G, but heavily cued) When you wish learners to produce original analyses where you are unable to predict the answers: Short-answer questions (G) Long-answer question (essay) (G) Report (G) Project (G) Case study (G) Logs, diaries (G) Video (G)
Synthesis To produce a unique communication	Essay outline (G) Essay (G) Compose music (G) Write poetry (G) Report (G) Project (G) Case study (G) Logs, diaries (G) Video (G)
To produce a plan	Outline a plan (G) Write a plan (G)
Create a set of abstract relations (NB: identifying relations is analysis) Formulate hypotheses	Short-answer questions (G)
Evaluation	Multiple-choice questions (one or more correct answers) (R) True/false (R) Matching (R)

Short-answer questions (G)
Fill-in-the-blank questions (G, but heavily cued)
Essay (G)
Essay outline (G)
Report (G)

R = tests recognition of the correct answer
G = requires the student to generate the answer

PART THREE

Sources of assessment

Chapter 11

Self-assessment

INTRODUCTION

This chapter has strong links with Chapters 7 and 5. Chapter 7 explored the various types of responsibility students may adopt in the assessment process. In Chapter 5, we looked at possible kinds of student involvement in the generation and negotiation of assessment criteria. In this chapter, we consider the role students might play in assessing their own learning.

Self-assessment is not a method of assessment, but a source – the student is the assessor (or, more probably – as we shall discuss – 'an' assessor). This source may be used with different methods and instruments. Self-assessment can apply to any learning outcome, including products, performances and processes; you can use it, in one form or another, with students of all ages. The instruments used to support self-assessment can include open-ended self-reports, semi-structured reports, ratings or checklists – you can find examples elsewhere in the book.

Self-assessment does not appear much in the literature until the 1970s. It was stimulated then by the growing importance of reflection in some areas of professional practice and by the development of distance and open learning. Many hundreds of thousands of Open University students have, for example, acted as the sources of their own assessment by answering the 'SAQs' – self-assessment questions – in their course units. Using these questions, activities and exercises, accompanied by carefully prepared feedback, students can check their learning. You can also use these techniques in modified form in face-to-face teaching. For example, as part of lecture handouts, inviting students to answer questions before, during or after classes.

Self-assessment is now growing in importance and features strongly in some of the newer means of collecting, organizing and interpreting evidence of performance. We describe these in other chapters, including learning logs, journals, diaries, records of achievement, profiles and portfolios. Self-assessment is essential to the process of claiming credit for prior learning or experience. A report in *The Times Higher Education Supplement* (1997) of a survey into changing student assessment methods in Scotland found that nearly a quarter of the 300 replies related to self-assessment; this high proportion was considered a 'surprise'.

Writing originally in 1987, Rowntree claimed that the practice of self-assessment rarely extended beyond 'lip-service' and that its full potential had not been realized. Although much progress has been made since the first edition of Rowntree's book, his points are probably still valid. To be effective, self-assessment needs to be an integral part of a course. Both student and tutor need to take the results seriously and act accordingly (Rowntree, 1987). This chapter suggests some ways in which you might achieve this.

SELF-MARKING

Some writers distinguish 'self-marking' from 'self-assessment'. Self-marking involves the award of a mark, score or grade. There are three aspects of this, corresponding to the three main types of assessment introduced in Chapter 2. Students may be measuring their performance against:

- a set of criteria
- their own previous best
- the performance of others in their group.

The results of such self-marking only very rarely go forward unmoderated to count towards final assessment. In practice, self-marking is often a limited operation, such as checking the answers to multiple-choice questions or simple mathematics problems or spelling tests, where the criteria are pre-set and marking is unproblematical. Self-assessment, on the other hand, is wider in scope. For example, it could encompass student involvement in establishing assessment criteria, and then applying these to their work.

Research into self-marking

Although the results of self-marking are rarely significant in the final result, research is, none the less, positive about the value of this source of assessment, concluding it can be both reliable and valid. Andresen, *et al.* (1993) report that self-assessment has been shown to be capable of supplementing or completely replacing teacher assessment. Elsewhere, Boud (1989) concludes that 'most students generate marks that are reasonably consistent with marks given by staff', noting that weaker students tend to overmark, and stronger students do the opposite. Research evidence shows that self-assessment can be as reliable as other forms of assessment. It appears to be more accurate in sciences than arts, but this is probably because the criteria in sciences are usually more explicit (Brown, *et al.*, 1997).

Research in the vocational assessment area leads to similar conclusions. Mitchell and Sturton (1993) report that students' own assessments of their ability are as valid as the assessments of others, and the correlation between tutor and student marking is very good. If there is a bias, 'all of the research shows that candidates tend to under rather than over assess their capabilities'. Moving beyond vocational assessment and into schools, Mitchell and Sturton instance the finding of an evaluation of the use of Records of Achievement. This was that pupil 'modesty' – that is, underestimation of their achievement – was a problem. It was felt that students may carry over assumptions they have derived from norm-referenced assessment.

Research is thus positive about the quality of self-marking, that students seem as accurate as the other sources of assessment. There is, even so, a general reluctance in education to take student self-grading seriously. Boud (1989) has a neat rejoinder to those focusing only on the problems:

> Studies which have identified the unreliability of teacher marks have not led to calls for teacher grading to be abandoned, rather they lead to considerations of how the marking process can be made more reliable.

Despite all this, Brown, *et al.* (1997) argue that the main aim of self-assessment should be the improvement of student learning rather than summative assessment – and, one might add, the growth in student responsibility that might reasonably be expected to follow from self-assessment. This is the main emphasis we take in the rest of this chapter.

THE BENEFITS OF SELF-ASSESSMENT

As Brown, *et al.* (1997) argue, self-assessment is particularly important in promoting learning. Alverno College, in the USA, is often referred to in this context. At Alverno, the central function of assessment is to 'provide the student at each of the many stages in her development with a progressively fuller and more individual profile of her emerging combination of gifts, skills and styles so that she can become an independent learner.... Most important of all, she herself is training to become an expert assessor of her own abilities'. Students are thus required to demonstrate their self-assessment capacity (*Assessment at Alverno College*, 1979, quoted in Mitchell and Sturton, 1993). In this sense, self-assessment is necessary if the individual is to have the motivation and self-insight to go on learning, be able to set their own direction and measure their progress.

Other benefits claimed for self-assessment include that it:

- helps students identify what assessment criteria mean in practice
- prepares students for the reflection on their performance they will be required to practise in a number of professions (for example, teaching and nursing)
- helps students to consolidate or integrate learning gained across a number of modules, units, courses, or experiences.

The following extracts from drama students' diaries show some examples of students learning from self-assessment on their drama course.

> Because of limited space and audience position, Anne has changed her resting position after her solo. We worked fairly hard and John and I completely changed the pacing and our dance at the end. Although we liked the 'Errol Flynn'-type move at the end, Brenda [the choreographer] didn't. I couldn't understand this at first, but then realized it was out of character – too long and flowing and not 'beastish' enough.
>
> Mavis

> I got a lot out of tonight. My only wish is that I could go through the experience again – a constant feeling after each production. The part I like best is when I move down towards Angela; I become very aware of the music, 'my' sound, and really feel that I respond and dance better with it.
>
> Jane

> Another weakness I now have under better control is my hatred of being criticized. At first I took any form of criticism very personally and was especially upset when it came from someone in the group – John for example. Now, instead of snapping back, I can control my emotions. I still don't like it, but I can now look at myself more objectively.... The drama course tends to make you very aware of your own strengths and weaknesses. There is nowhere to hide.... The group is such, however, that everyone will try to help you sort out your problems.
>
> Tim

IMPLEMENTATION

It is as well to be aware of the difficulties in implementing self-assessment. Depending on their previous educational experiences, students (and particularly older students) may have grown dependent on the assessments of others. It can be frightening to students in these circumstances to have to make judgements about their own work. Teachers may be uneasy, too, doubting students' readiness to take this degree of responsibility. These attitudes need to be addressed as self-assessment needs more than compliance from students and tutors if its potential is to be realized (see Chapter 7). Both tutors and students may need considerable support at first, including support from peers. Extrinsic incentives may also be needed, such as (for students) making self-assessment a course requirement, awarding marks for self-assessment, allocating time in class and treating the results as being worthy of discussion.

External incentives are not, however, sufficient. According to Kohn (1993, quoted in Boud, 1995a), you should follow two general principles. First, every comment you make on assignments should be designed to build the authority of the student – that is, their capacity for self-determination. In terms of self-assessment, this means helping students to develop their own standards and their own judgements of performance against these standards. Second, your interventions should develop students' intrinsic motivation, so they become more deeply involved in what they are doing, rather than just seeking to please. Thus, the strategy should be to lead students from extrinsic to intrinsic motivation for self-assessment.

Students should be prepared for self-assessment as part of their induction. It is best introduced early in a year, course or programme, when students are more likely to be open to what may be a new approach. You should base self-assessment on specific tasks that the students have completed – such as a project or a painting; or on events they have experienced – such as a field trip or a production – rather than making it too ambitious or general. The instruments students use should also be specific, precise and unambiguous – self-assessment is best kept simple, especially at the start.

In many ways, there is nothing special about self-assessment. All the other assessment principles covered elsewhere in this book also apply, including the availability of explicit criteria, the use of appropriate methods and instruments of assessment, and openness in procedures.

Progressive development of self-assessment

Sound self-assessment is usually developed over an extended period of time, by means of regular practice accompanied by feedback. One useful idea is to ask students to complete a self-assessment sheet for each assigment, commenting on such points as:

- the strengths of this piece of work
- how I could improve it
- the grade it deserves
- what I would have to do to turn it into a higher grade
- what I would like your comments on.

Unfortunately, there seems to be no generally agreed model for the progressive development of various types or levels of self-assessment (though Brown, *et al.*,

1997, quote Hatton and Smith). The framework of dimensions and continua introduced in Chapter 7 can be adapted for use in self-assessment. The quality of students' reflection can be deepened by using indicators for dimensions relevant to planning and undertaking assessment developed in association with the students.

Finally, self-assessment needs to be fully integrated within the students' subjects of study. It should not be relegated to a fringe area of the curriculum. Emphasis placed on self-assessment in 'hard' as well as 'soft' subjects makes the point to students that it has status and is worth persevering with. Teachers working in teams, using common practices, can help students experience the twin benefits of enhanced subject learning and the development of a generic self-assessment capability.

CONCLUSION

We have concentrated in this chapter on self-assessment. This source of assessment should not, however, be treated in practice as being self-contained. It should be orchestrated together with other sources. It could, for example, lead to peer and tutor assessment via the following sequence:

- students assess their own work
- they then assess the work of a peer
- in pairs, the students give and receive one another's feedback
- they compare their own self-assessment with that of their peer, discussing particularly any differences between the judgements
- students then decide, as individuals, what to do in the light of the discussion
- work is submitted to the tutor, perhaps with the student's own earlier self-assessment and that of their peer.

KEY ACTION POINTS

- Integrate self-assessment within your assessment design and into the curriculum.
- Prepare students fully.
- Introduce incentives, if necessary.
- Provide explicit assessment criteria.
- Consider using a self-assessment sheet to accompany assignments.

Chapter 12

Peer assessment

INTRODUCTION

'Peers' are people of equal status, power or situation. For the purposes of our discussion, peers share the status of 'student'. They may differ from one another in other ways – for example, age, social status and prior experience. Peer assessment implies an element of mutuality.

As with self-assessment, peer assessment has two aspects, related to two of the main purposes of assessment:

- making formal estimates of the quality of other students' work
- giving and receiving feedback for learning.

The first of these we shall call 'peer marking', the second 'peer assessment'.

As with self-assessment, the term refers to the source of the assessment – in this case, a peer or peers. You can use peer assessment in a very wide range of curriculum activities, both those resulting in products (for example, written assignments, objects, performances) and for processes (for example, participation in discussion or in a project). Peers of any age can assess one another. As with other types of assessment, the criteria may be given (as is often the case in peer marking) or devised by/negotiated with the students.

Much research has been carried out on peer assessment, but it is difficult to generalize given the number of variables involved, including subject area and local context.

In this chapter we consider:

- the benefits of peer assessment
- how to implement peer assessment and peer marking
- peer assessment of processes.

THE BENEFITS OF PEER ASSESSMENT

According to Falchikov (1995, p160):

> The overwhelming view, arrived at after observing the results of over 20 years of peer assessment studies, is that peer assessment is generally a useful, reliable and valid exercise.

As with self-assessment, variations between students and tutor are no greater than those between tutors.

Peers are much better placed to judge some assessment tasks than is a tutor. In conventional educational contexts, they spend much more time with their colleagues than does the tutor. Knowledge of their peers gained via interaction can be particularly important in assessing process skills, such as the performance of members of a group working together on a project or a production over a sustained time period.

By means of peer assessment, students are likely to develop a better understanding of what is looked for in their work as they become familiar with criteria when they have to apply them. Via peer assessment, students can be helped to meet the demands of more formal assessments. For example, formative comments from a peer can indicate changes that need to be made to an essay before it is submitted to the tutor for summative assessment.

Peer assessment can be a useful way of covering curriculum ground or of giving further practice in course- or subject-related skills. Each student, for example, could be asked to answer a question, solve a problem or undertake an exercise and then pass this to another student for assessment and feedback. Each student would thus become familiar with two areas, which are the question they answer and the question they assess.

Students learn collaborative skills by working with one another. They may also develop other interpersonal skills by, for example, giving feedback to peers. They benefit from seeing the variety of approaches taken to assignments and to their subsequent assessment.

Peer assessment may also save tutorial time. For example, instead of assessing assignments, the tutor may moderate the results of peer assessment. As with other aspects of assessment, we lack data on whether or not time savings can be expected from this approach. One study quoted in Brown, *et al.* (1997) suggests that peer assessment took only a third of the time, but the methods used here may also have involved group rather than individual assessment. It could be that the tutor spends much the same amount of time when using peer assessment, but uses it differently and perhaps more productively.

HOW TO IMPLEMENT PEER ASSESSMENT

In the introduction to this chapter, we distinguished the broader concept of 'peer assessment' from the more specific 'peer marking'. In the latter, the student allocates a mark or grade to their colleague's work. We look first at how to introduce and maintain peer assessment.

Peer assessment

First, some general points that apply whenever a process is being introduced that may be unfamiliar to students. Careful induction is needed, including an explanation of the rationale of peer assessment and the benefits students might expect. 'Added value' is important here as students will not be enthusiastic if the benefits seem to apply only to the tutor – they may feel they are being short-changed. Students need time to acquire the skills of peer assessment. As with self-assessment, students need to practise it, starting with relatively specific and short-term activities and moving on to the more complicated and sustained ones. You may need to work with students on the principles and characteristics of good feedback, for these are at the heart of peer assessment (see Chapter 6).

Setting up peer assessment has much in common with preparing for other assessment arrangements. Procedures are best kept simple. You should monitor peer assessment and evaluate the results, using these to inform any changes. It is a good idea to talk to colleagues who have successful experience of implementing peer assessment.

For peer assessment to succeed, clear criteria must be available (see Chapters 5 and 9). These can be given or created by or with the students. Another variation is for the students to turn a list of criteria into a checklist or rating scale (see the examples in Chapters 5 and 9). Generally, the more involved students are in setting criteria, the better their assessments will be as they will then be familiar with, and committed to, these criteria. You might use the following sequence:

- individuals draft criteria
- pairs compare drafts and agree one list
- pairs join with others in small groups and agree a group list
- the list is compared with the tutor's
- a final joint list of criteria is agreed
- individuals assess their own work using the list
- pairs assess one another's work using the list
- individuals redraft their work as necessary
- work is assessed by the tutor to the same set of criteria
- pairs or groups discuss the tutor's feedback and action plan accordingly.

This is a relatively elaborate process that you could use for major pieces of work as it includes assessment from the three sources of self, peer and tutor. You can shorten or adapt the list as necessary to suit your circumstances. You could also extend it to include the generation and use of a marking scheme as well as the criteria, and develop model answers or select these from previous student assignments. This may seem a complicated and time-consuming process, but it can generate considerable student commitment and understanding, and save time later. (See also Figure 5.1 in Chapter 5.)

You will need to consider the logistics of peer assessment. In some contexts, peer assessment is both valid and easy to arrange – as in cases of presentations and exhibitions or poster sessions.

Peer marking

You will generally find it easier to use peer assessment for formative feedback than for summative (or part summative) assessment. Students are more receptive to giving and receiving formative peer feedback than to allocating marks or grades. They may be reluctant to judge their peers and also feel that is the tutor's job, not theirs, to assess summatively. Also, some tutors are reluctant to see students significantly involved in marking. So, peer marking has to be approached carefully if the result is to count towards a credit. (Less formal peer marking – for example, when students exchange answers to multiple-choice questions – is a different matter, and is relatively easy to set up.)

Nevertheless, you may decide to incorporate peer marking into an assessment strategy. This could be said to be a preparation for life, as we have, on occasions, to judge the work of our colleagues who may also be our friends. As pointed out earlier, in some circumstances, peers are the most logical source of assessment, such as when they form the audience for a presentation or where they have been working together on a group project and the team process is to be assessed (see Chapter 26). Another reason for responding to the challenge is that if peer assessment results never influence summative assessment, students may not take this source of assessment seriously.

The following ideas may help with implementation:

- ensure that students are provided with agreed criteria
- require them, as one of the rules of peer assessment, to explain and justify their marks according to these criteria
- incorporate an appeal system (perhaps a group of students, with the tutor as the final arbiter)
- ask students to sign their assessment to ensure a sense of responsibility (although students in some studies say that anonymity means they can be more honest).

PEER ASSESSMENT OF PROCESSES

Peers are frequently used as a source of assessment of processes, such as those involved in a group of students working together on a project or to make a group presentation. Peer assessment can take two forms:

- assessment by the group of how the group worked
- assessment of individuals within a group.

Figure 12.1 (from Brown, *et al.*, 1997) is a checklist aid for the former, with an emphasis on formative rather than summative assessment.

Criteria to assess the performance of individuals within a group might include:

- attendance
- acceptance of a fair share of the work
- generation of ideas
- keeping the group focused on objectives
- fulfilment of a specific role, such as data collection
- constructive criticism
- problem solving
- supporting others.

A checklist based on such criteria could be completed by each member of the group on each of the other members. The group and/or the tutor could then collate the results. Alternatively, the group could – as a group – discuss each item and agree a decision on the rating for each individual group member. The results could then be discussed and moderated as necessary (see Chapter 26 for assessing individual contributions to a group project).

CONCLUSION

In peer assessment, the role of the tutor shifts towards that of external examiner, moderator and monitor of the process. As with the external examiner, the tutor is usually the final arbiter. Thus, fears that peer assessment means the abrogation of the tutor's authority are ill founded.

Most of our meetings were confused	1 2 3 4 5	Most of out meetings were well organized
We often got side-tracked	1 2 3 4 5	We stuck to the task most of the time
We didn't listen to each other	1 2 3 4 5	We did listen to each other
Some talked too much and some did not talk enough	1 2 3 4 5	We all contributed to the discussion
We did not think through our ideas sufficiently	1 2 3 4 5	We thought through our ideas well
Some got aggressive and some got upset	1 2 3 4 5	We were able to argue and discuss without rancour
Most of us seemed to be bored by the discussion	1 2 3 4 5	Most of us seemed to enjoy the discussion
Most of us did not improve our discussion skills	1 2 3 4 5	Most of us did improve our discussion skills
Most of did not learn much	1 2 3 4 5	Most of us did learn through our group work

Note: the discussion is more important than the rating.

How could the group have worked better?

Name _____ Group _____

Thank you for your views.
There will be an opportunity to discuss the overall reactions of the group
at our next meeting.

Figure 12.1 *How our group worked (based on Gibbs, 1992)*
Source: Brown *et al.*, 1997

KEY ACTION POINTS

- Be clear about your reasons for using peer assessment and the benefits you expect.
- Select appropriate assessment tasks.
- Ensure clear assessment criteria (and other instruments) are available.
- Brief students carefully, especially if they are unfamiliar with peer assessment or have used it unsuccessfully.
- Start simply, helping students build the necessary skills gradually.
- Monitor the progress of peer assessment, adapting arrangements as necessary.
- Consider the implications for your own role.

Chapter 13

Using computers in assessment

INTRODUCTION

When the words 'computer' and 'assessment' are heard together, it is easy to assume that this is just a reference to a set of multiple-choice questions delivered by a computer. Much less is heard of the many other ways in which computers can help in assessment. For this reason, this chapter is rather more wideranging than the others in the book. We shall, for example, have something to say about using a computer to type out your tests and manage assessment generally.

HOW COMPUTERS CAN BE USED

In Table 13.1, we identify 11 broad assessment functions in which computers can be helpful. Only four of these involve delivering and marking the assessment. This illustrates the considerable potential of computers in assessment, even in areas where it is difficult – or pointless – to use a computer for marking.

We shall now look at each of these functions further.

Process text, data and figures

The most mundane use of the computer is that of preparing assessments. These may need words, graphics, tables, figures and so on – things that are quickly produced using computers and can be modified easily after testing or for use on a subsequent occasion. For the tutor, the personal computer becomes a rich depository of proven assessment materials, ready to be quickly reworked for new purposes. In some systems, stored assessments may be downloaded by learners or by other tutors, banishing the chore of printing, collating and circulating materials. Many Internet-based courses have assessments of this type.

Table 13.1 *Some uses of computers in assessment*

Function	Some examples
Process text, data and figures	Typing assessments using a word processor Storing assessments on a computer
Manage assessment	Storing assessment results Storing learner profiles Analysing assessment results (such as with a spreadsheet program) Issuing timetables, attendance lists, results tables
Deliver assessments (no computer marking)	Tutors or learners printing out a test from a computer Tutors or learners downloading a test over the Internet
Mark assessments	Using an optical mark reader (OMR) to take in students' answers, mark and print out results; feedback may also be given
Deliver and mark assessments	Delivering the assessment by computer; learners inputting their answers at a terminal; the computer marking the work; feedback may also be given
Create assessments	Using a specialized program, such as Question Mark, to write a test in a computer-deliverable format
Create assessment answers	Learners using a computer to create their answers – say, word processing an essay, preparing a spreadsheet
Submit assessments	Learners using an intranet or the Internet to submit their work to their tutors
Provide feedback	As part of computer marking (see above) Storing a set of feedback comments – tutor selecting which ones to print for which learners
Self-assessment with marking and feedback	Computer holding diagnostic and formative tests that learners do to check their own progress
Report assessment results	A computer holds a profile form into which teachers can type comments for individual learners. The completed forms can be printed out and sent to whoever needs them

Manage assessment

Computers can also be used to help manage assessment by storing data on learners, assessments completed and their results. More importantly, such stored data can be quickly analysed in order to give tutors information on the performance of their learners and of their assessments.

The need for help with storing data has become more pressing as a result of the twin influences of worsening tutor:learner ratios and the increasing use of verbose forms of assessment, such as profiles and portfolios. This has led to the development of special computer programs to record and manipulate assessment data. For example, the National Extension College's *NVQ Organizer* series helps in assessing skills, preparing action plans for learners, mapping learners' progress onto the national standards and producing records for assessment and verification.

However, much can be done without the use of specialized software. For example, marks can be analysed using a spreadsheet program as shown in Table 13.2, where the highest and lowest marks, averages and means are calculated by the spreadsheet. The correlation between the two sets of marks is given, too. This can be used to help decide whether or not two separate assessments have, broadly, given consistent results for each learner. That is, have learners who have scored highly on one assessment also scored highly on the other? Graphical illustrations of results can also be prepared, as shown in Figure 13.1. Here, each dot represents the two marks of one learner. For example, the dot furthest to the right is the learner with an exam mark of 91 and a course mark of 76. These can be useful in helping you get a feel for the spread of results on a test or for

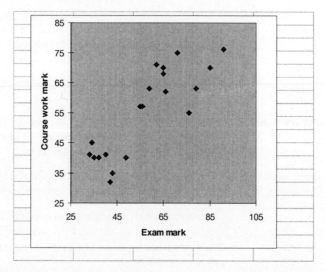

Figure 13.1 *Graph showing the spread of marks from Table 13.2*

Table 13.2 *Using a spreadsheet to analyse marks*

Candidate	Exam mark	Coursework mark
1.	42	32
2.	65	70
3.	76	55
4.	34	45
5.	85	70
6.	33	41
7.	56	57
8.	79	63
9.	91	76
10.	35	40
11.	65	68
12.	71	75
13.	62	71
14.	66	62
15.	43	35
16.	49	40
17.	55	57
18.	59	63
19.	40	41
20.	37	40
Highest mark	91	76
Lowest mark	33	32
Average mark	57.15	55.05
Mean mark	57.50	57.00
Correlation between the exam and coursework marks	0.85	

how results on one test compare with those on another. Diagrams of this type are particularly helpful when discussing results with colleagues – it is easier for everyone to concentrate on the overall picture when the detailed learner-by-learner figures have been removed.

The more powerful database programs offer features that allow for the tracking of individuals and student groups. Complicated reports, formatted to your requirements, can also be produced. However, whereas most personal computers have a spreadsheet program provided within the cost of the initial purchase, good database programs cost several hundred pounds.

Before investing in such software, you need to be clear that the benefits it can bring are worth the money you are paying, including the costs of learning to use the program before it can do anything of value to you. It probably makes more sense to start by using your spreadsheet as a database. Once you have reached the limits of what a spreadsheet database can do, you will be well primed to judge which database you need next. Generally, database programs can take in data prepared on spreadsheets, so, in making the transition between the two programs, you do not have to retype your records.

Deliver assessments (no computer marking)

Printing and circulating assessments can be tedious and expensive. In some situations, security considerations leave you with no choice. In other situations – such as when administering skills tests or using take-away tests – they can be stored in a computer and accessed by learners when they need them. The assessment itself may not require the use of a computer, so the learner just prints a copy and takes it away. This method of distribution makes great sense with widely dispersed learner groups, as is the case with courses run over the Internet and with learners thousand of miles apart. Even single-site courses can benefit from this approach. For example, a lecturer may need to hand out assessments to 200 students, but only 150 turn up to the relevant lecture. The lecturer hardly wants the remaining 50 to search them out to request the assessment. Far better to put it on a server and leave the students to download it.

Mark assessments

Often computers are used to mark assessments that learners have completed elsewhere. Where this is the case, learners indicate their choice of answer on a form that can be read by an OMR machine. These machines can read hundreds or thousands of sheets per hour, depending on the size of machine. Once the data has been read, it is processed by the computer, using the answers previously entered by a tutor. Learner results, feedback and analyses of performance can then be printed out.

Deliver and mark assessments

Potentially, the most powerful use of computers is to deliver the assessment and to mark it. To do this, the computer must be able to store the questions (and any associated stimulus material) and present them to the learners. Learners need to be able to input their responses in some form that the computer can process in order to award a mark. This presents no difficulty when the questions are multiple-choice ones. However, several other question formats (Peel, 1994) can be used including:

- putting a list in order
- displaying a question, followed at five-second intervals by each of the answer options (this makes it more difficult to deduce the correct answer by comparing the options)
- fill-in-the-blank questions – they present problems in terms of defining what is and is not an acceptable answer
- matching text to images
- presenting an image where clicking on a particular part of the image presents a particular answer.

Programs for preparing, displaying and marking such questions are discussed next.

Create assessments

In addition to using generic word processing programs to type in assessments, specialized programs are available to create computer-administered tests. These programs are relatively easy to use and guarantee you a test that will work when the learners try it.

Perhaps the best-known program of this type is Question Mark. This offers seven types of question: multiple choice; push button, where learners click the button against the correct answer; multiple response, which can be used to put items in order; hot spot, where an image is presented and learners have to click the spot representing the correct response; numerical input; and text match for short answers. The seventh 'question type' is actually the display of instructions: no response is permissible. (Nicol, nd)

Examine is another program designed for tutors wishing to create on-line assessments. It supports six question types: multiple choice, multiple selection, numeric, true/false, multiple true/false and comment – that is, questions that collect comments from learners, but which are not marked.

Questions are prepared using text files, so it is possible to convert your existing questions to Examine format quite simply. When used with Microcosm (a hypertext system), hot spots in Examine can take learners to Microcosm text, so allowing them to move between learning and assessment at will (Brailsford, 1994).

Various other systems, including EQL Interactive Assessor, and DIADS, are described by Brown *et al.* (1997).

This is a rapidly developing area about which it can be hard to find information. One directory of software was published in 1994 (NCET 1994), but has not been updated since. The journal *Active Learning* is also a good source of current activity in computer-based assessment.

Create assessment answers

The use of computers by learners to do their assessments is rapidly increasing. Learners are often encouraged to use a computer to prepare their answers – for example, to word process their assignment or display their data using spreadsheet tables and graphics. Where all learners are using such programs, you need to consider the following:

- should the nature of the assessment task take advantage of the functions offered by the computer?
- how does the use of a computer in this way affect the marking scheme?

For example, when setting a question that involves data, should you stipulate that this is to be displayed using a spreadsheet program?

More problematical is the situation when not all learners have access to a computer to present their work. Here, you have to be careful that the marking scheme does not advantage those who do have computer access.

Computers are also increasingly used to obtain information via the Internet for use in assessments. Again, you have to consider how this affects the task that you set and those who lack Internet access. (A powerful example of this happened to one of our sons who had been asked to do a project on bridges. Within minutes of searching on the Internet, he found a major site on bridges with details and pictures of bridges from all over the world. When setting the project, it had not occurred to the tutor that any students would have access to such a resource.)

Submit assessments

A very straightforward use of computers in assessment is for the submission of student work. Generally, this involves word processed work, such as essays and reports. These can be attached to e-mail messages for sending to a centre or the tutor. Reports of this approach imply that marking is done on paper and the work returned to the learner by post. However, it is feasible to mark an assignment on screen and e-mail it back to the learner. Various methods are available for the physical marks, such as:

- tutors underline any words they wish to comment on; comments are then placed as footnotes or are on a separate sheet
- tutors underline any words they wish to comment on; comments then follow in square brackets
- if student and tutor share a word processing system with a revisions facility (this allows a reader to see a document both as it was and as it is after changes), a tutor can type comments straight into the learner's work. These

comments will appear, clearly distinguished in a bright colour, on the student's computer screen.

Provide feedback

There is widespread agreement that feedback is important in learning. This is acknowledged in tutor marking every time we provide written comments or, when time permits, discuss an assessment with a learner. Worsening tutor:student ratios have led to tutors looking for more efficient ways to give feedback. For example, some tutors create a word processed comment bank as they mark. Each comment is numbered, so, instead of having to write out a given comment many times, they can just refer a student to a comment by number (Brown, *et al.*, 1994). Another use of such comment banks occurs when tutors extract from the bank just those comments that apply to any one student. These extracted comments are pasted into a new document, creating 'personalized' feedback sheets from a common resource.

Such straightforward uses of computers both eases the assessment load and increases the quality of feedback for students. Such feedback banks can be extended to produce reports and profiles (Lloyd-Jones *et al.*, 1992).

When the computer is doing the marking, feedback can be automated using comment banks stored by the marking program. Various programs are available for this purpose, including TIPS (Habeshaw, Gibbs and Habeshaw, 1993); the Open University fast feedback system (Baker 1983); and the National Extension College MAIL system (Freeman, 1983).

Self-assessment with marking and feedback

Computers can be used to provide self-assessment. Learners are provided with questions, grouped by topic. According to learners' performance on a topic, they are provided with feedback on how much they know and what action they should take next.

Report assessment results

Finally, computers can be used to communicate results to whoever needs them. This can be done at quite a simple level by storing report formats in a computer and then typing comments and results in to them. This leads to attractive printouts and ensures that the report is safely filed in the computer.

A more sophisticated approach is to initially store the results in a database. Then, with no further typing, different reports for different purposes can be generated from the same data. Also, once the data is in a database, you can carry out complicated analyses and printout summary data, such as histograms and line diagrams.

139

The advantages of computers in assessment

Does computer assessment work? Bull (1994) reminds us that '...there are no rules. What may work in one subject may be inappropriate in another', so it is hard to generalize about the role of computers in assessment. However, Bull notes that one aim – to increase efficiency – may be hard to achieve as 'The current level of development of computer-based assessment means that efficiency gains in terms of staff time tend to be long term.' The potential is there, though: 'Computer-based assessment has greater potential than paper-based systems for access and flexibility for both students and tutors and for effective management, collation and transfer of assessment information.'

The National Council for Educational Training (NCET), now called the British Educational Communications and Technology Agency (BECTA), also found (NCET 1996) that IT was valuable in assessment, making assessment information more accessible, reducing administration and enhancing the quality of reports.

When evaluating his own development project, Stephens (1994) reached similar conclusions. He found that computer assessment had proved worth while, but the development time needed was considerable. He concluded that computer assessment 'allows staff to concentrate on assisting students with problems and relieves some aspects of onerous repetitive marking... [it] often requires more than individual effort. It requires institutions to support activities that deliver appropriate training and support to individual staff....'

When considering the time needed to set up computer assessment, it is useful to remember that (with appropriate copyright permission) published banks of questions are often highly suitable for computer storage. Also, working in a team (sometimes across institutions) can spread the load and give you access to assessment items prepared by other teachers.

In the more limited area of assessing multiple-choice questions by computer, Brown *et al.* (1997) identify 17 advantages over pencil and paper marking. These include such factors as being able to allow students more than one attempt at a question, preventing plagiarism by randomizing the questions, accurate marking and relieving staff of the need to mark.

GUIDES TO DEVELOPING COMPUTER ASSESSMENT

Most of the skill in designing a good test for computer delivery lies in designing a good test *per se*, so our advice in the other chapters of this book is highly relevant to computer assessment. However, on top of these assessment skills, each system will require some additional learning time before it can deliver any benefits.

Some guides to developing objective questions for computer-based assessment exist. *Better Testing: A computerized guide to writing objective tests* (Clarkson and Danner, 1994) has been reviewed in *Active Learning*. The University of Aberdeen also publishes two self-teaching tutorials entitled *Setting Effective Objective Tests* and *Efficient and Effective Examination Using Computer-assisted Assessment*. These are based on using Question Mark, but also deal with the general principles involved.

KEY ACTION POINTS

- Consider which of the 11 uses (see Table 13.1) might be useful to you now.
- Identify which of these you can carry out with your current skills, equipment and time – work on these to start with.
- For uses that require more time to develop than you can afford, look for colleagues and institutions with whom you could collaborate to produce something useful to you all.

PART FOUR

Using assessment methods

Chapter 14

Objective tests

INTRODUCTION

In this chapter, we look at the nature of objective tests, when to use them and how to write reliable and valid questions. (We discussed the meaning of the term 'objective' in Chapter 9.)

As mentioned in Chapter 9, the word 'objective' in the term 'objective questions' refers to the method of marking the questions. That is, objective questions can be marked without any judgement being made on the part of the marker. The marking is an entirely mechanical process and so can be done by computer. In no sense does the term 'objective tests' imply that such tests are any more objective in their assessment of learners than any other possible tests. Nor does the term imply that the teacher's choice of what to test is any less subjective than for any other assessment method.

The main types of objective test are:

- multiple-choice questions
- true/false
- matching.

These are described later in this chapter.

WHEN TO USE OBJECTIVE TESTS AND WHY

There are three circumstances in which objective tests are particularly valuable:

- when you need to sample a wide range of course content
- when you want to use the time taken to mark tests more efficiently
- to diagnose learning difficulties.

Let us now look at each of these in more detail.

To sample a wide range of course content

Objective tests are frequently used to assess what learners know and what they can do (in the mental sense) and to produce a score. Their particular value in assessment of this type lies in the fact that learners can be tested on a large number of points in a short time. (In Chapter 1 we mentioned that one way to improve the reliability of a test is to increase the number of questions. With most other question types this is not practicable because the test becomes too long for the learners.)

The other great benefit of objective tests is that administering the questions yields information that can be used to improve the questions. (We do not discuss methods for analysing questions in this book, but good accounts can be found elsewhere, such as Ward, 1981.) Objective tests can therefore reach very high levels of reliability and validity – something that is often elusive with other question types.

In general, objective tests are used to assess at the lower levels of Bloom's hierarchy – that is, knowledge, comprehension and application. This fact, though, is not an intrinsic characteristic of objective tests. It merely reflects the difficulty of setting questions at the higher levels. For example, to set a synthesis question would require the presentation of a complicated scenario with disparate elements and the objective questions might then present a range of supposed syntheses of the information. The learner would have to say which was the best synthesis. Such a question might take hours to construct.

To use time efficiently

Generally, an objective test requires less learner time than any other way of testing the same range of material. Objective tests, then, make efficient use of learners' time.

The tests can also be efficient from the teacher's viewpoint as they can be marked by machine. Even if hand-marked, the marking will take less time than if the questions were in some other format. However, objective tests do take longer to create, so teachers can only expect to save time if they can share the burden of creating questions or use the questions many times. Where time is saved for teachers, they can then concentrate on activities that are more productive than routine marking.

To diagnose learning difficulties

In addition to using objective tests to assess learners, they can be very effective in diagnosing learners' problems. Their power to do this lies in the distractors.

If each distractor is chosen to represent a common mistake or misunderstanding, then an analysis of a learner's errors tells the teacher what the nature of the learner's problem is. The teaching can then be adjusted accordingly. For example, in the following question, each of the distractors reveals something about how the learner has tackled the problem. (As before, the asterisk indicates the correct answer.)

What is the value of 2^3?

A   6   (error suggests the learner calculated 2 x 3 = 6)
B   5   (error suggests the learner calculated 2 + 3 = 5)
C* 8
D   9   (error suggests the learner calculated 3 x 3 = 9)

LIMITATIONS OF OBJECTIVE TESTS

The one serious limitation of objective tests for knowledge is that they can only test recognition of facts and not the recall of them. For example, compare the following two questions. In the first, a learner who cannot recall the dates might still recognize them when scanning the four options. In the second case, there is no data that could jog the learner's memory. Effectively, the second question is more difficult to answer. (This is a phenomenon we all experience. For example, when we forget a name and someone else says 'Do you mean...?' we often immediately say, 'Yes, that's the one.')

What were the dates of the Second World War?

A   1940–1945
B* 1939–1945
C   1938–1946
D   1938–1944

What were the dates of the Second World War?

The other limitations of objective tests are of less substance. The objection that learners can guess the answers has little force. First, they can guess answers on any type of test. Second, if they 'guess' the correct answer, it suggests that they suspected its correctness. Third, if guessing is considered to be a problem, the marks can be adjusted to take account of this. (See Ward, 1981, pp40–41 for details of how to do this.)

Finally, it is often said that objective tests are 'easy' and only test the lower levels of Bloom's hierarchy (knowledge and comprehension). In response to these objections, we would suggest that objective tests are as easy or as hard as one wishes to make them. For example, is the following question easy? (We have deliberately not shown the key in this instance.)

What is the meaning of the word romic?

A   Connected with Rome.
B   A phonetic system.
C   A type of rambling walk.
D   A Romanian dialect.

EXAMPLES OF TESTING AT THE FOUR LEVELS

How a question is worded can determine the level the question tests at. Below there are four questions on Ohm's Law. Each tests at a different level in Bloom's hierarchy.

The first just requires visual recognition of the formula for Ohm's Law. This is $V = IR$. Learners can get this right by recognizing it even if they do not understand what the symbols mean. So, this first question just tests the recall of knowledge – that is, the lowest level in the Bloom hierarchy.

What is the correct form of Ohm's Law?

A $VR = I$
B* $V = IR$
C $I = R/V$
D $R = VI$.

The second question is a test of comprehension as the answer does not involve rote recall of facts. Instead, the learner has to consider the relationships implied in $V = IR$ and work out that doubling V will double I.

If the voltage applied to a circuit is doubled, what will happen to the current?

A* It will double.
B   It will halve.
C   It will stay the same.
D   It will square.

The third question requires the learner to calculate a voltage given a current and a resistance. All calculation questions are tests of application as the learner is using method or a formula to find what will happen in a particular case.

A current of 4 amps flows through a circuit with a resistance of 20Ω. What is the voltage across the circuit?

A   5 volts
B   4 volts

C   16 volts
D*   80 volts.

The final example is that of an analysis question on Ohm's Law. Analysis involves such tasks as finding out what principles are at work in a given situation. The question in this example provides some data that are not consistent with Ohm's Law. The learner has to work out (analyse) what the explanation might be.

> The following measurements were taken in a circuit containing one resistor. Each set of results was taken twice.
>
> (1) $V = 20, I = 2$; (2) $V = 30, I = 1.5$
> (2) $V = 40, I = 1.33$.
>
> Which of the following is the most likely explanation?
>
> A   the results are just what Ohm's Law predicts
> B   there is a poor connection in the circuit
> C*   the resistor is changing value as the current changes
> D   the high voltages are affecting the meter.

Which test, when?

Most objective questions use the multiple-choice format. There are good theoretical reasons for preferring multiple-choice questions to true/false as the more distractors a question has, the lower the chance of a learner guessing the answer. (With random guessing, a learner would select the correct answer 50 per cent of the time with true/false questions, but only 25 per cent of the time with a four-option multiple-choice question.)

One approach to selecting the best type of question is the system shown in Figure 14.1. This algorithm helps you to find the most powerful question format given the restrictions and opportunities inherent in the topic to be assessed. The method suggests that you first consider whether or not the topic involves relating factors. If it does, this strongly suggests using a matching question. If the question is not about relating factors, then you should consider how many distractors you will be able to generate. If you can find three or four, then you could write a multiple-choice question. If, however, you only have two outcomes, then you have no option but to choose the true/false format. If none of these formats is suitable, then that suggests your topic is not suitable for an objective question and you will need to consider one of the other formats discussed in Chapter 9.

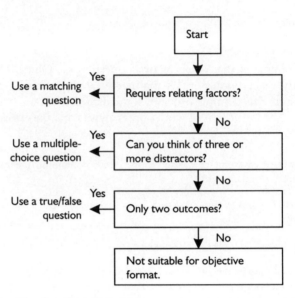

Figure 14.1 *Choosing the question type*

THE STRUCTURE OF MULTIPLE-CHOICE QUESTIONS

Stem and options

Each multiple-choice question contains a stem and a series of options. The correct option is called the key; the incorrect options are called distractors. For example:

What is the correct form of Ohm's Law?   ← Stem
A   VR = I   ← Distractor
B*   V = IR   ← Key
C   I = R/V   ← Distractor
D   R = VI.   ← Distractor

The stem can be a question or an incomplete statement, as in the following two examples:

Which of the following is a hardwood tree?   ← Question
A   Larch
B*   Oak
C   Spruce
D   Scots pine.
An example of a hardwood tree is: ← Incomplete statement

A   Larch
B*   Oak
C   Spruce
D   Scots pine.

The wording of the stem is crucial because if it is confusing, the question will fail to test what it sets out to. In general, the statement form produces shorter, clearer stems, but sometimes the question form is clearer (a comprehensive list of stem wordings appears in Gronlund, 1968, pp28–9).

Correct versus best answers

So far, all the examples that we have used have had just one correct answer. However, questions can have more than one correct answer, as in:

Which of the following are hardwood trees?

A   Larch
B*   Oak
C   Spruce
D   Scots pine
E*   Elm
F*   Mahogany.

Occasionally, the learner is asked to make a judgement as to which is the best rather than the absolutely correct answer, as in the question below. However, teachers will usually wish to explore why a learner has chosen such an option, in which case a different question format is needed. The problems that arise here can be illustrated by the following question.

The best wood to use for fencing posts is:

A   Larch
B   Oak
C   Spruce
D   Scots pine
E   Elm
F   Mahogany.

Learners might tick 'oak' on the grounds that posts made of oak will outlast posts made of any of the other listed woods. On the other hand, oak is extremely expensive, so some learners might tick some other, cheaper wood, arguing that 'best' would be the good value-for-money option. Such a question, then, might be better suited to a matching format where it would be possible for learners to reveal their thinking.

General guidelines for options

Given that increasing the number of distractors reduces the chances of simply guessing the key correctly, it is good practice to have three or more distractors. However, distractors are of no use if they do not distract, so there is no point in padding out a list of two or three distractors with another one or two that are trivial or obviously wrong. Few learners will choose such distractors, so the question will effectively have only the original two or three distractors.

You may not be able to find three distractors for all your questions. It is then quite acceptable for your test to have questions with differing numbers of distractors. However, this creates a problem if you wish to apply a mathematical correction for guessing (Ward, 1981). Unfortunately, such guessing corrections can only be applied if every question in the test has the same number of distractors. This is a serious, but immovable handicap.

General guidelines for distractors

Usually, distractors represent common misconceptions and errors that learners make. So, when writing questions, your main source of distractors is yourself as you recall the errors that your learners frequently make. Indeed, generating a list of common errors is a good way of getting ideas for questions. Provided you use these sorts of errors, then you can be sure that you have used plausible mistakes for your distractors. Plausibility is essential as an implausible distractor is unlikely to be chosen.

One useful aspect of distractors is that they can control the level of difficulty of a question. This is illustrated by the following two questions where we have deliberately omitted the keys. You will probably find the first question easy to get right, but the second less so. This is because the degree of difference between the options in the first question is wide, while, in the second question, the degree of difference is narrow. This illustrates a general rule to apply when constructing multiple-choice questions: to make the question harder, narrow the differences between the options; to make it easier, widen the differences.

Which of the following is the tallest building?

A   St Paul's Cathedral
B   The Empire State Building
C   The Kremlin
D   The Sydney Opera House.

Which of the following is the tallest building?

A   The Eiffel Tower
B   The Empire State Building
C   Canary Wharf
D   The Sears Tower.

DESIGNING MULTIPLE-CHOICE QUESTIONS

This section draws on the 16 rules recommended by Gronlund (1968). We have simplified these a little, ignoring some of his more rarefied rules and consolidating others. In this way we have brought our total down to ten rules.

Rule 1: measure important outcomes only

While this rule risks stating the obvious, we have all seen (or even experienced) tests that break it. A test should only test what is important, but there is always a risk that a test is constructed around what is easy to test. Often this turns out to include many of the more trivial items on a course. Equally, a test should not examine learners on the obscure parts of a course. So, effectively, this rule says, if it is important, test it; otherwise ignore it.

Provided that you use a test specification table (these are discussed in Chapter 16) as the basis for your test and sample from it in an appropriate way, then this rule will be superfluous. However, if you are constructing a test in some less systematic way, then this rule becomes critical.

Rule 2: write a clear stem

A fair (and reliable) question needs to be capable of being readily understood by the target group of learners. This means taking care over the stem. It helps if you can write a stem that can be understood without having to read the options, such as 'What is the chemical formula for hydrogen sulphide?' This allows learners to think about the problem and then check their answer against the options.

A stem should pose one clear problem and include as much of the option wording as possible. For example, the following question has a stem that is meaningless on its own ('businesses mostly close') and words repeated in each option that do not need to be there.

Businesses mostly close:
A*   because they run out of cash
B   because they are unprofitable
C   because of fraud
D   because their markets disappear.

The question would be much clearer rewritten as follows:

The main reason that businesses close is because:
A*   they run out of cash
B   they are unprofitable

C   of fraud
D   their markets disappear.

A particular issue in stem wording is the use of negatives. Generally, a stem with a negative will prove harder for learners to understand than one without. So, negatives are best avoided. For example, the following question is hard to answer because of the negative stem.

Which one of the following symphonies was not written by Mozart?
A   the *Linz*
B*   the *Eroica*
C   the *Prague*
D   the *Jupiter*.

There are many ways of rewriting this question to avoid the negative stem. One possibility would be:

Which one of the following symphonies was written by Mozart?
A*   the *Linz*
B   the *Eroica*
C   the *Pathetic*
D   the *First of May*.

Just occasionally, the core of what is to be tested concerns something negative. In this case, the negative may have to be used. For example:

When someone is hurt in an accident, you should not:
A   talk to them
B*   give them something to drink
C   cover them with a blanket
D   ask them if they are in pain.

Rule 3: ensure that the grammar of the term matches that of the options

If the grammar of the stem is not consistent with that of the options, then the correct answer may be apparent without any knowledge of the subject matter. In the following example, it is clear that C is the correct answer as the stem ends in 'an' so requiring the next word to start with a vowel.

A test that has a fixed number of answers is called an:
A   Multiple-choice test
B   True/false test
C*   Objective test
D   Short-answer test.

Rule 4: avoid verbal clues in the stem to the correct answer

There are many ways in which the stem can contain clues to the expected answer. For example, in the following question, the use of the word 'days' in the stem suggests that B is the correct answer as the other options do not refer to days. (We have not shown any of the options as being the key as our point is valid irrespective of whether B is or is not the key.)

How many days' notice must a customer give to withdraw money from a super-saver account?
A One week
B 28 days
C A month
D Three months.

Rule 5: distractors must be plausible

When writing multiple-choice tests, it is often hard to find sufficient, good distractors. You can be tempted to use almost anything in desperation. However, if a distractor is rarely chosen by learners, then it is clearly not plausible and might as well not be there.

In the following question, there is really only a key and two distractors. No one would ever choose option B.

In a double rainbow, which is the innermost colour of the outer rainbow?
A Red
B Black
C Violet
D* Blue.

Rule 6: avoid 'all of the above' and 'none of the above'

In the following question, many trainee doctors will know that benzodiazepines and beta-blockers are used to treat anxiety. They may be less sure about beta-adrenergic antagonists. However, the option 'All of the above' coupled with two fairly definite anxiety drugs will suggest to some learners that beta-adrenergic antagonists are also used to treat anxiety. Hence, learners plump for D using their partial knowledge of the subject together with clues within the question's structure. Generally, any question containing 'all of the above' has this weakness.

Which of the following are used to treat anxiety?
A Benzodiazepines
B Beta-adrenergic antagonists

C   Beta-blockers
D* All of the above.

There are similar problems with 'none of the above'. In the following question, the fact that B is clearly wrong provides a hint that all the options other than D are wrong. Even if learners know that A, B and C are all incorrect, this does not tell us that they know which countries are in the European Union. Hence 'none of the above' is of dubious value in multiple-choice questions.

> Which of the following countries are within the European Union?
> A   Turkey
> B   Argentina
> C   Latvia
> D* None of the above.

Rule 7: vary the length of the correct answer

When writing questions, there is a natural tendency for the correct answer to be longer than the other options. This arises from the need to qualify the correct answer more carefully than the distractors. For example, in the following question there is a sense that A must be correct because of its very careful wording.

> Multiple-choice tests should be used:
> A* to test knowledge when there are several plausible answers
> B   when there are two answers
> C   to test knowledge
> D   because they save time.

Ideally, you should keep all options within one question to a comparable length. Where this is difficult to achieve, you should try to vary the length of the correct answers in comparison to the distractors across a test as a whole. This ensures that learners cannot spot the correct answers solely from their length.

Rule 8: avoid making the correct answer less definite

If the correct answer has lots of conditions attached to it, it can appear more plausible and, hence, be guessed to be right.

> Essays are a good assessment method for:
> A   Knowledge
> B   Application
> C* Higher order skills, provided students are confident writers and tutors have plenty of marking time
> D   Arts subjects.

Rule 9: vary the position of the correct answer

If the keys to the first eight questions in a test of ten questions are in positions A, B, C, D, A, B, C, D then learners will assume that the correct answers to questions 9 and 10 are A and B respectively. To overcome this problem, the keys should be randomly distributed across A to D (or however many options each question has).

Rule 10: make sure each multiple-choice question is independent of others in the test

Sometimes the stem of one question contains information that is of help in answering another question. For example, the second question below can be answered using the information in the stem of the first question. This makes the second question useless as it only tests the learner's ability to see the answer further up the test paper.

Given that $a^2 - b^2 = (a + b)(a - b)$, what is $1,001^2 - 1,000^2$?

A   1
B   2
C* 2001
D   1,001,000

What is $a^2 - b^2$?

A $2(a - b)$
B* $(a + b)(a - b)$
C $(a + b)(a + b)$
D $(a - b)(a - b)$

A similar problem occurs when learners can only answer one question provided they know the answer to another one. In this case, learners who cannot answer the first may not be able to answer the second and so are penalized twice. For example, the second question below is unlikely to be answered correctly by someone who could not answer the first question.

When should you prune a shrub that flowers on the current year's growth?

A* Immediately after flowering
B   Immediately before flowering
C   In early spring
D   In the autumn.

When should you prune Forsythia?

A   In February
B   In August
C* In May
D   In November.

If each question in a test is to carry its full weight, it needs to be independent of all the others. In this way, the learner's performance on the question tells you something about the learner. On the other hand, where a question is linked to one or more other questions, the learner's answer will not provide you with new information about them.

TRUE/FALSE QUESTIONS

This section draws on the rules recommended by Gronlund (1968).

True/false questions are a form of reduced multiple-choice question and are generally used when it is impossible to create any distractors other than the simple negative of the thing to be tested. In other words, every true/false question is implicitly of the form:

Which of the following is true?

A   Statement A
B   The opposite of statement A.

Generally, then, true/false questions are used as a last resort. Their sole virtue lies in their simplicity, but, in all other respects, the multiple-choice or matching formats provide a more powerful test of the learner's knowledge and understanding.

Much of the good practice described above for the design of multiple-choice questions also applies to true/false questions. In particular, rules 1, 2, 4 and 9 for multiple-choice questions apply directly to true/false ones. There are, though, some special points that arise in the construction of true/false questions.

Rule 1: only one significant point in each question

When true/false questions can be construed as making more than one statement, then they become ambiguous and difficult to answer. For example, does the question below mean that all pubs serve both beer and wine or that some pubs serve beer and some pubs serve wine or that some pubs serve both? In the first case, the answer would be 'false' and in the second 'true'.

Pubs serve beer and wine.
True ☐   False ☐

Such a question would be better asked as three separate questions:

Some pubs serve only beer.
True ☐   False ☐

Some pubs serve only wine.
True ☐   False ☐

Some pubs serve both wine and beer.
True ☐   False ☐

Rule 2: the statement should be unambiguously true or false

Often the first draft of a set of objective questions will be tried out on colleagues. If some of them start debating whether a statement is true or false, then it is not clear enough for a test question. For example, the statement:

Alcohol is good for your health.
True ☐   False ☐

will provoke endless debate whereas the statement below is less debatable:

Moderate alcohol consumption can reduce the risk of heart attacks.
True* ☐   False ☐

Rule 3: aim for short statements in clear English

This rule needs to be interpreted with care as the complexity of the statement and its language should match the level of the course. However, whatever the level, the aim should be to create questions that test for what has been learnt rather than the ability to decipher an unnecessarily complicated question. The following is an extreme example of how not to write a true/false question.

In the recent past, doctors used to say that alcohol was a health risk, but more recent research has shown that it has some beneficial effects, although it can still be harmful. Nowadays it is fair to say that moderate alcohol consumption can reduce the risk of heart attacks.
True* ☐   False ☐

Rule 4: avoid negative statements where possible

The points we made about the use of negatives in multiple-choice questions also apply to true/false questions. The question:

Glass is not a solid.

True* ☐   False ☐

is better phrased as follows because it is clearer without a negative and knowing what glass is not is no indication that the learner knows what it is.

Glass is a supercooled liquid.

True* ☐   False ☐

Rule 5: ensure that questions dealing with opinions are genuinely true/false

An opinion is neither true nor false, so statements of opinion cannot, by themselves, be the stem of a true/false question. However, you can ask true/false questions about the source of an opinion and about the distinction between fact and opinion. For example, the following is an acceptable true/false question:

Mme de Pompadour said 'Après nous le déluge.'

True* ☐   False ☐

whereas, the following is not because it cannot be said to be objectively true or false:

Verdi wrote better operas than Mozart.

True ☐   False ☐

Other true/false formats

We have illustrated the rules for constructing true/false questions using examples in the form of sentences only. More complicated true/false questions can be set using a diagram or a piece of text as a source and then asking questions about it. For example, the following questions are based on a piece of our own text from the beginning of this chapter.

Read the following text and then answer the questions below.

The word 'objective' in the term 'objective tests' refers to the method of marking the questions. That is, objective questions can be marked without any judgement being made on the part of the marker. The marking is an entirely mechanical process and so can be done by computer. In no sense does the term 'objective tests' imply that such tests are any more objective in their assessment of learners than any other possible tests. Nor does the term imply that the teacher's choice of what to test is any less subjective than for any other assessment method.

An objective test can be set without the use of any judgement.
True ☐   False* ☐

Markers do not have to use their judgement in objective tests.
True* ☐   False ☐

Objective tests can be marked by machine.
True* ☐   False ☐

MATCHING QUESTIONS

Matching questions are essentially a series of multiple-choice questions all on the same topic and presented as one compound question. For example, in the question below, there are effectively five multiple-choice questions (the five items in List 1). Each question has the six options in List 2. So, this question could have been presented as 5 multiple-choice questions, each with 6 options, making a total of 30 lines of question material. Clearly, the more compact matching question format is preferable in this instance.

To answer the question below (which would be presented with a series of blanks in the leftmost column), the learner has to select an item from List 2 that best matches the item in List 1.

List 1, below, gives a number of woodworking tasks. For each item in List 1, choose the best saw type from List 2. Write the letter in the saw type column.

Each item in List 2 may be used once, more than once or not at all.

Correct answers	List 1	List 2
E	1. Cutting timber with the grain.	A Coping saw
B	2. Cutting timber across the grain.	B Cross-cut saw
D	3. All-round sawing.	C Dovetail saw
F	4. Cutting joints.	D Panel saw
C	5. Cutting fine joints.	E Rip saw
		F Tenon saw

The items in the first list of a matching question are called 'premises', while the items in the second list are called 'responses'.

Rules for constructing matching questions

This section draws on the rules recommended by Gronlund (1968) and Ward (1981).

Rule 1: the premises list must be homogeneous

As each of the premises is to share the same distractors (the list of responses), then each of the premises must refer to the same subject matter. In the example above, the subject matter is 'sawing wood', which gives us a homogenous list of premises.

Rule 2: each response must be a plausible distractor for every premise

When learners look at a list of responses to match to a given premise, they should not find that a particular response is ruled out by the nature of the premise. In general, provided the premises list is homogenous, this will not be a problem. If it is a problem, you may be able to resolve it by choosing other responses. If that does not work, then your premises list is probably less homogenous than you thought and you may need to split your matching question into two or more questions.

Rule 3: ensure that the two lists contain different numbers of items

Writers often design matching questions where each item in the responses list is used just once. With equal numbers of items in the premises and responses lists, learners can work out the final match by elimination. To prevent learners from doing this, the responses list often contains at least one more item than the premises list.

However, if you tell learners that each response may be used once, more than once or not at all, you remove the possibility of answering the question by elimination. As with all types of question, anything that you can do to inhibit guessing is worth while.

Rule 4: keep the premises and responses short

Matching questions are inherently complicated and place a premium on the learner's short-term memory capacity. To avoid overloading learners with information, it is best to keep both the premises and responses short. If that proves impossible, then it is worth considering using another question format instead.

KEY ACTION POINTS

- Use objective tests when you wish to sample a wide range of course content.
- Use objective tests to diagnose learning difficulties.
- Use objective tests at any of the first four levels of Bloom's hierarchy.
- Use a matching question when you are testing the learners' capacity to relate factors.

- Use a multiple-choice question when you can think of several distractors.
- Use a true/false question when you cannot find enough distractors for a multiple-choice format.
- Observe the ten rules for multiple-choice question design.
- Observe the five rules for true/false question design.
- Observe the four rules for matching question design.

Chapter 15

Short-answer questions

INTRODUCTION

Some texts treat short-answer questions as a form of objective test on the grounds that very little judgement is needed on the part of the marker. Such an approach leads to too much emphasis being placed on one-word response questions that, while important, make up only a part of the rich range of short-answer questions.

For our purposes, then, we will define short-answer questions as those that require the learner to produce answers of, generally, fewer than 50 words and do not require the construction of paragraphs.

Typical forms of the short-answer question include:

- filling in a blank(s)
- producing a list
- writing one-sentence answers
- completing a table
- completing a diagram.

All these question types share two main characteristics. First, they require only a very limited writing capacity on the part of the learner. Second, the questions are constructed so as to constrain the likely form and range of the answers. The first characteristic is designed to help the learner, the second to help the marker.

We have only given the answers to the questions in this chapter where they are essential to an understanding of the question design point being made.

WHEN TO USE SHORT-ANSWER QUESTIONS AND WHY

You have seen that objective questions only require the learner to recognize correct answers. All short-answer questions require both recall and construction on the part of the learner. Thus, short-answer questions test a wider range of skills, in a more demanding way, than do the objective ones. Compare, for example, the two questions below on the Frutiger typeface. Identifying C as the correct answer and then writing 'C' is less demanding than recalling the words 'sans serif' and then writing them down correctly.

(Multiple-choice version)

Frutiger is an example of:

A   a serif typeface
B   a bold typeface
C* a sans serif typeface
D   a decorative typeface.

(Short-answer version)

Frutiger is an example of a _____ typeface.

So, the value of short-answer questions lies in their ability to test recall and the fact that they require the construction of simple answers. Wherever these two abilities are important, the short-answer question gains over the objective format. For example, employees working in the despatch section of a builder's merchant need to know the names of a very wide range of items. If their knowledge was tested with objective questions, it might later transpire that they could not recall the right names when faced with a customer. A test using short-answer questions would be a better replication of the ability to recall these items when working with customers.

However, the advantages of short-answer questions need to be balanced with their disadvantages, of which there are two main ones:

- the wide range of possible answers
- determining acceptable variations of the correct answer.

We discuss these two problems below.

The range of answers

First, even the simplest short-answer question can result in a range of acceptable answers. For example, the short-answer question about a typeface above was

Planning and Implementing Assessment

intended to produce the response 'sans serif', but might well produce responses such as 'clear', 'modern' or even 'attractive'. So, what is on the surface a very simple question with a very obvious answer, proves to be more complicated. This is the hidden trap in short-answer questions. They look simple, they look simple to write, yet, without taking great care in their wording and structure, they can be vague and complicated.

The problem of marking

If we take steps to design a question in order to focus the range of likely answers on to what we intended to test, we still have a problem. Different learners may express the same correct answer in different ways. Even when they all know the right words, they may spell them in a variety of ways. As the questions become more complicated, interpreting the answers becomes more and more difficult. In the following question, the required responses are 'carbon' and 'decorative items'. However, learners could correctly put the name of almost any material (other than iron) into the first blank and there are many ways of filling the second, such as garden gates.

Wrought iron has a low _____ content and is used for _____ _____ .

Of course, we could rephrase the two examples we have used in order to narrow the range of likely answers. In general, though, the problem can at best be minimized, never eliminated.

Problems of automating marking

These two problems conspire to create other difficulties when you wish to use computers to mark such tests. Whereas computers can readily mark objective questions with total accuracy (see Chapter 13), it is much harder to create watertight marking regimes for short-answer questions. So, when you move from objective questions to short-answer ones, there are gains and losses. As ever in assessment, the solution to the question of which type of assessment to use often turns out to be 'as wide a range as you can'.

THE STRUCTURE OF SHORT-ANSWER QUESTIONS

There are many possible structures for short-answer questions. Some of these are discussed below.

Fill-in-the-blank questions

We have met an example of this type above:

Wrought iron has a low _____ content and is used for _____ _____.

Questions of this type vary from a single sentence with a single blank to a short paragraph with perhaps ten or more blanks.

When constructing questions of this type, each blank represents a word, but the length of the blank is not normally proportional to the length of the answer. (If the answers are to be written over the blanks, then every blank has to be long enough to accommodate the longest sensible response.) Definite and indefinite articles need careful consideration and, if they are required in the response, they need their own blanks.

Consider the three examples below. In the first, there are two blanks for 'an engineer'. This format avoids the too-helpful cue of the 'an' given in the second version. The third version is confusing as the single blank after 'was' leads the learner to assume that only one word is needed.

Brunel was _____ _____ who built _____ and _____.

Brunel was an _____ who built _____ and _____.

Brunel was _____ who built _____ and _____.

With fill-in-the-blank questions, you need to decide whether or not you are going to provide a list of words to be used. If you do provide a list, it is good practice to make it at least one word longer than the number of blanks, so that the final blank cannot be completed by elimination. One advantage of giving the words to be used is that a blank need no longer imply just one word. For example, in the question below, the first blank is for 'an engineer' (two words) and the second is for 'bridges' or 'railways.'

Use words from the list below to complete the following statement:

Brunel was _____ who built _____ and _____.

List of words: railways, cathedrals, an architect, an engineer, bridges.

Another advantage of giving the list of words is that the question becomes fully machine markable. You can even eliminate the risk of spelling mistakes by setting up the program so that the learners are required to drag words from the list into the blanks.

One word of caution, though – once you provide the words, you are no longer testing the learners' capacity to recall the answer themselves. As with objective questions, you are just testing their capacity to recognize the answer.

Lists

Another useful form of short-answer question is one that requires the learner to list a number of items. This format is designed to:

- clearly show how many responses are required
- constrain the length of those responses.

Constraining the length helps learners who are uncomfortable with writing extensive prose and makes the answer easier to mark.

> Name three features to be found in a modern car that help protect its passengers in the event of an accident.
>
> 1. _____
> 2. _____
> 3. _____

A variation on this is to give students a list of items to put in order or to rank. Generally, though, such questions can be put into an objective format, which, because it is easier to mark, is to be preferred.

Sentence answers

Some questions ask the student to write one or more sentences. In some cases this is because the ability to write sentences is being tested. In other cases, the sentence format has been chosen solely for convenience.

The sentence form is often essential in the teaching of languages. Here, what is being tested is the capacity to write the sentence, so no other test format will do. Examples of this type are:

> Write, in French, 'I need to buy two return tickets to London.'
>
> Rewrite the following as one sentence.
>
> 'This is Mr Jones. I told you about his work yesterday.'

Such questions raise the usual problem of marking as there will be a range of legitimate answers. The question setter needs to decide what is and is not acceptable.

Apart from cases such as the above, the sentence answers can usually be reworded in order to narrow the range of responses, making marking easier. For example, the first question below invites a rambling response, which will prove difficult to mark. If the point of the question is to find out whether or not the learner knows at least two of the causes of acid rain, then the second version of the question is preferable. It makes it clear to the learner what response is required and will produce a response in a form that is easier to mark.

Explain why rain is often acid.

_____

Give two reasons for rain often being acid.

1. _____
2. _____

In summary, then, we are suggesting that the sentence format short-answer question needs restrained use. On most occasions, some other question format will be better.

Complete a table

Lawyers use the term 'fact management' to describe a skill that is needed by solicitors and barristers. This skill involves taking the mass of material that forms a case and organizing it in a way that makes it accessible and enables conclusions to be drawn from it. The process of fact management includes such skills as categorizing, tabulating, constructing databases and analysis. Many subjects could benefit from the teaching of these skills. One way of promoting them is to directly require their use in assessment. In other words, rather than just asking for factual responses, questions can ask for the same information to be presented in an organized form. Tables are one way of doing both this and encouraging learners to think in terms of categories and relationships.

The following question is an example of how a tabular short-answer format can be used to test the learner's ability to classify objects. Questions in this format can be both demanding yet straightforward to mark.

There are many ways in which you can classify the 52 cards in a pack of playing cards. One method, by colour, is shown in the first row of the table below. Think of four other methods and then fill in the remaining rows of the table.

Characteristic	Groups formed from this characteristic	Number of groups
Colour	Red cards Black cards	2

(Based on an idea in Jeffrey, 1968)

Tables can also be used as a device to structure the learner's answer in order to make it easier to mark. For this reason, a tabular approach is often used for self-assessment questions. An example of a tabulated short-answer format appears below. When structuring a question in this way, you have to consider the effect of that structuring on what is being tested, which is that the format makes the task of analysing the problem easier. One great merit of tabular formats for questions on processes or calculations is that they help reveal where the learner has gone wrong and so aid the diagnosis of learning difficulties.

In the table below are examples of three types of decision facing a mail order clothing company that sells casual and sportswear for adults. In the column alongside these examples, write down the information you think would be needed for these decisions and note whether it would be obtained externally or internally.

Decision type	Example	Information needed
Strategic	Whether or not to expand into the children's clothing market.	
Tactical	Product position, price, quality.	
	Market segment choice.	
Operational	Progress on promotional activities.	
	Sizing decisions.	

Source: NEC CIM Advanced Certificate in Marketing: Management Information for Marketing and Sales, p4.

Complete a diagram

The final format that we consider is completing a diagram. Learners can be asked to:

- add labels (a test of knowledge or comprehension)
- add missing parts (a test of knowledge, comprehension or application)
- put parts into their correct order (a test of knowledge, comprehension, application or analysis)
- add lines or other means of showing relationships (a test of comprehension, application or analysis).

When used to test for knowledge of the names of parts, as in Figure 15.1, the test setting is much more realistic than other forms of pencil and paper testing. A diagram is therefore an excellent method for testing this type of knowledge.

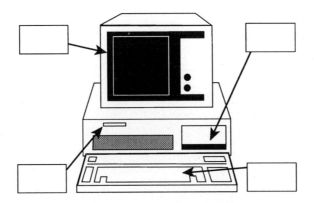

Figure 15.1 *Using a diagram question to test knowledge*

Diagrams can be used to test much more demanding material higher up the Bloom taxonomy, as in the following question testing application. Many students are initially puzzled by the verbal expression of such problems. For example, for many students in the early stages of learning probability, the following question is quite difficult.

> A botanist is sent 3 rare seeds from a plant-hunting expedition. She knows from the work of other researchers that one-quarter of seeds of this type germinate. She sows all three seeds. What is the probability that she will get
>
> 0 plants?
> 1 plant?
> 2 plants?
> or 3 plants?

Their difficulty lies in not knowing how to model the problem. By providing a diagram, it becomes clear to students what type of calculation is required. So, with the aid of the diagram overleaf, the problem becomes much more manageable. For example, they can see that in the '2nd seed' column they need to insert the probability of a seed being no good into the first empty box. Of course, a diagram also makes the problem easier and so you would not provide one if you wished to test the higher-level skill of modelling this problem.

CHOOSING THE TYPE OF QUESTION

With ingenuity, any of the forms of question that we have discussed can probably be used to test material at any of the six levels in Bloom's hierarchy. However, certain question formats lend themselves more readily to certain levels in the hierarchy. These are summarized in Table 15.1. The table suggests

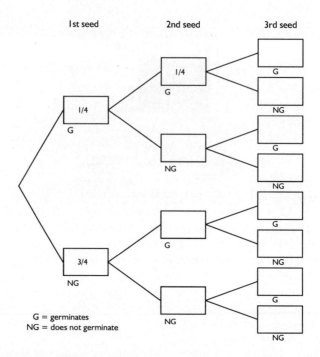

1st seed   2nd seed   3rd seed

G = germinates
NG = does not germinate

when each method is highly appropriate, useful or of little value. The few blank entries correspond to situations where the format is probably unusable. In many cases, short-answer questions can only be asked about some initial data (such as a paragraph of text or a diagram). Where this is generally the case, we have indicated this with a '+'. Table 15.1 should be read in conjunction with Figure 10.3 of Chapter 10, when it can be seen that there are many other ways of assessing the six levels of the hierarchy.

Table 15.1 *Some potential uses of short-answer formats*

Type	Knowledge	Comprehension	Application	Analysis	Synthesis	Evaluation
Fill-in-the-blank	●●●	●●●+	●+	●+		●+
Producing a list	●	●●●		●+	●+	●●+
One sentence answers	●●	●●	●●	●●+	+	●●+
Completing a table	●●●	●●●	●●●	●●●+	●●●+	●●+
Completing a diagram	●●●	●●●	●●●	●●●+		

Key
● = of little value; ●● useful; ●●● highly appropriate
+ = format usually requires some data, such as a paragraph of text, a table or a
    diagram, on which to base the question

WRITING SHORT-ANSWER QUESTIONS

Writing questions is easy. Writing ones that will produce the responses that you anticipate is hard. There are, though, three steps that aid the writing of good short-answer questions:

- choose a specific scenario for your question
- write down the answer that you hope the learners will give, together with any other acceptable answers
- write the question.

The key point here is that you think of the answers before the question. This focuses your thinking on the specific learning that you wish the learners to display. Once you are clear about this, you can then shape a question that matches the desired answer.

The need for the specific scenario

Suppose we wish to set a question that tests the learner's understanding of the marketing concepts of new and existing products in new and existing markets. Learners would show understanding of this if they could categorize products in this way. To illustrate the problem of setting questions of this type, we might first try the question in the format below.

Give an example of each of the following:
1. existing product in existing market _____
2. existing product in new market _____
3. new product in existing market _____
4. new product in new market _____

However, this could generate millions of answers and, without knowledge of the background to the learner's answer, it would be hard to judge what was new and what was existing.

Clearly, then, to make this type of question work, we need to base it on a specific scenario. This allows us to predict likely answers. A possible scenario for this topic might be as follows:

A plant nursery supplies young trees to three local authorities in its area.

The need to think about the required answers

Now the scenario is clear, we can think about the answers we wish learners to give and the acceptable alternatives. The purpose of the question is to get them to give examples of the four categories of product/market. Our preferred answers might be as follows.

	Existing Markets	New Markets
Existing Products	Young trees	Other local authorities Garden centres
New Products	Shrubs Older trees	Other local authorities Garden centres

Think of the question

If the answer required is as above, we can now frame the wording that is likely to yield something like this. Our version is below. Notice that we have amended the scenario to make it clear that its location is not suitable for opening up as a garden centre. Also, by inserting 'Young trees', we have given an indication of the way in which the table should be completed. The format and the indicative answer help to focus the students' responses in a manageable way.

A plant nursery supplies young trees to three local authorities in its area. It is in a remote location, unsuitable for development as a garden centre. The nursery's management is reviewing options for expanding the business via its strength as a nursery. Complete the table below to show the major ways in which they might do this.

	Existing Markets	New Markets
Existing Products	Young trees	
New Products		

SUMMARY

In this chapter, we have looked at one of the commonest question formats: the short answer. We have shown that its apparent simplicity is deceptive as writing good short-answer questions is by no means easy. Questions can all too easily be ambiguous or ask for something other than what the teacher intended. We have reviewed a variety of short-answer formats (others are possible) to illustrate the uses of some of the key types and their methods of construction. Finally, we have looked at how to construct questions by working backwards from the answer that you hope to see.

In the next chapter, we move to the other extreme and discuss long-answer formats.

KEY ACTION POINTS

- Use short-answer questions when you wish to sample a wide range of a syllabus.
- Use short-answer questions when you do not have enough time to prepare objective questions (but remember that the short-answer ones will take longer to mark).
- Choose from fill-in-the-blank, lists, sentence answers, tables to be completed and diagrams to be completed formats.
- To write a question, first write down the answer that you wish students to give – this will guide you to the best format to use and to a clear wording of your question.
- 'Questions' are often clearer if they are phrased as statements.

Chapter 16

Exams and tests

INTRODUCTION

In this chapter, we look at written examinations and tests. Neither term is easy to define as there are many types of exam and test. Gronlund (1968) seems to use the word 'test' to mean both tests and exams, while Habeshaw, *et al.* (1993) use both terms, but do not explain the difference between them. Brown *et al.*, (1997) avoid the word 'test', but Rowntree (1987) uses both terms extensively, although often in specialized contexts, such as objective, oral, personality and intelligence tests.

Custom and practice, then, are not much help here, so we will attempt a working distinction.

Exam	*Test*
• primary purpose is summative	• primary purpose is summative
• taken at the end of a course	• taken at some specified point within a course
• specific questions set, usually covering the whole course	• specific questions set. they may cover the course so far or just a selection of topics, such as those that have been difficult for students
• a mark or grade summarizes performance on the exam, which is a proxy for performance on the course	• there may be a mark or grade to summarize progress
• no formative feedback	• formative feedback to help learners improve their performance and plan their study

We suggest that exams tend to be summative, to come at the end of courses and yield a single mark or grade. On the other hand, tests tend to be formative and may appear at any point in a course. Feedback from tests is usually designed to help learners focus on their weaknesses.

This chapter concentrates on the design of exams and tests as a whole, rather than on how to write particular questions. We have chosen this approach as we have already discussed question design in depth in Chapters 14 and 15.

TYPES OF EXAM

There are four basic forms of written examination (Race, 1995; Lloyd-Jones *et al.*, 1992):

- closed-book exams
- open-book exams
- take-away topics
- take-away questions.

Each type is capable of variations, so the characteristics listed in Table 16.1 are only indicative. However, the variations between the types are significant as each type needs to be used when it is right for the circumstances.

Table 16.1 *Types of exam*

Exam types	Indicative characteristics	What they put a premium on
Closed-book exams	Fixed time period No use of notes or textbooks Choice of questions	Working at speed Knowledge Exam technique
Open-book exams	Fixed time period Can use own notes and textbooks Choice of questions	Retrieval skills Synthesis skills
Take-away topics	Topic set in advance to allow for preparation Fixed time period when the exam is taken	Retrieval skills Selecting information
Take-away questions	Question set in advance to allow for preparation Fixed time period when the exam is taken	Retrieval skills Selecting information

Closed-book exams usually have a fixed time period and may or may not include a choice of questions. They are good for testing knowledge, comprehension, application (of the paper and pencil variety) and analysis. It is harder to test synthesis and evaluation simply because it is difficult to set sufficiently complicated questions with data that is wide-ranging enough in a time-limited exam. Affective and interpersonal skills cannot be tested at all by written exams.

The open-book exam allows more searching questions to be asked, such as those emphasizing information retrieval and the manipulation of information. Factual questions make less sense in an open-book exam.

Where the topic of a question (or even the actual question) is announced in advance, learners have no shortage of time to gather information. Indeed, they are likely to arrive at the exam with too much information, so, again, the exam is a test of being able to organize and select information.

This discussion shows that the four types of exam are not simply options that can be used to vary the assessment method. Rather, they are methods from which to select according to what you wish to assess. If the focus is on memory and application, then the closed-book exam is the one to choose. If the focus in on a higher-level task based on the sources used on the course, then the open-book type is appropriate. If you wish to test the skill of investigating a wide range of sources as the basis for questions of the analytical or evaluative type, then one of the take-away formats is best.

Some texts argue that you should choose whichever exam format is least stressful for your students. While good advice in theory, in practice changing from one exam format to another may well also change the range of learning that is tested.

WHY USE EXAMS?

In a survey at Lancaster University 'exams were almost universally disliked' (Brown and Knight, 1994), so why should we consider using them? Race (1995) suggests three strong reasons for using exams:

- they are economical
- they are fair in that all students do the same task in the same way
- you can be certain that it is the learner's own work.

Exams are also widely regarded as being objective and credible (Lloyd-Jones *et al.* 1992, p 119).

There can, though, be a technical problem when candidates are allowed a choice of questions. Once different candidates answer different questions, it becomes difficult to compare the performance of candidates (Lloyd-Jones *et al.*, 1992). These authors raise this point in the context of public examinations where, they argue, 'not all candidates have covered identical syllabuses with identical teachers' and so 'a choice of questions is offered.' However, most teachers who set exams do so for cohorts of learners who have followed just one syllabus and so there is no necessity to offer a choice of questions.

Various authors have raised other objections to exams. Some of these objections can be circumnavigated. Race (1995) suggests that we should see it as a disadvantage that 'students get little or no feedback about the detail of their performance'. That is usually true, but it just indicates that where feedback is of importance, an exam is not the approach to choose. He also points out that 'badly set exams encourage surface learning', but we find it hard to reject an assessment method on the grounds that it is possible to use it badly. That would be true of all assessment methods and so is no aid in choosing between methods. More critically, Race suggests that 'technique is too important. Exams tend to measure how good students are at answering exam questions, rather than how well they have learned'. It is hard, though, to imagine any assessment method that does not have a technique to be mastered that goes along with it. There is a technique to answering multiple-choice questions, just as there is to preparing a portfolio. Also, whatever the technique, students should always be given adequate practice of it. So, in response to this last criticism, we would argue that you should use as wide a range of assessment methods as possible so that the weaknesses of any one method will be less able to bias the outcome. Students should also be given extensive practice (with feedback) on all the methods that they will experience.

CONSTRUCTING AN EXAM

An exam should reflect the syllabus to be tested or, if the exam is only one of several assessment methods, it should reflect a defined part of the syllabus. However, it is easy to fall back on asking knowledge questions and, in the process, test only one aspect of a syllabus. One Schools Council research project found that around 55–60 per cent of several 'O'-level exams were devoted to knowledge. In the case of one geography exam, only 6 per cent of the marks were for application (Lloyd-Jones et al., 1992).

For simplicity, in describing the method of designing an exam, we will consider the case where one exam is used to test the whole of a syllabus. The principles are easily extended to cases with several assessments.

The first step is to identify the spread of the content of the syllabus between topics. An example of this spread for the first half of a leadership course run by the British Institute of Innkeeping (BII) is shown in Table 16.2. This shows the topics in the course and their relative weights over the first three Bloom levels. For example, the first topic, the service profit chain, takes up 25 per cent of the syllabus, so it will be worth about 25 per cent of the marks. Within this topic, the marks need to be split so that knowledge of the service profit chain receives 18 per cent and comprehension of it receives 7 per cent.

These weightings – which show the relative importance of each topic and each type of learning – should be reflected in the exam marking.

Table 16.2 *Exam specification table: step 1, topic weighting (in percentages)*

Knowledge type	Service profit chain	Setting business objectives	Motivation	Reward	Leadership	Totals
Knowledge	18	18	0	11	7	54
Comprehension	7	14	0	0	7	28
Application	0	0	18	0	0	18
Totals	25	32	18	11	14	100

Once you have a table in a form similar to that of Table 16.2, you can then decide how many questions are needed in each cell and what type of questions they should be. The type of question is chosen using the principles discussed in Chapter 10. There are, of course, many different exams that could be set to meet the requirements of Table 16.2. The particular format chosen by the Institute is shown in Table 16.3. (This illustrates the practical difficulties of examining. Ideally, some of the skills here – such as leadership – should be tested at the workplace. However, the realities of the industry constrain the Institute to testing just the learners' knowledge and understanding of leadership.)

The format in Table 16.3 is generic – it shows the format of an exam, but not the particular questions for a particular exam. We can set any number of exams to the format of Table 16.3, knowing that each one will:

- have exactly the same distribution of marks between topics and levels
- will have sampled topics in exactly the same proportions each time.

Results from exams constructed in this way can be compared with each other (assuming equivalent marking schemes are used each time), enabling standards to be monitored over time.

MARKING SCHEMES

All the care taken in preparing an exam specification table and setting questions to match it will be wasted if equal care is not taken over marking. The purpose of a marking scheme is to ensure that the marker marks the question that was set. Any well-designed question should have a definable set of acceptable answers. It is the marker's job to award marks for these, and not for other possible answers. In this way, students are tested against the questions and on

Table 16.3 *Exam specification table: step 2, question format*

Knowledge type	Service profit chain	Setting business objectives	Motivation	Reward	Leadership	Totals
Knowledge	1 x short answer (3 responses) = 3 marks	1 x short answer (3 responses) = 3 marks	None	1 x short answer (3 responses) = 3 marks	1 x short answer (3 responses) = 3 marks	12 (52.17%)
Comprehension	1 x MCQ/ matching question = 2 marks	1 x MCQ/ matching question = 2 marks	None	None	1 x MCQ/ matching question = 2 marks	6 (26.09%)
Application	None	None	1 x short answer (scenario) = 5 marks	None	None	5 (21.74%)
Totals	5 (21.74%)	5 (21.74%)	5 (21.74%)	3 (13.04%)	5 (21.74%)	23 (100%)

a consistent basis. The need for consistency is paramount in any assessment. If different markers use different criteria, then the results will have little meaning.

It is not the purpose of a marking scheme to provide detailed feedback to students on their performance. Indeed, where detailed feedback is the main need, marks are of little importance and can even be a distraction for learners.

The first step in writing a marking scheme for a question is to write out the answer that you expect to receive. (In the case of long-answer questions, you might just list the points that you expect the answer to include.) This makes you aware of:

- what you will award marks for
- alternative answers that will be acceptable.

Also, attempting to write out the answer often reveals weaknesses in the questions. One of the authors of this book uses the following workshop exercise when training teachers to write questions. Individuals or small groups write what they think is a well-phrased question. Groups then swap questions and write out what they think is a good answer. These answers are then presented to the whole workshop. Frequently, the question setters are astounded at how their question has been interpreted. The moral of this exercise is:

- first, write your answer
- then, decide what question you need to ask in order to obtain that answer.

In general, the types of detail that need to be included in a marking scheme depend on the question format, not the topic. For example, for a multiple-choice question, you need to specify the correct answer(s), the number of marks and whether or not there is a penalty for incorrect answers. Typical generalized criteria of this type for a range of question formats are given in Table 16.4. (Generalized criteria for some of the longer-answer formats have been discussed in Chapter 9.)

Table 16.4 *Typical marking criteria*

Types of questions	Typical marking criteria
Multiple- choice, true/false, matching questions	Which answer(s) is(are) correct How many marks a correct answer carries Whether or not there is a penalty for selecting a wrong answer
Fill-in-the-blanks questions	Which word or words must appear in each blank How many marks there are for each blank Permitted variations for each blank An indication of the accuracy required, such as, do misspellings matter?
Short-answer questions	Which points must be included in the answer. There are usually specific words that must appear How many marks there are for each point Permitted variations for each point An indication of the accuracy required – do misspellings matter?
Application questions	Usually marking schemes for application questions award most of the marks to showing understanding of: The principles of the method When to apply it – that is, carrying out its steps in the correct order To what to apply it – that is, using the data in the question correctly What the result means Getting the right answer will usually only merit a small proportion of the marks. Minor mistakes (say, arithmetical ones) are not usually heavily penalized.

Example of a marking scheme for an application

Marking schemes for knowledge and comprehension are fairly straightforward as you can list the items to be tested and decide how many marks to award to each one. Marking schemes for application are more difficult, so we will illustrate the principles by means of the following example.

A very typical application question format is that of a calculation. In Table 16.5 is a possible marking scheme for the following question.

A coin is tossed 200 times, giving 120 heads and 80 tails. Use a method of your choice to test at the 5 per cent level whether or not it is a fair coin.

Creating the marking scheme involves two steps. First, identifying all the steps in the correct application of the method. Second, deciding how many marks to allocate to each step. There are many justifiable ways of allocating the marks, but, given that this is a test of application, no marking scheme should penalize arithmetical mistakes too much. In our example, candidates can gain 10 out of 12 marks, whatever arithmetical mistakes they make.

Table 16.5 *An example of a marking scheme for the chi squared question*

Stage	Marks	Performance required
1. Method chosen	2	Chi squared formula stated (1 mark) Hypothesis stated (1 mark)
2. Data selection	2	Observed frequencies identified as 200 and 120 (1 mark) Expected frequencies identified as 100 and 100 (1 mark)
3. Data inputting	1	Data from step 2 inserted into correct positions in the formula (1 mark)
4. Step selection	2	Steps of calculation carried out in correct order (2 marks)
5. Step working	2	Calculations arithmetically correct (2 marks)
6. Result	1	Correct value of chi squared found, given the data used in step 2 (1 mark)
7. Interpretation	2	Correct conclusion reached, given the chi squared valued found (2 marks)

Tips on marking schemes

The better your marking scheme, the easier the task of marking becomes and the less re-marking is needed. When writing your scheme, it helps to:

- prepare a model answer
- award marks only for things that are present or absent
- write the scheme assuming that your reader is an inexperienced marker
- pilot the scheme.
  (Adapted from Brown, Race and Smith, 1996.)

Strategies for marking

'On balance it is better to mark answers to each question than answers in each paper' (Brown *et al.*, 1997). This neatly summarizes the heart of marking strategies. We assume that you already have your detailed criteria before you start your marking. In that case, the aim of your marking is to apply those criteria systematically to each paper. As the criteria will be question-specific, you are more likely to evenly apply the criteria for, say, question 1 to all papers if you mark all the question 1 answers together. Even with this approach, though, you may find that issues arise about interpreting your criteria. In anticipation of this, it can help to:

* pick out a few excellent answers first and mark these against the criteria
* repeat for a few very poor answers
* review and annotate your criteria in the light of this trial run
* mark all the questions against the annotated criteria
* continue to annotate the criteria as you go along to remind yourself of how you are interpreting them.

(See Brown, Bull and Pendlebury, 1997 for some further ideas on how to ensure consistency in your marking.)

THE MEANING OF MARKS

Implicit in our discussion of exams have been three assumptions, which are that:

* exams will normally be criterion-referenced
* the result will be some form of overall grade or mark summarizing a candidate's performance on a course or part of a course
* feedback is not the main purpose of a marking scheme.

We need to discuss the first of these two points before asking 'What does the mark mean?'

We have said that exams will normally be criterion-referenced – and we are tempted to write should normally be criterion-referenced. Marks and grades from norm-referenced tests and exams are hard to interpret (see Chapter 2). The sole function of such assessments is to allocate a fixed number of places to the best of a larger group of contenders. Thus, it can make sense to set, say, entrance exams for an institution that can take 100 people a year and to simply allocate the places to the 100 best-performing candidates. Where this is done, though, the minimum standard for admission will vary from year to year. That may or may not be acceptable to the institution, but they should at least be aware of this. The alternative in this instance is to set a criterion-referenced exam with a pass mark that represents the minimum standard for admission. If more than 100 applicants meet this standard, 100 can be chosen from them using additional criteria.

Having disposed of the lack of meaning of the norm-referenced exam – and offered a way of avoiding such exams – we can now ask 'What does the mark mean?' for criterion-referenced exams. What we say here assumes that:

- an exam specification table has been drawn up
- in setting questions to match the table, the total syllabus content has been sampled in a representative manner.

These two provisos are essential if the exam is not to be biased towards certain areas of the syllabus.

Having ensured a representative paper, we can consider what, say, a mark of 60 per cent means. On the surface, it seems to say that the candidate has mastered 60 per cent of the course. However, does this mean that the candidate has mastered 60 per cent of the learning outcomes and knows nothing of the remaining 40 per cent or does it mean that the candidate has reached the 60 per cent level for each outcome or what? The answer is that we don't know.

The problem is illustrated by the two candidates in Table 16.6. Both have achieved results of 60 per cent. The first knows nothing about topic 3 and, on the other two topics has scored most marks at the knowledge and comprehension level. The second candidate has a fairly even spread of marks across all topics and all levels. So, even when all candidates do the same questions, similar marks may hide very different achievements.

Table 16.6 *Performance of two candidates scoring 60 per cent in an exam (maximum possible scores in square brackets)*

Knowledge type	Topic 1	%	Topic 2	%	Topic 3	%	Total (marks)	Total (%)
Candidate 1								
Knowledge	18	[20]	10	[12]	0	[8]		
Comprehension	10	[15]	8	[9]	0	[6]		
Application	12	[15]	2	[9]	0	[6]		
Totals	40	[50]	20	[30]	0	[20]	60	[100]
Candidate 2								
Knowledge	10	[20]	6	[12]	6	[8]		
Comprehension	9	[15]	5	[9]	5	[6]		
Application	9	[15]	5	[9]	5	[6]		
Totals	28	[50]	16	[30]	16	[20]	60	[100]

It is possible to refine the marking structure for an exam by requiring a minimum level of performance on all topics or on a certain number of topics. Consider how the two candidates with 60 per cent each would fare under a system that required half the marks on every topic to be awarded before a pass would be given. Candidate 1 would fail; candidate 2 would pass. Given that exams seek to summarize performance on the whole of a syllabus, this is a more representative result than the straight measure of 60 per cent. Rightly, it can be argued that, using the second marking system, candidate 1 gets no credit for what they know on topics 1 and 2. All this also illustrates the importance of telling students how many marks each question carries and how the total or pass mark is computed. Without this knowledge, candidates can spend too much time on certain questions at the expense of others.

Having said all this about marking schemes, we need finally to mention that, if recording what learners know is the aim of assessment, profiling is more appropriate than examinations (see Chapter 3).

TESTS

In the lists at the beginning of this chapter, we suggested that the primary purpose of tests is diagnostic or formative. They can be summative, but it is the features of the diagnostic or formative test that we shall pursue here.

Diagnostic and formative tests seek to answer the questions 'What should the learner study next?', 'Why is the learner finding ... difficult?' 'How might the learner study differently?' Tests need to be designed in specific ways if they are to answer such questions.

Test design differs from exam design in two fundamental ways:

- the focus is usually much narrower (perhaps one week's work)
- there may be several questions on the same topic, each designed to probe a different aspect of understanding.

For example, the test in Table 16.7 explores increasingly difficult cases of simple addition. Those questions that are answered incorrectly tell the teacher what sorts of misunderstandings the learner has and the teaching can then be adjusted accordingly. (In practice, this test should have two or three questions of each type so that it can distinguish between an occasional slip and a more persistent misunderstanding.)

Deciding on the sample

When constructing a test, you have to sample from all the possible items that you could test. The principles of sampling vary according to the type of test.

Table 16.7   *Diagnosing understanding of simple addition*

Question	Tests
1. 3 + 5 =?	Addition of single-digit numbers – no carry
2. 7 + 4 =?	Addition of single-digit numbers with carry
3. 8 + 2 =?	Addition of single-digit numbers with carry, leaving zero in the units column.
4. 12 + 5 =?	Addition of double-digit number and single-digit number – no carry.
5. 14 + 7 =?	Addition of double-digit number and single-digit numbers – with carry
6. 12 + 13 =?	Addition of two double-digit numbers – no carry
7.15 + 17 =?	Addition of two double-digit numbers – with carry

Sampling for progress tests

Progress tests are designed to help learners find out what they do and do not know. Usually a progress test refers to a defined part of a course – a topic or last week's work, say. The test needs to validly sample the stated area of work. This can be done by creating a test specification table in the same manner as an exam specification table (see Table 16.2). In this sense, the test is a mini exam.

However, while a progress test may produce an overall mark, it is more important to produce formative feedback that tells learners what they have mastered, what they don't know, what types of mistakes they are making and so on. This is usually best achieved by means of a large number of short questions rather than few longer ones as shorter questions pinpoint difficulties more precisely.

Sampling for diagnostic tests

Diagnostic tests do not need to sample a topic or a period of work – they can simply focus on known areas of difficulty for learners in general in order to reveal the difficulties of learners in particular.

So, to construct a diagnostic test, you need to start from a list of all the common problems that learners have with the topic or topics of the test. For example, a French language test might explore common mistakes with gender or the agreement of past participles. In other words, while exams and progress tests are based on representative samples of the syllabus, diagnostic tests are based on representative samples of errors and difficulties. Straightforward topics are therefore absent or under-represented.

PREPARING FOR EXAMS AND TESTS

Preparation for exams can be divided into three parts:

- preparation well in advance
- revision
- the day itself.

Preparation in advance

Students need to be clear about the structure of the test or exam that they are going to take. For example, they need to know how many papers there are and how much time is allowed for them. As mentioned above, under Marking schemes, they need to know how marks are awarded and how the final result is calculated. For example, do they have to achieve a certain minimum score on several papers?

Then, for each paper, they need to know:

- the time allowed
- what types of questions are asked
- how many questions
- what choice of questions is allowed
- how marks are allocated for each question
- what form of examination each represents (for example, open-book exam).

There are various documents in which this sort of information can be found. Students should be encouraged to delve into past papers, marking schemes and examiners' reports (which often include an analysis of the strengths and weaknesses of students' work and examples from scripts). Indeed, as students should be taught how to take exams and tests, teachers can usefully guide students through such documents.

Analysis of these sources should help students to identify common problems they should avoid. For example, avoid:

- not answering the question
- missing key concepts, or failing to define them or show understanding of them
- ignoring the course and its content
- poor selection of content (for example, including content irrelevant to the question)
- poor time allocation to the various questions
- ignoring the exam paper's instructions (for example, on how many questions to answer in each section)
- illegibility

- failure to eliminate small errors (for example, by not leaving time to read through answers)
- unclear sentences and paragraph organization.

Revision

Students also need to be taught how to revise. Often they just read and re-read their notes, as if to memorize a subject is to understand it. In fact, revision always needs to be an active process, one in which students use the knowledge and so acquire understanding. For example, students need to answer questions (even ones they set for themselves), solve problems, put material into their own words and so on. There will need to be some memory work, too, such as selecting and memorizing quotations. Revision is also an opportunity to sort out all notes and fill in any gaps.

Students need to be clear about all relevant aspects of the exam paper as this does affect their performance. They need to be given plenty of opportunity to be familiar with the paper, including:

- its structure
- likely sections
- choices open to students
- whether or not questions are seen in advance
- question formats (sometimes, for example, there is a set of multiple-choice questions)
- materials that can be taken into the exam room (for example, set texts, calculator).

Another important aspect of the revision stage is drawing up a timetable to ensure all topics are covered. Questions need to be anticipated and answers practised, by, for example, completing them in outline. It may be a good idea to undertake a mock exam or a cut-down version of this because, like a soloist practising before a concert, just to work through sample sections should be sufficient.

Students who need further help could consult Henderson (1993).

The day of the exam

All practical arrangements need to be thought through and made in advance. This includes double-checking the date, place, equipment needed (and its current condition), travel route and likely travel time. Students need to take spares (pens, pencils, batteries).

Students should arrive for the exam rested but ready for action. This might mean taking some exercise first or whatever preparatory routine helps the individual reach readiness for peak performance.

Once at the exam desk, students should scan the whole paper and make any preliminary decisions about which questions to answer (and which to avoid). Selected questions should be tackled positively, for example by:

- underlining key words
- jotting down key points.

For some students, it is a good idea to plan all their answers first, but without allowing this to take up too much time. Others warm up by answering a question on which they feel adequately prepared, but no more than this, leaving their strongest questions to later. Students need to pay attention to time passing, allowing time for reading all their questions through at the end and making any necessary modifications. This, once again, emphasizes the need for practice at exams and tests.

It is also desirable to allow short pauses for relaxation. Care needs to be given to clarity of handwriting and layout, checking that syntax is straightforward and diagrams are easy to understand. In exam answers, quality is usually more important than quantity.

Students need a contingency plan if, despite their efforts, time runs out. Available time may need to be reallocated, to ensure that the required number of questions is attempted and the maximum possible marks accumulated. It is much easier to pick up marks quickly by leaving an outline of a new question than polishing one that is already very good. A contingency plan is also needed for panic. For example, should a question prove more difficult than expected, it may be as well to leave it and move on to another.

KEY ACTION POINTS

- Decide whether or not you need an exam or a test (see the listings at the beginning of this chapter).
- Decide which type of exam you need: open-book, take-away topics or take-away question formats.
- Construct an exam specification table before deciding which questions to set. Write out the marking criteria for each question – the format of these vary with the type of question (see Table 16.4).
- Decide how the pass mark (or other interpretation of the results) is to be defined.
- Decide which type of test you need – such as progress or diagnostic.
- For a test, sample appropriately according to the function of the test.
- Ensure students are well prepared for exams and tests.

Chapter 17

Extended written work

INTRODUCTION

Assignments often require students to respond in writing. Responses range on a continuum from a word or phrase through a sentence or paragraph right through to theses of tens of thousands of words. The challenges placed on students thus vary greatly, both in terms of the amount of content students have to generate and the ways in which they are required to organize it.

Chapter 15 covers the setting and marking of short-answers questions, defined as those which require the learner to produce answers of fewer than 50 words and do not require the construction of paragraphs. To these we might add the linked short answers that Brown, *et al.* (1997) call 'modified essay questions'. These consist of lists of points and short paragraphs (see their examples on pp77–80). Such questions can be a very useful compromise between short-answer and full essay questions and are particularly suitable for testing the students' capacity to select evidence and give brief and clear explanations. The questions indicate the structure of answer required and focus students on the necessary subject content. They are easier to mark than more open-ended written assignments and are more reliable – though they usually take more time to set.

However, our concern in this chapter is with extended written work. The essay has always been the most frequently used assessment of an extended written nature, so we start with that. We then consider other types of extended written assignment before discussing how to give feedback on such work. We then look at how students can be prepared for extended writing assignments.

THE ESSAY

What is an 'essay'?

The term 'essay' has been used in its modern meaning of 'a short prose composition on any subject' for around 400 years, but the core meaning of the word is a trial, a test, an experiment (apparently the word is still used in this sense in philately). One of the definitions given in *The Chambers Dictionary* (1993) is an attempt, a tentative effort; it logs meanings of 'a first draft, a trial, an experiment' as archaic, but it is interesting to see that the origins suggest a much less polished product than the one we currently associate with the word.

The history of the word 'essay' thus suggests that the student should try out ideas, draft something, examine a topic without necessarily coming to firm or final conclusions. The related word 'assay' implies a bold attempt at something difficult, adventurously doing one's best.

The Latin root verb 'exagere' has as one of its meanings 'to bring to perfection', suggesting both the initial drafting and testing out of ideas and the working up of these into something more finished and worthy of public inspection. In later centuries the word 'essay' has come to be associated with only the finished pieces of work, the elegant, often slight creations of sophisticated writers in fashionable periodicals. This suggestion still hangs over students today – essays are supposed to have a smooth trajectory and a perfect finish – the feel of an experiment, a bold attempt at something having largely been lost.

In a useful chapter, Stefani and Nicol (1997) discuss the difficulties students have in 'understanding what an essay is, how it is to be used to represent disciplinary thinking, or how it is produced'. They quote research that shows that until they have these necessary background understandings students will be unable to produce reliably good essays. They also draw attention to the differences between tutors' and students' conceptions of essays.

Different types of essay

Essay questions vary considerably in nature and in the demands they make on students. At one extreme they are very open, while at the other students are given full details of the required framework of each part of their essay. Different types of essay are suitable for assessing different aspects of student learning and different course outcomes.

The demand made on students is indicated largely in the key verb contained in the question. The verb indicates to the student the required level of treatment of the topic. An instruction such as 'describe' or 'give an account of' suggests a treatment towards the bottom end of Bloom's taxonomy. Verbs such as 'discuss', 'explain' and 'analyse' require more complicated levels of processing of data. The higher levels are suggested by words such as 'assess', 'judge' or 'evaluate' as these require the student to critique or justify a case. So, essays can require the competent but pedestrian presentation of other peoples' ideas through to original, personal material and interpretation.

Such levels can only be approximate, but the question setter needs to choose a verb carefully and, if necessary, amplify what is required by further comment. Students may need help in identifying the level of interpretation required by a key verb. Several books offer direct guidance on this (see, for example, Henderson, 1993; Lewis, 1993; and Brown, *et al.*,1997) in the References and further reading section at the end of the book.

As well as the key verb, students need to look carefully at the concepts in the essay question. This is the content area the verb operates on. In the following, for example, students need to notice 'role of government', 'intervening' and 'the economy' as key concepts:

Justify the role of government in intervening in the economy.

Students would need to define these concepts, or at least make clear the interpretation they were using. Note also the key verb 'justify', indicating that students should give adequate grounds for their conclusions – an outcome towards the top of Bloom's taxonomy.

One of the strengths of the essay form is its flexibility – questions can take any number of forms, including:

- a quotation to discuss
- an argument to challenge or explain
- a case to argue or solve
- two situations to compare or contrast.

What essays test

Students have to work out the purpose of the specific question and its boundaries. They have to identify any issues underlying the question, decide what counts as information and where this might be found. They have to select relevant material and organize this clearly, often within a particular word limit. This will require them to decide on priorities for inclusion. They have to attend to the needs of their reader and this has implications for style and presentation. Students have to develop a range of skills – collecting and organizing information, planning and time management, drafting, using comments and presenting their work attractively.

The traditional essay tends to be open-ended with its purpose in need of definition, its audience unspecified and its assessment criteria implicit. The more confident, articulate and adventurous students might relish these challenges, but others struggle.

Problems with essays and how to overcome them

In this section, we look at the demands the essay form makes, both on students and assessors, and how these can be met.

The essay poses difficulties for students. First, essays take a long time to write. Second, to write effective essays, students need a set of techniques specific to the form. Some students are good at writing essays, some poor. Thus, some students produce well-structured essays whatever the topic, while others – even when their knowledge of the essay topic is good – find this difficult. As an assessor you thus have to decide whether you wish to test primarily understanding of the content or the students' ability to write an essay or some mixture of the two. Setting too many essays, as with any other assessment method, is likely to be limiting. Students who write good essays will be rewarded again and again, and students who write bad essays will never do well. To overcome this you can:

- vary the forms of written assignment set
- test by means other than writing
- set clear criteria
- help students improve their essay-writing skills (see the books recommended in the References and further reading section at the end of the book).

Essays also present you – the tutor – with challenges. While they are easy to set, essays are time-consuming to mark (thus reversing the position with multiple-choice tests, which are time-consuming to set, but quick to mark). As we saw in Chapter 3, marker variability is also an issue, so low reliability is a potential problem. As Brown, *et al*. (1997, p65) remind us, 'differences in marks can owe more to variations among examiners than to the performance of students'. To overcome this, you need a manageable number of clear criteria that markers can hold in their minds while assessing. Getting assessors together to mark sample scripts and discuss the results can also help standardize their performance.

OTHER FORMS OF EXTENDED WRITING

Essays are rarely used in life outside education. They are thus a rather artificial form – we do not communicate with one another via essays. This explains the increased attention being given to other forms of extended written assignment.

The report is becoming increasingly popular. The word derives from 'to carry back' as the individual is set the task of 'carrying back' (to a sponsor or client) information and, often, recommendations as to action. This suggests its two advantages over the traditional essay. First, there is usually a more realistic audience than the tutor. This might be a 'real' audience, such as a manager in a company where the student is on work placement; or the audience might be simulated. Second, and linked to this, there is usually a realistic context. Reports examine a situation, consider alternative ways forward and make recommendations for action. Students often perceive this as more practical and worth while than an academic essay – motivation is generated as a result of relevance.

Reports have their own format – usually including an introduction or terms of reference, method(s) used, data collected and its interpretation, conclusions, recommendations, references, appendices. This provides a firmer structure for the student than the traditional essay and it makes marking easier (marks can be allocated to each section against criteria – see Chapter 9).

Reports often also include visual displays of information – charts, graphs, designs, illustrations. These present a wider-ranging challenge to students and the variety can be motivating. Presenting a report to a real audience can also bring home to students the need for clarity and good presentation in their work. Other aspects of the required format, such as a word limit, also seem less arbitrary when presented in the context of the requirements of a particular audience.

Other formats for extended writing also incorporate an audience and real-life demands. Students could, for example, be asked to produce a review for a newspaper or write a paper for a journal or magazine. Other possibilities include summaries, annotated bibliographies, briefing papers or case study notes. Diaries and learning logs are covered in Chapter 22 and portfolios can require an extended written component (see Chapter 24).

Essays are usually completed by individuals on their own. Other forms of extended writing could require group work as well as individual contributions. The stage of research or data collection could, for example, occupy a group – some carrying out library research, others interviews, others surveys. Each section of the subsequent report could then be the responsibility of a particular individual, though others in the group could give support, for example by commenting on drafts (see Chapter 26 on group assessment).

The greater the variety of contexts and formats, the greater the likelihood that students will develop the transferable skills of writing.

GIVING FEEDBACK ON WRITTEN ASSIGNMENTS

Giving feedback has been covered in Chapter 6, but here some further points that are relevant to giving feedback on extended written work.

By definition, extended written work takes students time and effort. Some of this may be misdirected if, for example, students set off down a blind alley or misinterpret the question. Hence, formative feedback might be particularly useful, say, after students have produced a plan or an initial draft. Even a brief steer can help students produce work that reflects their ability rather than some unfortunate mistake.

The nature and extent of feedback will obviously vary according to the students, their stage of development, the curriculum area and the nature of the task. Students generally need an overview supported by marginal comments or comments at the end of the assignment, which may be linked to marginal numbers or letters. Care should be taken not to overburden the student with too much comment.

You may decide to circulate general feedback notes on an assignment, based on marking all the students' work. These may include examples of good and bad practice, probably omitting the names of the students concerned (and reproduced only with their permission). You can also elaborate feedback in face-to-face sessions.

Pre-prepared sheets, such as those shown in Chapter 5, can also ease the job of giving feedback. Another possibility is to use computer banks of standard comments, personalized as necessary (see Chapter 13).

Your job is made easier if students word process their essays and generally take care regarding the presentation of their work.

HELPING STUDENTS PREPARE FOR WRITTEN ASSIGNMENTS

Students need to be clear about a number of things:

- the purpose of the particular assignment
- its audience – whether real or simulated – and any other aspects of context
- the meaning of the question (especially, if it is an essay, of the key verb and concepts)
- what information might be relevant and where it might be found
- any details of the required structure for the answer.

The length of answer is often specified. Students need guidance on what this means. For example, are references included in the word length, and what about appendices? Students sometimes make elaborate attempts to circumvent word limits, even including frequent or lengthy footnotes that, in fact, contain substantive content. Students need to be clear what the position is, the rationale for this (for example, to help students focus, help tutors mark) and any penalties that apply for ignoring word limits. You then need to operate the system consistently.

Writing extended pieces of work involves many stages, over a period of time. Students may need help with time management – for example to ensure time is available for the important later stages of drafting, getting comments and redrafting, and attending to presentation (Chapter 25 gives advice on goal setting and planning a timetable).

One way to prepare students is to keep previous examples of written work (with their authors' permission). If possible, these should cover a range of levels of performance and types of assignment. You can also use these in an assessment exercise, to familiarize students with assessment criteria for such work. For this, you need a number of attempts at the same assignment. Students then read the scripts and rank them. The results are discussed and the actual marks revealed. This kind of exercise helps students to develop, over time, an awareness of what the criteria mean in practice.

Resources aimed at students who need help with extended written assignments are listed in the References and further reading section at the end of the book.

KEY ACTION POINTS

- Ensure you and the students understand and agree the criteria for essays – both generally and for specific titles.
- Decide what you want each essay to assess.
- In setting essay questions, ensure both the key verb(s) and key concept(s) are clearly stated.
- Vary the forms in which you set extended written work.
- Where possible, incorporate a real-life task and audience for students' writing.
- Where appropriate, set written work to be completed by groups of students.
- Help your students with writing skills.
- Give students formative feedback on their work in draft (where appropriate).
- Give students good feedback on their work, using pre-prepared sheets and other methods that economize on time.
- Encourage (or require) students to present their work clearly and attractively.

Chapter 18

Assessment of oral work and class participation

INTRODUCTION

Oral assessment is growing in importance. In this chapter we cover the:

- presentation
- viva
- crit
- consultation.

The last three forms are mainly associated with higher education, but if you are working in another sector you could nevertheless find that they are useful forms of oral assessment, suitably adapted.

We also explore a neglected area – assessment of the students' oral participation in classwork. We end with some comments on how students can be prepared for oral assessment.

PRESENTATIONS

Definition

Presentations require students, individually or as a group, to communicate a body of information to an audience. The topic can be almost anything and the information presented may be more or less extensive. The audience for the presentation might comprise other students from the same year or different years to the presenting student(s), the tutor and people from outside the formal educational context (such as those in a workplace or local community).

Assessing presentations

Presentations are a rich source of assessment. Many skills are needed to plan and give an effective presentation, including subject skills (grasp of key concepts, ability to select content) and the more generic skills relating to communication. We discussed in Chapter 9 some of the difficulties in designing assessments involving presentations – in particular, the need for clarity in what is being assessed (for example, subject knowledge, presentation skills or a mixture of the two). In this chapter, we focus on presentation skills themselves rather than the knowledge students might demonstrate using a presentation as a vehicle.

Assessment of presentation skills can be global or focus on one or two aspects in more depth. In a well-designed curriculum, students might move from the general, to various specific aspects, and then back to the general. In this section, we start with the assessment of general 'presentation skills' and then move on to look at assessing specific aspects.

Global assessment of presentations
Using presentations, you can assess:

- the identification of an issue or manageable area
- relevant selection of content
- structuring and organization of material
- time management, both before and during the presentation
- appropriate use of illustrations
- documentation of sources
- handling of questions from the audience
- manner of delivery, including clarity of speech and body language.

Figure 18.1 is an example of a form asking students to assess their peers on a wide range of presentation skills. These are grouped under the two main headings of 'delivery' and 'content'. Within 'delivery', the students are asked to comment on the aspects of voice, body language and use of visual aids; under 'content', on the introduction, main part of the presentation and conclusion. There are, of course, many other ways of organizing these basic aspects of a presentation (see, for example, the criteria set out in Chapter 9).

Assessment of specific aspects
Alternatively, assessment can focus on one or two aspects in detail – such as the introduction, voice, handling of questions. You might choose, for example, to assess the clarity of the explanations given in a presentation. Brown, *et al.* (1997) list four key ingredients of this, based on research:

Figure 18.1 *Example of a presentation skills assessment form used by students at the University of Lincolnshire and Humberside*

Presentation skills peer assessment form – delivery

Assessing individual performance

This form is used to assess individual performance in the group presentation. Each student in the presentation group gives this form to a student in the audience who is assessing only the performance of the student who gave them the form. At the end of the presentation, the observer student returns the completed form to the student being assessed.

Student being observed

Student observing

Rate the delivery of the presenter as poor, OK or excellent for each aspect listed, Use the comments box for suggestions or advice on possible improvement.

Delivery	Poor	OK	Excellent

Voice: *did the presenter*

make sure everyone could hear?

control the pace (not too fast/slow)?

speak clearly?

convey confidence and control?

sound spontaneous and relaxed?

not read out from notes?

avoid being too familiar (using slang etc)?

Body language: *did the presenter*

maintain good, relaxed posture?

establish and keep eye contact?

face the audience?

Figure 18.1 *cont.*

	Poor	OK	Excellent

look as if he/she was enjoying the talk?

avoid distracting mannerisms or habits?

refer only occasionally to notes?

Visual aids: *did the presenter*

ensure the room had the equipment needed?

make sure everyone could see?

use well selected examples?

bring the examples in at appropriate points?

remove them as soon as finished with?

avoid looking at the screen too often?

use appropriate and clear handouts?

Comment

File this peer assessment of your presentation delivery at the end of your portfolio behind the Presentation skills assessment feedback sheet.

Figure 18.1 *cont.*

Presentations skills peer assessment form – content

Assessing the entire presentation

This form is used to assess the group presentation as a whole for its content and structure. It is not for assessing individual performance. One student in the audience completes it and each member of the assessed group must have a copy of it for their own portfolio.

Name

Topic

Date

Rate the content of the talk poor, OK or excellent for each aspect listed, Use the comments box for suggestions or advice on possible improvement.

Overall content

	Poor	OK	Excellent

Introduction: *did it*

grab audience attention?

link the audience and the topic?

describe the presentation's specific purpose?

say where questions would be accepted?

Main presentation: *did it*

state the main sub-topics?

clearly signal each sub-topic?

have no extraneous content (padding)?

use recaps appropriately?

make smooth transitions?

Figure 18.1 *cont.*

	Poor	OK	Excellent

have clear supporting material?

have a logical pattern?

Conclusion: *did it*

sum up the message of the talk?

provide a clearly organised finish?

allow questions?

deal with questions clearly and quickly?

Comment

File this peer assessment of your presentation at the end of your portfolio under the Presentation skills assessment feedback sheet.

- signposts – statements that indicate the content
- frames – statements that indicate the beginning and ending of subtopics
- foci – statements and gestures that highlight the important points of the talk
- links – statements that connect the different parts of the talk and connect the talk to the listeners' experience and knowledge.

You could build criteria around these four aspects of explaining.

Assessment of the group and individuals within it

Assessment may be of a group presentation. Additionally, you may reserve some of the marks for the performance of individuals within the group. In this case, you need criteria for the contributions individuals make to the work of the group – whether in defined roles (for example, data analysis, drafting) or generally (such as, attendance, contribution of ideas). This is discussed in Chapter 26.

Conclusion

However presentations are assessed, the general principles of good assessment outlined elsewhere in this book apply, including:

- a manageable number of criteria (are there too many, for example, in Figure 18.1?)
- criteria that can be understood by students (here Figure 18.1 seems acceptable).

THE VIVA

Definition

'Viva' is a contraction of the Latin phrase 'viva voce', which literally means 'by or with the living voice, by oral testimony'. Hence, its current meaning of an oral examination, usually in higher education. The term implies a formal assessment, otherwise other nouns – such as 'tutorial' or 'discussion' – would be used.

What it assesses

The viva is generally used in conjunction with other work previously undertaken by the student, whether individually or as part of a group. You might, for example, read an assignment but grade it only after a viva has been carried out.

The viva is traditionally associated with major pieces of work at a high academic level, such as a dissertation or thesis, but it can also be used for other purposes, such as assessing a portfolio. In a viva you can follow up issues in more depth, clarify difficult or complicated areas and, particularly, resolve doubts and reservations concerning the candidate's work. It enables you to check the authenticity of the student's work (and it can do this very effectively and economically). You can also use a viva to make decisions about cases that are, for whatever reason, borderline or present difficulties – for example, students who scored highly for coursework but performed poorly in an examination.

Students tend to view vivas negatively, perhaps because of their association with decisions of a pass or fail nature, but the viva can also be used more positively as an opportunity to decide between pass and distinction. It gives students a further route that they can use to demonstrate their ability. Vivas can also be an effective way of assessing group projects and deciding how marks should be allocated to different group members.

Vivas assess a range of skills, including verbal fluency, the ability to deploy depth of knowledge and the capacity to respond under pressure. As with other assessment methods, it has the useful secondary function of alerting tutors to aspects of the learning environment requiring attention.

How to implement a viva

As with all assessment methods vivas have their problems. Students can find them very stressful, so assessors need to strike the right balance between relaxation and challenge. Vivas also risk being either assessor-dominated or led by the student's agenda, thus being either too structured or too formless. You need to ensure that there is a balance between specific questions and student-initiated discussion. You also need to be aware of the 'halo effect', which is when a student's strength or weakness in one topic or skill (for example, body language or verbal fluency) leads you to ignore others.

You can overcome these potential drawbacks, as shown in Table 18.1.

Table 18.1 *Difficulties with vivas and how to overcome them*

Potential problems	Ways to resolve them
Student nerves	Give practice (eg, via role playing)
Too structured/unstructured	Use a framework of questions
Halo effect	Keep to criteria; compare with colleagues

Conducting an effective viva begins with the preparation. You need to be thoroughly familiar with the work on which the viva is based. If, as is often the case, this work is substantial, your preparation may take some time. If it is a thesis, several days' work might be involved. The following sequence will help you engage effectively with the student's work:

- get a clear overview of what the student is trying to achieve (this should have been agreed in advance with a tutor)
- consider what questions the student might reasonably be expected to address, given their brief
- read the study selectively to assess how successful the student has been in meeting their agenda and whether or not the key questions have been addressed
- make full use of introductions, conclusions and summaries within the thesis to analyse the student's approach to the topic
- scrutinize the sources for relevance, currency and completeness
- then read the whole study, noting points of detail that may form the basis of discussion in the viva (and probably of feedback to the student by other means, such as written comments)
- make an assessment, linking this to your detailed comments.

For more on assessing theses, see Johnston (1997 – listed in the References and further reading section at the end of the book).

Vivas usually involve more than one assessor (often termed 'examiner') and, for theses, one of the assessors will be external. The student's tutor will also be involved, but often as an observer rather than an assessor. The assessors should meet in advance to agree the approach they will take to the viva – the questions they will ask, the issues they will raise and how these will be divided between the assessors. If several students are being examined, fairness needs to be considered – that is, each student should be given the same opportunities, which usually means the vivas should be of the same length and the questions should be of a similar level of challenge.

THE CRIT

Definition

The term 'crit' (short for 'criticism') is used in subjects such as design, where students are required to present their ideas for collective criticism and comment. It has emerged naturally as a form of assessment based on the likely future professional role of responding to a client's brief. Thus, a class of architecture students may present their work (as individuals or subgroups) to students and staff during the course of several hours or even days. This could carry a significant proportion of the course credit marks and form a powerful summative assessment experience.

What it assesses

A crit tests all the aspects of presentation we looked at earlier, but it puts particular emphasis on the visual component and on the students' capacity to respond to questions and criticism. Students are put in a challenging situation, simulating what, for many, will become an important part of their professional lives. It also offers a showcase for the students' work, publicly affirming its importance. Because of its many valuable ingredients, the process could be exploited by other subject areas.

How to implement a crit

The difficulties associated with this method of assessment are similar to those mentioned above in relation to presentations and vivas. Most important is probably the degree of pressure students are under and the wide range of skills they need, both subject-related and transferable. The keys to the success of crits are:

- ensuring that there are opportunities for the students to practise the required skills several times during their course
- the development of public criteria used (and understood) by those assessing (often students as well as tutors)
- careful management of the event by the tutor
- thorough preparation by all concerned
- agreed procedures (including how and when the result, and associated feedback, will be given).

Only the students who perform are usually assessed. However, as an interesting extension of this form of assessment, you might also choose to look at the way the audience carries out its role. For example, students can be 'difficult', interrupting, putting unpopular peers under unfair pressure, failing to concentrate or just not attending. Acting as responsible and responsive members of an audience can be translated into criteria and also assessed, and students may need to practise this. You might consider that the skills of being a good member of an audience are as necessary outside education as the skills of presentation. As a tutor/assessor, you also need to set a good example as a role model, by listening, asking sound questions and giving good feedback.

THE CONSULTATION

Definition

The consultation is another form of oral assessment. Brown, *et al.* (1997) define consultations as 'conversations with a purpose that usually take place between a professional and a client' in areas such as architecture, medicine and engineering.

What it assesses

Again, the assessment situation here seeks to get as close as possible to real-life contexts. You can test a wide range of skills, including many we have looked at under presentations, vivas and crits, but, in addition a consultation tests students' abilities to:

- establish rapport with a client
- avoid unnecessary technical language
- answer questions clearly
- gain essential information from the client as to their requirements
- listen to what the client says
- draw appropriate conclusions from what the client says
- check understanding
- ensure the consultation has a shape (for example, an introduction to establish the agenda and a summary of agreed follow-up action).

PARTICIPATION IN CLASSWORK

Assessing participation

We have been looking at oral assessment situations that seek to mimic the real world – the presentation, crit, consultation. However, we also ask students to take part in certain learning experiences, such as lectures, seminars, workshops and tutorials. These require varying degrees of oral contribution – minimal, for example in a lecture, significant in a tutorial. In practice, this opportunity is often wasted, with 'participation' being interpreted merely as 'attendance' and the only thing that is assessed is an associated end product, such as an essay or laboratory report. As we know, most students take seriously only what is assessed and if their oral performance in class is not assessed, they are not likely to deem it necessary to develop the necessary skills.

In this section, we show how to make more use of course experiences by assessing students' participation in them. To do this, we use the vehicle of the seminar. However, the principles can also be applied to any form of class or laboratory work, for students of any age.

The seminar

The word 'seminar' now means little more than a class in which discussion takes place, is more or less organized and under the direction of someone – usually a tutor. In the past, a seminar usually meant a small class of, say, between 8 and 16 participants; now the word is often used to describe much larger gatherings.

The origins of the word suggest something more exciting than students usually now experience. The word comes from the Latin 'semen', which means seed. Linked words are 'seminal' and 'seminary'. The connection between all these words and the root can be seen. A seminary is a place for breeding ideas (a seed plot) and 'propagating' young men and women who will later be 'transplanted'. A 'seminal' idea is the first development (seed) of an important or influential idea. Hence, the seminar should be a place in which such ideas are generated and fostered. The word implies interaction between those present so as to produce insights of a quality that is likely to be higher than any one person could develop on their own.

Sadly, theory and practice are often far apart. In theory, seminars are opportunities for all students to contribute to the cut and thrust of discussion. This suggests the need for performance in a wide range of communication skills, in and through a particular subject area. The usual pattern is for students to take responsibility, either individually or within a team, for leading discussion within a seminar series. In practice, however, only a small proportion of the group usually takes part in the seminars or, worse, the seminar degenerates into a lecture by the tutor and loses its essential point as a learning vehicle. Even the students' written inputs – intended to stimulate group discussion – can become yet one more inert input. There are various reasons for this – the disinclination of students, lack of student preparation, the tutor's need to 'cover the syllabus'.

The situation could be transformed – and the ideal of the seminar recreated – by assessing all aspects of student participation in what is supposed to be an interactive learning experience. Thus, not only students' written work, but also their communication skills, could be assessed.

Assessment criteria for participation in seminars

Attention is usually focused on the performance of giving or reading a paper. Criteria for this can be adapted from those given above under Presentations (see also the example in Brown, *et al.*, 1994, p42). However, it is a mistake to limit participation in seminars to the rare occasions of giving a paper. Other forms of participation are both equally important and more neglected. The essence of a seminar is a shared experience to which all present contribute.

Criteria following from this are multifaceted and distinct from those involved in delivering a paper. They might include:

- frequency of oral contribution
- length of oral contribution
- relevance of oral contribution
- variety of oral contribution (for example, asks a variety of questions, explains, interprets, gives examples)
- clarity, conciseness of language
- capacity to listen to others and build on their contributions
- capacity to involve others and encourage them to take part
- capacity to use language to progress the discussion of a topic and build the social cohesion of the group.

You could involve students in identifying the criteria. You could, for example, ask them to define what makes a good seminar and use their ideas as a basis for constructing criteria (see Chapter 5). This process should improve students' understanding of the purpose of such events, and their subsequent participation in them.

Recording performance against the criteria

A difficulty with assessing classwork is that it leaves no record. One solution is to video or tape record classroom performance, but this can lead to artificiality and the end result must be of good quality. Another drawback is that analysing the resulting tapes can be very time-consuming.

You could turn the criteria into an observation schedule. This is a listing of the various forms of student behaviour, such as 'asks question', 'introduces a new idea'. An observer then records examples of these as they occur. If the seminar is student-run, then the tutor can complete these forms. Alternatively (or as well) a colleague could be involved. Observation schedules help overcome the halo effect and create evidence to support the assessment result. A less demanding device is a rating schedule, examples of which can be found in Chapters 5 and 9.

Conclusion

Participation in seminars is thus complicated and operates at many different levels. In addition, you need to assess the academic content of the students' contributions. The complexity should not, however, mean that we do not try to assess at least some of the main dimensions of performance. If oral communication skills are important, it is worth while investing time in identifying and assessing them properly. As students usually spend hours of their contact time in seminars (and similar forms of classwork) it ought to be possible, progressively, to assess the component parts, much in the way suggested earlier for presentations.

PREPARING STUDENTS FOR ORAL ASSESSMENT

Preparing for assessment generally is covered in Chapter 25, but this section makes some points specific to oral assessment.

As with all assessment methods, students may need more induction into, and preparation for, oral assessment than we might suppose. As we saw with seminars above, students (and some tutors) may have only a vague idea of what a seminar is intended to contribute to learning, or perceptions may differ to the point of incompatibility. Stefani and Nicol (1997, p139) make a similar point about tutorials:

> It is remarkably common to hear tutors complain about students' lack of participation in tutorials, and it is also common to hear students indicate that they don't really know what is expected of them in a tutorial.

Hence the need for explicit information, discussion and clarification whenever a particular method is introduced.

Most of the methods covered in this chapter need extensive preparatory work. If, for example, students are to be assessed by viva they will need to re-read the material forming the basis for the oral assessment, for example a dissertation or portfolio. They should also anticipate what questions the assessors might ask and, particularly, consider any contentious points or areas in which they feel their work is uncertain. It might be worth collecting further material on these – introducing fresh, relevant ideas based on further work can make a significant difference to the assessment result. Setting up a role play of a viva can also be useful. If the tutor cannot arrange this, students might be encouraged to get their friends to help. A role play might lead to a discussion of such points as listening to the assessors' questions, talking for an appropriate length of time, body language and the need to take the initiative on occasions, for example when invited to ask questions or make any final comments.

Similar kinds of preparatory work can be undertaken for crits and consultations, depending on the exact forms these methods take in any given situation.

Students need to establish whether they are to be assessed only for the performance (for example, the presentation) or their preparatory work and associated documents are also to be included.

If the assessment is of a group performance, students need to know what procedures will govern any overall group assessment mark and the marks for individuals (see Chapters 12 and 26 on peer assessment and group assessment).

KEY ACTION POINTS

- Decide the balance in the assessment between oral skills and subject content.
- Determine assessment criteria.
- Choose an appropriate method of oral assessment.
- Decide whether you are assessing a group performance, individual performances or both.
- Familiarize yourself with any associated student work (for example, written work, art objects).
- Agree an approach to the assessment with other assessors (if appropriate).
- Plan the detail of the assessment event, especially if this is complicated.
- Decide how you will record evidence for the assessment.
- Prepare any necessary schedules or forms.
- Help students prepare for the assessment.

Chapter 19

Performance tests

INTRODUCTION

Among a list of areas in which performance tests may be needed, Gronlund (1971) lists the following:

- skills – a wide range, including communication, laboratory experiments, artistic/expressive arts, sport
- work habits – such as use of time and equipment at work, group work
- scientific attitudes – for example, open-mindedness, preparedness to experiment.

Performance assessments are thus relevant across the curriculum – from sport to chemistry, dance to nursing. They offer the benefits of authenticity (the student is seen directly performing), involvement (performing can be a powerful stimulus to motivation, particularly when an audience is present) and easy access to sources of assessment other than a tutor.

In this chapter, we look first at performance tests generally, then consider three in more detail:

- practical work in science subjects
- practical activity that might be assessed as part of a work placement
- posters and exhibitions.

Chapter 18 covers oral performance, including group or individual presentations, vivas and seminars.

TYPES OF PERFORMANCE TEST

Degrees of naturalism

The term 'performance tests' covers a wide range of assessment situations. As usual, we can view this as a spectrum. At one end are naturalistic situations. This is where students are actually performing in a real-life context – examples are in nursing and teacher training, where students are, for at least some of the time, carrying out the full range of responsibilities of the role, although another professional may also be present. Such assessment may be complicated, focusing on many different skills – both practical and interpersonal – each of which may be further subdivided. You cannot predict exactly what might happen in such contexts and this, too, puts them in the 'naturalistic' category.

At the other end of the spectrum is the assessment of performance in artificial circumstances – such as in a laboratory or classroom – where these are not the usual environments in which the performance takes place. These tests usually focus on just one or two practical skills, such as making a particular weld or using a piece of equipment.

In between these two extremes are situations that seek, in different ways and to varying degrees, to simulate real life. Examples include:

- in-tray exercises in management education, in which students are asked to respond to a selection of documents a manager might receive in a given time period (such as letters, memos, financial statements, agendas)
- assessment for life saving awards that, as well as including more artificial tests (such as administering resuscitation), simulate particular situations of danger in water to which students must respond
- driving tests, which involve driving on public roads (but not motorways or in the dark).

While there is a general preference now for more naturalistic assessment, there are occasions when this is difficult or dangerous or where it does not allow sufficient focus on a particular skill. You have to strike a balance between authenticity and a degree of control. In some situations, lives may be at risk if complete realism is achieved. For example, a trainee nurse cannot safely be allowed to undertake some activities unsupervised. One solution is to create an environment with the appropriate degree of control – such as skills laboratories in which nurses practise such potentially dangerous skills as giving injections.

In vocational assessment, the distinction is sometimes drawn between primary or direct evidence of performance (such as that gained by observing the student) and secondary or indirect evidence (such as a product or a statement from a third party).

One further type of performance test stands on its own – the artistic event.

A play, musical or dance does not seek to replicate the real world (not, at least in any direct or simple way). Such events have to be judged by criteria appropriate to the particular art form. These may be complicated and implicit. The process of creation itself may also be assessed. Productions may be elaborate and multifaceted, involving many people: writers, actors, singers, orchestral performers, lighting and stage crews and so on.

Where performance assessment is not essential

In the above examples, the objectives of the curriculum require that student performances are sampled and judged – that is, you cannot validly assess the desired outcomes without involving the students in observable activity. However, you can also use performance as a method of assessment where other methods would serve as well, and where the main assessment focus is elsewhere, for example on subject knowledge. An example of this might be learning a poem. The student may be required to learn a poem (and assessed on this), but assessment may also be via a performance (reciting the poem to the teacher or class). In this case, the performance itself is incidental as what you are assessing is the student's capacity to remember the words in the correct order. You could test this in other ways — such as asking the student to write down the words – but you may choose the performance option because it is more interesting to students. In situations like this, you need to remember what it is you are testing, as the criteria must flow from that. In our example, criteria important to reading poetry as a performance (tone, emphasis and so on) would not strictly be relevant at all.

You can, of course, assess both performance and knowledge. Performance tests of various kinds are now increasingly being incorporated into many aspects of the curriculum. For example, to develop transferable skills and in response to employer/societal demands. As was pointed out in Chapter 9 (in the discussion of presentations), you need to be clear about exactly what you are assessing – the performance itself or something else.

Helping students to prepare for performance assessments

The general points made in Chapter 25 all apply here, too. Students need the following information:

- the practical work they are required to do
- under what conditions assessment will take place (including the facilities and equipment that will be available)
- how, when and by whom their work will be assessed
- what proportion of their assessment mark the performance represents
- what criteria are to be used.

Students will usually need an opportunity to practise before the assessment and accompanying feedback, which may come from direct observation, video or audio recording.

SCIENTIFIC AND LABORATORY WORK

Much of this section draws on Chapter 7 of Brown, *et al.* (1997). The level of treatment is most relevant to those working in higher education, although if you are involved at another level (for example, 'A' level) you should still find the information helpful, but may need to adapt it for use in your situation.

Current problems

In Chapter 3 we commented on the gap that often exists between espoused and actual practice. One aspect of this is the difference between statements of curriculum intention and actual assessment arrangements – that is, the statements stress higher-level learning, while the assessment stays at the lower levels of Bloom's taxonomy. This can often be seen in the scientific subjects. Brown, *et al.* (1997, pp100–2) quote a study of first-year laboratory classes in chemistry that showed:

- every one of the 22 departments questioned relied heavily on written work for the assessment of practical work
- none assessed practical work directly
- only 6 made explicit the aims and objectives of the individual experiments
- the overwhelming majority of experiments were at low levels in Bloom's taxonomy.

In these instances, the full range of necessary scientific activity is left unassessed. Brown, *et al.* offer a useful taxonomy against which courses can be compared. This moves through the following hierarchy:

- simple demonstration – to show theoretical principles
- exercise – tightly structured experiments designed to lead to well-known results
- structured enquiry, requiring some student initiative and developing procedural and interpretative skills
- open-ended enquiry, requiring students to use their initiative in identifying and formulating problems, designing experiments and interpreting the results
- major projects that may be chosen by the student or presented by industrial or other clients.

The higher-level skills – which appear in syllabuses, but seem neglected by assessment strategies – resemble those of the research scientist (Brown, *et al.*, 1997).

You can use alternative taxonomies. The value of the exercise lies in its focus on the outcomes represented by practical laboratory work, and in its enabling you to check whether or not:

- these are varied and progressive
- the assessment strategy is testing the full range of outcomes.

Audit

Brown, *et al.* (1997) suggest that you should start with an audit of laboratory practice – cross-referencing learning outcomes, content and assessment methods. They have a useful list of objectives for lab work (p101), but not all these need to be assessed every time. The audit may show that:

- some outcomes are not assessed
- some assessments can be dropped – for example, where the learning outcomes are overassessed.

In the light of this, you may need to make changes, such as those we discuss in the next section.

Assessing laboratory work

Here we consider a range of different instruments and methods for assessing laboratory work, in particular:

- a standard laboratory report marking sheet
- an observation checklist
- assessment methods that replicate the ways in which scientists actually work
- the structured mini-practical.

The laboratory report marking sheet

Using a standard laboratory report marking sheet for each experiment has a number of benefits. It helps ensure a consistent approach across a department – students can see in advance the criteria against which their work is assessed, and marking can be quicker (see Figure 19.1 for an example). Gibbs suggests that the teacher fills in the 'guidelines' and 'maximum marks' columns before students do the work. The 'guidelines' column indicates what the student should concentrate on in that section/area and so equates to a statement of assessment criteria. Students can thus see in advance how marks will be allocated, and for what. Students return the form with their report. The teacher uses it to allocate marks (in the fourth column) and to give feedback to the student by writing comments against the different sections/areas in the fifth column. The emphasis can be varied for each experiment, to ensure variety and progression.

Laboratory marking sheet

Student's name:

Title of experiment:

Date:

Section/area	Guidelines	Maximum mark	Your mark	Feedback
Introduction				
Background				
Method				
Equipment				
Results				
Analysis				
Conclusion				
Accuracy				
Presentation				

Total mark:

Overall comments:

Figure 19.1 *Example of a laboratory report sheet (based on Gibbs, et al., 1986)*

The observation checklist

Many courses seek to induct students into the scientific way of working. This requires the assessment of process. A checklist is the best instrument for this as it reflects whatever is considered important in scientific method. You might include items such as the following:

- watches attentively
- takes the lead
- reads instructions
- ask peers questions
- responds to questions
- asks demonstrator for clarification
- checks apparatus is working properly.

You can turn this into an observation schedule, on which each instance of the particular behaviour is ticked as it occurs during a given period. Alternatively, you can turn it into a rating scale, such as those shown in Chapters 5 and 9. The observation can be carried out by a tutor, demonstrator or the students themselves. As with other assessment methods, students need to know not only the criteria but also to appreciate why they are important.

Working like a scientist

Gibbs, *et al.* (1986) suggest ways of improving the assessment of laboratory work, based on the working methods of 'real' scientists. Scientists make notes as they go; students are usually asked to submit their laboratory reports later. This leads to polished work, but the time might have been better spent. Also, students sometimes work in too leisurely a way, instead of with the concentration of the scientist. To avoid this, students can be asked to submit:

- 'instant lab reports'
- completed handouts
- a lab notebook, capturing data, ideas and thoughts as they come, and aiding the interpretation of results.

These methods encourage better observation and keep students in a proactive frame of mind. Students may need support, including suggested headings and some examples of completed work. You need to think about the assessment criteria. For example, neatness is unlikely to be a priority. You may require the reports, handouts or notebook to be handed in periodically, say every few weeks. You might decide to run occasional seminars or tutorials based on students' work. Students can be encouraged to share the content of their notebooks – for example, in the final few minutes of a practical class.

The structured mini-practical

Brown, *et al.* (1997) describe structured mini-practicals to be used in laboratory-based subjects, but also in other areas of the curriculum, such as social work and law.

A series of assessment stations is designed, each with a five-minute task. This means that in 2 hours, with 4 rest periods, 20 students can be assessed on 20 different tasks. Brown, *et al.* give examples of the application of this form of assessment from medicine – taking readings from an EEG, interpreting a radiograph, identifying a malfunctioning heart from an audio recording, taking a patient's history, identifying tissues.

These mini-practicals can sample a wide range of behaviours. They require careful design and planning, but assessment is immediate and feedback fast. Assessors may need training – for example, in observation skills and keeping strictly to timing. You can use these practicals for summative or formative assessment.

Other assessment ideas

Brown, *et al.* (1997) give a list of other assessment ideas, based on points made by Chris Butcher of the University of Leeds. The list includes:

- getting students to write a learning diary to encourage reflection on laboratory work
- asking students to draft laboratory reports then exchange them with a peer for editing
- varying the audience for a report – for example, readers of a popular scientific journal or students at a different educational stage or level – as well as the usual audience of the tutor
- asking students to draw up some advice for younger colleagues about to undertake the course – for example, problems they might meet and how to resolve them or two things to do before a laboratory session
- running a group poster session for a new group of students to show the range of work carried out in a semester.

Brown, *et al.* also suggest ways of integrating the teaching of theory and practice, such as:

- designing laboratory tasks during lectures
- holding theory sessions in the laboratory
- using laboratory time to finish reports and answer quizzes based on the lectures.

WORK-BASED LEARNING

Introduction

Work-based learning is not a method of assessment, but, rather, a context within which various assessment methods may be used. We discuss it here because of its growing importance. The study 'Graduates' work: Organizational change and students' attributes' (Harvey, *et al.*, 1997) identifies experience of work placement as the single most important element in helping graduates prepare for their subsequent lives. If there were to be a single recommendation to be made as a result of the research, it would be to encourage all undergraduate programmes to offer students an option of a year-long work placement and employers to be less reluctant about providing placement opportunities. The many benefits include the:

- chance to integrate theory and practice
- opportunity to work in contexts that are not narrowly educational
- chance to get feedback from a range of sources.

However, to be valuable, the work placement needs to be properly organized. This involves assessment in the broadest sense – that of students receiving feedback on their performance. Yet, much workplace activity is unsystematic and, as a result, opportunities for distinctive kinds of learning are lost.

So far, we have referred to work placements that take place as part of a degree course. Increasingly, however, they take place during other phases of education, particularly secondary education. Thus, if you are working in an area of education where work placements occur, please do adapt what follows to suit your own circumstances.

In this section, we use a number of terms interchangeably, namely, work-based learning, work experience, work placement. Similarly, we intend no distinction between 'workplace' and 'work-based'.

Types of work-based learning

Brown, *et al.* (1997) talk of four categories of work experience, in a descending order of specificity:

- vocational training – for example nursing or teaching
- structured work experience – not necessarily related to specific vocational expertise
- semi-structured work experience – less systematic and more informal than the previous category

- random work experience – where there is no clear, pre-determined expectation of student or employer (this may be a deliberate choice, but, often, work-based learning drifts into this category as a result of uncertain purpose or poor planning).

At the 'Developing graduate employability' conference held in Hull in January 1998, Peter Hawkins distinguished the following ways of providing work experience:

- traditional provision involving larger employers – for example, sandwich courses
- placements – often government-funded, to meet the needs of the smaller business
- project work – curriculum-based
- voluntary/community work
- part-time work – while studying
- work in the home and social activity
- simulated work experience – including the use of technology to create a virtual work placement
- involvement in the work of other people in employment – for example, via mentoring or work shadowing.

Hawkins predicted a dramatic growth in simulated experience, as the only way to provide work-based learning opportunities for all who need them.

However we define work experience, the boundaries between the various categories will be hazy and some students will move between different types of work experience.

Possible assessment methods

Many different possible sources, instruments and methods exist for assessing work-based learning. These are covered elsewhere in this book, as indicated below. Selection will be determined by:

- the purpose of the experience – assessment of a final teaching practice, for example, will probably need to be more rigorous and time-consuming than that of a short period in the workplace to gain experience
- the outcome of the experience – for example, assessment of the presentation of the results of a project carried out on behalf of the employer will differ from assessment of a learning log.

Assessment methods may include:

- specific performance tests, such as those discussed earlier in this chapter
- a presentation – for example, to the employer or to the student's peers on return to college (see Chapter 18)
- a poster session – see later in this chapter
- the completion of a project – see Chapter 20
- the views of different assessment sources on the student's performance in the workplace – sources could include the student, tutor, mentor in the workplace; see Chapters 11 and 12)
- a report linking learning in the placement to the student's other coursework – see Chapter 17
- learning logs, diaries or journals or extracts from these – see Chapter 22.

You could combine these methods to give a more complete assessment. Learning contracts may be used to tailor combinations of assessment methods to suit particular circumstances. Tasks could be completed, either by an individual or a group (see Chapter 26).

Work-based learning is an excellent opportunity to found assessment on tasks with high validity. Students can help employers solve authentic work problems, for example, by acting in a consultancy role. The audiences for assessment can be realistic and varied, including different groups within the workplace itself and other students (for example, current students and those about to go on work experience).

How to implement the assessment of work-based learning

Work-based learning needs careful implementation. It requires a partnership, and the expectations of all the partners need to be considered. This is particularly important as one of the partners – the employer – is external to, and outside the control of, the educational partner. Employers have their own requirements and expectations and these will not be primarily educational. Hence, the need for negotiation.

Usually, the educational institution takes the lead. A guide to work placement can inform negotiation. This might include purposes, roles, responsibilities and procedures (such as the frequency of visits by a tutor). The guide could conclude with a contract that all sign to indicate their agreement. Continued support may be needed, both by student and the employer, and arrangements for this should be agreed.

Students need information on:

- the work placement – both generally and on their particular placement
- assessment arrangements
- how the work experience links to other aspects of their course
- whom to contact if and when they are in difficulty, and how to make contact.

Students should have the opportunity for formative assessment and examples of previous student outcomes and assessments. Given the individual nature of work-based learning (differing students, differing employers, differing outcomes), a learning contract will often be a useful way of structuring and agreeing the assessment arrangements.

POSTERS AND EXHIBITIONS

Introduction

As we have seen, exhibitions have traditionally been used in areas of the curriculum such as art, design and architecture as a way of presenting students' work for assessment. The work presented or displayed might originate from an individual student or a group. The exhibition may stand alone or be accompanied by a brochure, a programme note or even an oral presentation. Assessment is usually summative, taking place at the end of a year or course. The work is displayed and usually a wider audience than just students and tutors is invited. Some exhibitions have a high public profile and can lead to commissions and employment. While exhibitions are traditionally associated with art, they are also sometimes used in other curriculum areas, such as geography and engineering. Similarly, while most exhibitions occur in further and higher education, there is no reason for not presenting the work of younger students in this way.

The poster session is in some ways related to the exhibition, though it is usually associated with different curriculum areas. The outcome of student work is displayed visually for an audience to comment on and, perhaps, assess. The audience may be one's peers or a wider group. The posters may represent the culmination of a very brief learning experience (for example, a two-hour session) or a much more sustained period (such as a semester). Most poster sessions fall into the former category, but they can easily form the basis of a more substantial event.

See also the section The crit, Chapter 18, as this has much in common with exhibitions and poster sessions.

Uses of exhibitions and poster sessions

Posters and exhibitions can be very engaging assessment events, both for students as their creators and for the audiences who view them and take part in associated activity. The public nature of these events puts pressure on students to produce work of quality, knowing that their peers and others will be viewing it. The needs of an audience, together with the associated deadlines, set a more realistic context for assessment than many other methods and are thus likely to lead to high validity (see Chapter 3 for more on the different aspects of this).

Poster sessions test students' capacity to present their findings concisely and attractively. What is displayed need not be limited to posters – photographs, models, drawings and accompanying text can all be included. In this, as in other ways, the boundary between 'exhibition' and 'poster session' is blurred.

Such sessions can also form a learning experience for those viewing or attending. The audience's knowledge can be furthered, their imagination stimulated. The sessions can thus form a springboard for further activity.

There are many possible applications and links with other student work. A poster session could, for example, accompany a presentation or a report; it could form the final part of a project; it could include the highlights of work produced over a particular period.

You can orchestrate a variety of assessment sources using this method. For example, students can provide their own assessment of their work, and peer and tutor assessment can also be used (see Chapter 12). The public nature of these events means that other audiences can also be involved in comment or even assessment. The assessment, by visitors/audience/clients/peers, can arise logically and feedback can be given quickly to the students. The involvement of several sources of assessment increases reliability via the process of triangulation (see Chapter 3).

The views of people outside the immediate learning environment can be particularly relevant if the session is designed to meet their needs. In a poster session exploring alternative ways of calming traffic in a village, for example, the responses of the residents themselves would be particularly important. On other occasions, skilled practitioners, potential clients or employers might attend, providing an excellent opportunity for students to gain up-to-date and credible feedback on their work. Equally, these multiple perspectives – self, peers, tutor, audience – may conflict and need reconciling, which is a challenge the students will often meet in their lives outside school and college.

How to implement exhibitions and poster sessions

Even small-scale, in-house events need to be planned. The following checklist covers aspects on which students may need to be clear. You can adapt this list to reflect the age and context of your own students.

When organizing exhibitions and poster sessions, the following factors need to be taken into account:

- the extent of the event – how many posters or pieces of work are involved
- the space available
- facilities and equipment available

- health and safety and legal requirements – these are especially important when the general public is involved
- access arrangments – including parking and signposting
- whether a presentation – or other form of oral input – is required or optional
- whether the students' presence is required and if so in what role – for example, to answer questions)
- what the criteria are for assessment – including what proportion of the total marks is to be given for appearance, layout and so on
- who assesses the students' work – as opposed to commenting more informally
- when the assessment takes place – it need not necessarily take place at the same time as the poster session or exhibition, in public.

Students could be involved in planning the event and confirming the arrangements with the tutor and any other people involved. They could be assessed for their participation in making such arrangements.

As with other forms of assessment, you can turn the criteria into a feedback form for students (see Chapter 5). Items on which feedback might be given for a poster session could include:

- clarity of purpose
- visual impact – clarity of design and use of illustration
- degree to which the poster is self-explanatory and communicates
- helpful level of detail
- information on the methods or process used
- justification for a conclusion and any recommendations
- appropriateness of language.

There might also be criteria for an accompanying presentation. The number and nature of criteria would vary according to the subject area, task and needs of the audience. An example of a feedback form for a poster session can be found in Gibbs (1992).

KEY ACTION POINTS

- Consider where performance tests might fit into your assessment strategy. In particular, consider their use for the application of skills in 'real-life' contexts, with audiences where possible.
- Choose tests at the appropriate point on the scale from naturalistic to artificial.
- Give necessary information to students covering the purpose of the tests, the conditions under which they will take place and the assessment criteria that will be used.

- Give students the necessary support in preparing for the assessment, including opportunities to practise.
- Prepare the necessary instruments, such as report sheets and observation checklists for use in laboratories and on work placements.
- Use a range of sources of assessment, including students and those outside the immediate educational context, such as employers.
- Agree the roles and responsibiities of all partners (especially for work-based learning); consider setting these out in a guide.
- Plan assessment arrangements carefully, particularly where these are likely to involve a range of assessment sources.

Chapter 20

Projects

INTRODUCTION

The term 'project' has no one fixed meaning. Projects occur in all parts of the curriculum and in a range of contexts, including the laboratory, library, studio, community. Some projects involve largely practical work, others focus on academic study or incorporate surveys and questionnaires. Projects are carried out by individuals and by groups at all stages of education. They are generally agreed to form a rich assessment resource, testing combinations of:

- subject knowledge
- process skills – such as interviewing
- transferable skills – such as time management and group working.

What, then, defines the essence of a project? We suggest three indicators:

- a move beyond the immediate educational context, from 'the classroom' into 'real life' – projects seek to develop applied learning
- student proactivity – for example, in choice of topic
- an extended time period for setting-up and completion.

Projects are thus by their nature more flexible than many other assessment situations. The methods of inquiry used will vary from project to project, as will the outcomes (for example, in length, scope, medium for presentation). Other assessment sources than the tutor may also be involved – for example the sponsor (an employer, perhaps) or those affected (such as the people in a community forming the subject of the project). Each project may be unique, which suggests the importance of negotiating and agreeing outcomes, parameters and criteria. Hence, learning contracts are often used within a project-based curriculum.

When assessing a project, you can focus on outcomes or process or a combination of the two. The outcomes of a project may take many different forms – a report, dissertation, model, computer program, an exhibition, a portfolio, an artefact, a presentation or poster session, for example (the assessment of these is covered in the chapters dealing with these various methods). You can base assessment of process on one or more sources, such as student accounts, peer assessment, tutor observation or any combination of these.

In this chapter, we focus mainly on projects in further and higher education. The general principles are the same, however, at all stages and if you are working, for example, in a school or as a trainer in industry, you can adapt the points to suit your own context.

HOW TO IMPLEMENT PROJECTS

Projects need careful implementation. Problems can include:

- students choosing projects that are too ambitious in scope, outcome or the amount of time needed
- vague assessment criteria
- projects drifting or losing their way
- individuals contributing unequally to group projects
- projects which are time-consuming to mark.

You can overcome all these potential problems by:

- helping students define their projects carefully and anticipating the resources they will need; time can be allocated within the curriculum for this planning
- holding strategically positioned meetings with students to review progress
- ensuring that the assessment criteria are sufficiently sharp
- using strategies to address unequal student contributions to group projects (see Chapter 26)
- involving sources other than the tutor (often they should be involved) in assessment (and see Chapter 27).

Carefully scheduled meetings with a tutor are particularly important. Sometimes students are left entirely on their own to complete their projects – perhaps on the assumption that they need no help or that it might distort the result or to economize on tutor time. In these circumstances, students receive no formative feedback and, thus, their project is assessed only summatively.

Regular meetings help keep projects on track, help students to produce their best work and provide opportunities to learn. Brown, *et al.* (1997) quote Wright's finding, that successful supervisors schedule regular and frequent meetings with their students and review progress at these times, too. Wright's work related to research supervision, but the same point applies to any form of project work. The meetings need not necessarily be long, but they do need an agenda and a focus, and students should prepare for them. Group rather than individual tutorials are often perfectly adequate if they focus on matters of common interest and are based on students' agendas.

Part of the initial plan should be a schedule or timetable, and you and the student should monitor this, especially as developing good time management is often one of the expressed aims of projects.

Whether they are working as individuals or groups, students can be encouraged to support one another. They may need help in developing the skills of giving and receiving feedback (see Chapter 6).

Points made elsewhere in this book apply to projects as to other forms of assessment. Particularly important with extended work in which the individual has to take the initiative are careful briefing, clear criteria and associated guidelines on how to proceed. Students working on their independent studies at the University of Lincolnshire and Humberside, for example, are provided with a reference guide, the contents of which we set out in Figure 20.1.

ASSESSMENT ISSUES

Three assessment issues are particularly relevant to projects:

- adopting a staged approach to assessment
- helping students to reflect on their learning
- achieving validity and reliability in project assessment.

Let us look at each of these in turn.

A staged approach to project assessment

We have pointed out the dangers of an 'all or nothing' summative assessment. In the previous section, we suggested ways in which students can be supported throughout their projects, including dividing projects into stages and holding regular progress meetings. You can extend this approach into the assessment arrangements. You could assess work at the completion of all or some of the stages. These could include:

- the definition of the problem or topic
- a literature search (or its equivalent)
- the formulation of an appropriate method to use to tackle the problem or topic

230

Reference Guide to the Planning and Production of an Independent Study

Contents

Figure 20.1 *The contents page of the* Reference Guide to the Planning and Production of an Independent Study *used by students at the University of Lincolnshire and Humberside*

- substantive content issues – understanding and interpretation of data, development of a conceptual framework
- the presentation and communication of findings.

You may need to negotiate the precise stages: not all projects lend themselves to this particular division.

Assessment of the work at each stage could be formative or summative. To assess each summatively might be too demanding in tutor workload and too constraining for students. One option is to assess the project proposal as a separate item from the finished product. This is both summative – testing the student's ability to formulate a sound proposal – and formative – in that it helps the student undertake the chosen project.

As an example, at one university, students undertake a unit in their second year of undergraduate study. This leads to the submission of a proposal for the independent study they will complete in their final year. The proposal is assessed and counts for 12 credit points. A student handbook explains the aims and rationale of the planning for independent study unit, its learning outcomes and how these are assessed. A format is supplied for the independent study proposal, of which the main sections are:

- proposed area/title
- aim/objectives of the study
- literature review
- methodology
- resources
- outline programme of work
- proposed form of assessment
- overall presentation of the proposal.

Each of these is expanded in the handbook, with indications of what might be covered.

Assessing reflection

A project may be the culmination of the students' course. It is also often seen, more or less explicitly, as a means by which students develop transferable skills. For these two reasons, you might build an element of personal reflection into the process and assess this. Continuing the example given above, in the planning for independent study unit at level 2 (worth 12 credit points), 30 per cent of the student's assessment is allocated to a 1000-word reflective critique covering topics such as:

- the student's aims and how far these were achieved

- problems the student encountered and how these were tackled
- how strengths were built on and weaknesses addressed.

In the independent study at level 3 (worth 24 credit points), 10 per cent of the student's assessment is allocated to a 1000-word critical evaluation of the independent study process, covering similar areas.

You can also assess reflective practice by means of an individual or group interview or viva. Sometimes questions on projects are set as part of a traditional exam. If so, the purpose of this needs to be clear. For example, it might be to move the student beyond the detail of the project to a consideration of its implications or to explore the strengths and weaknesses of the approach used.

Validity and reliability

Finally, how do projects perform against the twin goals of validity and reliability?

Projects often have high validity in relation to several of the areas addressed in Chapter 3 as they require the student to apply skills and knowledge in a real context. Reliability is more complicated. The variety of projects – one of their strengths – might be a weakness when it comes to reliability. On the other hand, projects (like essays) are often assessed against generic criteria. In this case, the ability to perform well in a project on one topic might also suggest the ability to perform well in a project on a different topic.

Figure 20.2 *General assessment criteria for independent study and criteria for a dissertation (University of Lincolnshire and Humberside)*

Assessment criteria

All independent studies must meet certain criteria which have been identified by the university. They require that:

- relevant literature is identified and reviewed
- there is appropriate contextualisation – for example, by setting the 'problem to be investigated' in both an academic context and its broader context (economic, regional, social, political, artistic, technical and so on)
- problems are effectively identified and solved
- appropriate aims and objectives are formulated
- appropriate data collection methods are identified and applied
- data is interpreted and related to relevant research
- the report is written and presented clearly in a form appropriate to the study
- there is good presentation of all aspects of the assessed work
- the report adheres to accepted academic conventions.

Figure 20.2 *cont.*

Assessment criteria for a dissertation

Section	Criteria
Abstract	Succinctly outlines: • the nature of the research • the research methodology • the results and/or main discussion • the conclusions and recommendations
Introduction	• describes the research problem • gives full background • includes limitations • clearly identifies the aims, objectives and hypothesis (if appropriate) • gives a brief introduction to the research methodology and justifies this choice • clearly identifies the theoretical framework • outlines the structure of the report
Main body	• uses a wide range of relevant texts to set the report into context of existing knowledge • covers the main threads of the study • covers the main investigative techniques used • clearly states and justifies data collection method(s) • presents results and/or main discussion clearly and logically • correctly presents any tables and comments on these as necessary • uses appropriate statistical techniques
Conclusions and recommendations	• draw together the main points in the report • refer back to the aims, objectives and hypothesis • set the research into wider context • clearly list appropriate recommendations • identify fruitful areas for further research (if appropriate)
Bibliography and references	• are correctly cited and listed according to the appropriate referencing system
Report overall	• communicates clearly in written and/or other forms of presentation • is carefully organised, creative and well presented • adheres to accepted academic conventions • demonstrates effective and appropriate information technology skills • communicates as a coherent and tightly-structured whole.

The likelihood of reliable assessment would be enhanced by clearly stating criteria that apply across all projects. Also, specific criteria applying to individual projects need to be clear and set at an appropriate level. Figure 20.2, following on from our earlier example, shows the general assessment criteria applied to all independent studies at one university. The specific criteria for a study taking the form of a dissertation are then shown. Students and tutors can negotiate within these frameworks.

You should give as much information as possible to guide students, such as any breakdown of marks. This also aids reliability in the subsequent assessment. If the project accounts for a significant proportion of the students' credit mark, you may need to involve a second marker, for example in borderline cases.

KEY ACTION POINTS

- Define the skills you wish to assess through a project.
- Decide whether you are assessing the product or process or both.
- Negotiate criteria with students as necessary; agree/explain any division of marks (for example, between different aspects of the project and between the group and individuals).
- Invest time early on agreeing a plan.
- Support students during the project – by means of progress meetings or interim assessments.
- Involve a range of sources of assessment where possible – for example, peers ,and employers as well as tutors.

Chapter 21

Assessing problem solving

INTRODUCTION

In this chapter, we look at assessing problem solving. We shall not discuss teaching problem solving as excellent accounts of appropriate teaching strategies can be found in various books (such as Brown *et al.*, 1997; Ausubel and Robinson, 1971; Glass and Holyoak, 1986; Gagné, 1970; and, very importantly, for mathematics, Polya, 1957).

Before discussing just what we mean by problem solving, we need to make the point that the term is often used to refer to mathematical problems. Calculations are a type of problem solving, but in this chapter we will look at a much wider interpretation of the term.

THE NATURE OF PROBLEMS

Exactly what a problem is can be hard to define, even though we all know one when we see it. Kahney (1986) sees problems as having two very simple characteristics:

- a person has a goal
- they are not able to reach it.

Other authors (for example, Glass and Holyoak, 1986) see a problem as having four components:

- a goal – that is, the solution you want
- objects – things you can use to reach the goal
- operations – permitted actions to reach the goal
- constraints – things you are forbidden from doing.

For example, in the case of the following simple statistical problem, these components are shown in square brackets.

Without using a calculator [constraint] calculate [operation] the probability of getting more than 75 heads when a coin is tossed 100 times [goal]. You may consult statistical tables [object].

From Kahney's two characteristics, he derives a definition of a problem and problem solving (1986): 'Whenever you have a goal which is blocked for any reason – lack of resources, lack of information, and so on – you have a problem. Whatever you do in order to achieve your goal is problem solving.'

Kahney's definition encapsulates the problem of discussing the assessment of problem solving. Problems include problems of living (such as 'I have been made redundant and I want another job'), mathematical problems (such as 'What is the highest common factor of 124 and 36?'), social problems (such as 'How can we reduce crime?') and business ones (such as 'Should we make a takeover bid for company X?'). From this wide range, we shall select two major categories of problems found in education and training:

- the mathematical, scientific and engineering type
- the social sciences and business type.

As Brown *et al.* (1997, p141) say, problems in the mathematical, scientific and engineering areas tend to be ones where 'methods and solutions are known to tutors'. To a lesser extent, this is also true of problems in the social sciences and in business. It is this 'known to tutors' factor that allows us to assess learner performance.

Another way of thinking about the 'known to tutors' factor is the concept of well- and ill-defined problems. 'In a *well-defined problem*, the solver is provided with all the information needed in order to solve the problem.' (Kahney, 1986, p20, author's italics). On the other hand 'An ill-defined problem, that is, an ill-structured problem, is one in which little or no information is provided...' (Kahney, 1986, p21).

It can be seen from Kahney's definitions (which are fully consistent with the views of other authors) that most problems in maths, science and engineering fall into the well-defined type whereas most problems in the social sciences and business fall into the ill-defined type.

PRINCIPLES OF PROBLEM SOLVING

A taxonomy of problem solving

When we wish to assess problem solving, we need to know which levels of learning are involved. Bloom's taxonomy is not very helpful here, except for simple problems where the learner applies an identified method. When that is the case, the learner needs to know (level 1) the method, comprehend it (level 2) and apply it (level 3).

A more helpful and extensive taxonomy of problem solving is suggested by Brown, Bull and Pendlebury (1997), based on the work of Plants, *et al.* (1980). They identify five categories of learning shown in Table 21.1. Each succeeding level moves further and further from 'methods known to tutors' and so becomes increasingly difficult to assess. It is not entirely clear, though, that this taxonomy is genuinely hierarchical or that it uniquely assigns a level to a problem. For example, solving a given problem may require diagnosis, the use of routines and interpretation. At what level, then, is this problem? So, while the model can help clarify ideas about the skills that are needed to solve a given problem, thereby indicating how it might be assessed, it may not be a sufficient model to guide the design of problem solving assessments.

Table 21.1 *A taxonomy of problem solving (based on Brown, et al., 1997, p144)*

Level	Learning activities	Examples
Routines	Using routine operations where the learner does not have to decide what to do	Converts °F to °C Finds the area under a curve
Diagnosis	Choosing the routine to use	When factorizing an expression, recognizes that the difference of two squares is a good method to use In a case study, chooses an approach that is well-matched to the nature of the problem
Strategy	Choosing a range of routines and deciding the order in which to use them	Chooses an overall treatment (that is, a combination of different therapies) for a patient with depression In a case study, brings together ideas from various sources, eg, marketing, economics and psychology

| Interpretation | Converting the problem into a form in which it can be solved | Given a verbal description of a problem, identifies variables and their values
Abstracts key factors from a lengthy case study |
| Generation | Creating new routines, rather than applying those that have been taught | In a case study, uses an innovative way of looking at the problem |

Stages in solving a problem

A more useful approach is perhaps that of Polya (1957), who offers a very simple model of the stages involved in solving any problem:

- understand the problem
- devise a plan
- carry out the plan
- look back – have I solved the problem?

Glass and Holyoak (1986) elaborate on this model to include the need to reformulate the problem if the initial plan does not work.

The power of Polya's approach when applied to assessment is its universality. Indeed, it is hard to envisage a satisfactory solution to any problem set for assessment that does not include each of the four stages. Here, then, we have the basis of a checklist for thinking about assessing any problem.

What are we trying to assess?

With this background to what problem solving is, we can now ask what it is that we wish to assess. A simple model for assessing problem solving is to use Polya's four stages and ask the following questions.

- Has the learner understood the problem?
- Has the learner devised an appropriate plan?
- Did the learner carry out the plan correctly?
- Did the learner evaluate the correctness or appropriateness of the result?

Here, we have the essentials of a set of generalized marking criteria that we can elaborate on for any given problem. We have used these as the basis for developing the initial criteria for the two problems shown in Table 21.2 in order to illustrate how Polya's ideas can be developed.

Table 21.2 *Deriving criteria for the stages of problem solving*

Stage	Solve $x^2 + x - 6 = 0$	Marketing case study
Understood the problem?	Shows that expects one or two answers of form $x = $ <number>	Shows that the essentials of what needs to be achieved have been identified
Devised an appropriate plan?	Recognizes that this is a quadratic equation Either uses the standard formula (clumsy solution) or looks for factors of 6 (best solution)	Plan addresses the core issues Plan is feasible Plan has a reasonable prospect of achieving the objective
Carried out the plan correctly?	Plan chosen at previous stage carried out correctly to yield $x = 2$ and $x = -3$	Steps in plan are clearly set out Time allocations are reasonable Resource allocations are reasonable (It is rarely possible to carry out the plan for assessment purposes.)
Evaluated the result?	Puts results back into the original equation to confirm them	The plan has been evaluated and its strengths and weaknesses identified

The first problem (Solve $x^2 + x - 6 = 0$) is routine (and, hence, well defined). Learners should recognize it as a request to solve a quadratic equation. Learners will know two methods of solving this, so, when they make their plan, they will need to choose between the methods. One method (the formula) is clumsy for such a simple case, while the other (looking for factors) is more elegant. The marking scheme might therefore penalize use of the formula as it is not a particularly appropriate plan.

The second problem is ill defined. It assumes that the learners are given a case study of a marketing problem and have to prepare a plan to solve the problem. In assessing this type of problem, we face two difficulties. First, there are probably many different, but equally good solutions – marketing is about imagination as much as it is about the systematic application of known methods. Second, learners cannot actually solve the problem – all they can do is describe how they would set about solving it. We just have to hope that writing good answers to questions is a reasonable indication of actual performance at work. Such a hope is probably optimistic. We might be better off assessing how the learners solve real problems at work (see the discussion of validity in Chapter 3).

For both these diverse problems, Polya's four steps seem helpful in prompting ideas for marking criteria.

Developing marking schemes

We have now established that Polya's stages provide a useful basis for structuring a marking scheme. They do not, however, give us enough detail to be a marking scheme in their own right, so we now need to consider that aspect in more detail.

In Table 21.3, we have expanded Polya's criteria (in the first column) to show the main types of error (in the second column) that learners might make at each stage in a typical problem. The shaded areas represent errors that will only occur with well-defined problems, while the unshaded areas generally apply to all types of problem. The first column reminds us what we are looking for in an assessment of problem solving – the ability to use the methods of problem solving. For example, in the case of a maths problem, we are not testing, say, the ability to make arithmetical calculations correctly. Important as arithmetical ability is, it should be tested separately from problem solving. In this way, the mark achieved in problem solving is not distorted by the learner's failings in arithmetic. That does not mean that marks cannot be deducted for arithmetical (or other non-problem solving) errors, but that the majority of marks should be awarded for problem solving itself.

In the second and third columns, we have set out typical errors and suggested how the marking system might respond to these.

You can choose to mark positively, awarding marks to each item that is present in the first column of Table 21.3, or negatively, by deducting marks for the errors in the second column.

Table 21.3 *Marking implications of errors in problem solving (the shaded areas represent errors that will only occur with well-defined problems, the unshaded areas generally apply to all types of problem)*

Problem-solving criteria	Errors	Marking implications
Problem understood	No attempt at solution because not understood Attempts to solve a different problem	These errors may lead to no marks being awarded for any part of the problem
Devised an appropriate plan, ie has chosen an appropriate strategy or method	Wrong method chosen	No marks for choice of method as this error will almost certainly negate all the rest of the work – it may be impossible to give any marks from here on

Table 21.3 *cont.*

	Method remembered incorrectly	Partial marks for choice of method – for subsequent stages, mark on the assumption that this was the correct method
	Useless strategy chosen; could never yield a solution	No marks for strategy – may not be possible to mark any stages beyond this one
	Poor strategy chosen, but could yield a solution	Partial marks for strategy – deduct marks for poor strategy; then mark using the learner's strategy
Carried out the plan correctly, ie used the method in the correct way, eg variables correctly matched to real-world data; data input correctly	Variables incorrectly matched	Award marks for items correctly input; then mark using the learner's data
	Data incorrectly inserted, eg wrong units used	Award marks for variables correctly used; then mark using the learner's assumptions (if feasible)
	Stages done in wrong order	Reduced marks for order of stages.
	Errors in application of stages	Reduced marks for application of stages
Evaluated the result – for correctness	No check Invalid method of checking Valid method, incorrectly done	All these errors would reduce the learner's mark for checking
– for meaning in the real world	No interpretation Invalid interpretation	Interpretation should be marked against the result the learner found. If this is correctly interpreted, full marks for interpretation can be awarded

Our discussion of problem solving has now established the essential nature of this skill and the key elements that we are looking for when assessing problem solving. We can now move on to look at some question and problem formats.

METHODS FOR ASSESSING PROBLEM SOLVING

A wide range of methods can be used to test problem-solving ability. The choice between them depends on the subject matter and the aspect of problem solving that you wish to focus on. The two principal methods are:

- calculate/solve/prove-type problems
- case studies.

The former are widely used in maths, sciences and engineering, while the latter appear in social sciences and business. All of these methods have been discussed elsewhere in this book, so we do not need to say much more about them.

Calculate/solve/prove

Generally, most problems of the calculate/solve/prove variety are tests of application or of analysis. In Figure 10.3 of Chapter 10, we listed the methods that can be used to test application. We have repeated these in Table 21.4, along with some comments on their relevance to calculate/solve/prove questions.

Table 21.4 *Methods for assessing calculate/solve/prove problems*

Methods	*Use for calculate/solve/prove problems*
Short-answer questions	Useful when you wish to check the correct result of each step, but do not wish to see the detailed working or reasoning
Fill-in-the-blank questions	Useful when you wish to check the correct result of each step, but do not wish to see the detailed working or reasoning
Create/do something	Useful when you wish to see the detailed reasoning and the results of each step in the method
Long-answer questions	Not of much value for calculate/solve/prove problems
Project	Not of much value for calculate/solve/prove problems
Case study	Not of much value for calculate/solve/prove problems

Your choice of method mainly depends on what you wish to mark. If you only wish to mark the outcome of each stage of a method, then fill-in-the-blank questions are ideal. The following question shows the use of the fill-in-the-blank formula for this purpose.

> How much will it cost to carpet a room 4 m x 3.5 m with carpet costing £15.00 per square metre? Write the results of your calculations in the spaces below.
>
> The area of the room is _____.
>
> The cost of the carpet for this area is _____.

The above format is not very helpful if you wish to give feedback on the student's errors as the nature of their errors may be hard to discern. Where you do wish to follow all their reasoning, then you need a freer answer format in which they write down every step in their thinking. If that is too free, then you can impose some structure by the way you word your question. The 'rare seed' example in Chapter 15 illustrates the principle. In its first form, without the diagram, students may have difficulty with the open format. The diagram creates a simpler, stepped version of the problem. This version also helps to reveal where students are going wrong and so gives more opportunity for formative feedback.

Methods for assessing subsets of problem-solving skills

There is a range of methods that can be used to assess an aspect of problem solving rather than solving a whole problem. When learners are asked to solve a whole problem, this might take them many hours. For example, a case study may need five to ten hours of work. Such time-consuming processes result in very few attempts to learn any one stage of problem solving. It can be more effective to provide situations in which one aspect of problem solving can be quickly tackled and assessed many times and a range of techniques is available to do this. Five such techniques are discussed in depth in Angelo and Cross (1993). These are summarized below.

Analytical memos
In this method, the learners are given a simulated problem that might occur in an organization and they have to write a memo (say one or two pages long) to a superior analysing the problem and proposing a solution. This method is particularly suitable for business studies and the social sciences. For example, the problem posed could be traffic congestion or a difficult pupil in a school.

Video recordings of process
Sometimes (particularly in formative assessment), the assessment is more

focused on how the learners tackle the problem (that is, process) than on the outcome. Process can be difficult to capture on paper, but easier to capture on videotape. Learners can record themselves in groups involved in a complicated process (such as diagnosing a patient's illness). Later, the groups can assess the steps in the process using criteria agreed when the problem was set.

Documented solutions

A particular difficulty in teaching problem solving is to get learners to reflect on the process. On the basis of the adage 'if it is important, assess it', this method encourages reflection. Learners are given a comparatively short problem to solve, but their solution must record their reasoning at every step. This assessment technique is particularly valuable as a diagnostic tool because it helps reveal the false thinking that led to errors in the solution. To encourage learners to reflect further on their work, they can be asked to give mini-presentations to explain their reasoning at each step. Others should then be encouraged to challenge this thinking or to give their own reasoning.

Problem recognition

Another difficulty students have in problem solving is recognizing the type of problem they have to solve. (Polya's (1957) many questions to help learners identify the nature of a problem remind us how difficult learners find this.) The method of problem recognition allows this one skill to be developed and assessed in isolation from the other aspects of problem solving. It involves presenting learners with a number of problems stated in a form in which they are only required to identify what type of problem each one is and the method they would use to solve it. The solution is not carried out. For example, ten statistical problems can be presented and the learners asked, 'What test would you use for each of these?' The method forces students to focus on the factors that identify the type of problem.

What's the principle?

This technique focuses on the principles being illustrated by given cases. This is another area of difficulty for learners. They may be able to solve problems presented as formal problems, but when presented with the complexity of a real-life problem, they are often unable to map it onto the principles and methods they know.

Learners are given a list of principles that they have been taught. They are then given a range of scenarios and have to identify which principles are at work in each scenario.

KEY ACTION POINTS

- Choose a taxonomy of problem solving before you decide how to assess a problem. This ensures that your assessment takes account of each step in the solution.
- Use the taxonomy in Table 21.1 when assessing progression in problem solving. Simple problems will match the early stages, while more complicated problems will match the later ones.
- Use the taxonomy in Table 21.2 when considering the steps within any one problem.
- Use marking schemes that anticipate likely errors and take into account the effects of following an error through the remaining stages of a problem.
- Promote problem-solving abilities by means of analytical memos, video recordings of process, documented solutions, problem recognition and what's the principle?

PART FIVE

Recording and reporting

Chapter 22

Recording, collecting and presenting evidence

INTRODUCTION

The subheadings in this chapter contain terms that are sometimes referred to as assessment methods, such as diaries and portfolios. We think that it is better to think of them as means by which students record and collect evidence. This could be evidence of process (how an aid for the disabled was designed; how a student planned an experiment) or of outcome (how well the aid worked; what the experimental results were).

In each case, though, the purpose of the diary or portfolio is to collect information that will help to demonstrate the achievement of some learning outcome that could have been assessed in some other way. For example, a nurse who is learning to write care plans may use a diary to record how she did this with a particular patient. She may also use the diary to reflect on what she did and its outcome. All this, though, is preparatory to the assessment question 'Is this nurse now fully able to write care plans?' It is unlikely that such a question can be answered merely from the diary.

Some of the methods described in this chapter also involve a possible conflict of purpose in that they may serve to both promote learning and assess it. This is particularly true of diaries, logs and journals. In these circumstances, there is a risk that the requirements for learning (such as openness and experimentation) will conflict with students' more cautious behaviour when being assessed (Chapter 1 discusses the purposes of assessment).

You can use the methods of recording, collecting and presenting evidence discussed in this chapter with students of any age. You may need to adapt the material to suit the level of sophistication of your own students and the context in which you and they are working.

DIARIES

Definition

The diary is a personal means for students to chart over time (for example, day-by-day, week-by-week or month-by-month) a selection of events on their learning programme, with reflections and, perhaps, analysis. The diary provides students with an opportunity to:

- reflect on their learning experiences – for example, in a class or in completing an assignment
- prepare themselves for a forthcoming learning experience
- integrate theory and practice
- comment on the environment in which they are learning – teacher, peers, materials, equipment and so on.

It also gives an opportunity for the tutor, and maybe other students, to respond, continuing a dialogue. The diary is an important tool in the preparation of some professionals (for example, in caring, nursing and social work).

When using diaries, you need to resolve a number of issues:

- the purpose of the diary
- whether the diary is used for formative and/or summative assessment
- if used as part of summative assessment, whether the diary is being assessed in itself or merely contributes to another assessment method
- who reads and who assesses the diary – several people may be involved
- whether the whole or part of the diary is read and assessed by the tutor.

The most important issue is the first as the purpose of the diary will guide decisions on the other issues. If the diary does not count towards formal credit marks, then it is likely that students will be more relaxed and feel less pressure to put in the 'right' things. On the other hand, not assessing the diary means that students may not take it seriously. Linking the diary to some other form of assessment is a sensible middle course.

Formative or summative?

Most commentators suggest that the diary is best used as a formative (or self-assessment) device. As the extracts at the end of this section (and in Chapter 11) suggest, it can be a fruitful vehicle for reflecting on learning, developing students' capacity to learn from experience. Students will be unlikely to learn from experience if they merely 'fake' their learning.

Learners can also use material within a diary as a source of contributory data to an assessment. For example, when writing a report or making a presentation on their work, learners may draw on their diaries both to remind themselves of what they did and to provide examples for quotation. For example, a diary of a work placement could illuminate a more formal report on a workplace project. Assignments can be set that require the learner to draw on authentic diary data. In some parts of the curriculum, the diary becomes a working document. In architecture, for example, it might include records of evolving work, sketches, comments, design ideas and responses from peers and tutors. With children at primary school, a diary of a field trip can be used to prepare subsequent displays and reports.

If you decide to assess diaries in themselves, you will need to consider how much of the diary students are to submit. As with portfolios, diaries compiled over a long period can be bulky to handle and difficult to assess. One solution is for tutors to read diaries regularly, while another is to ask students to submit sample entries, with explanatory comments.

Helping students keep a diary

Students find some aspects of keeping a diary difficult. Some write very abstractly, without including specific enough detail to illuminate their general statements. Others find the emphasis on reflection difficult. Students may be unclear about the function of the diary or lack the capacity to analyse and reflect or be afraid to do so. In these circumstances, the danger is that they retreat into purposeless, mechanical activity.

To avoid these sorts of problems, guidelines to students could cover:

- the purpose of the diary
- the audience – who reads it, who assesses it
- what to record and in how much detail
- style
- structure
- quantity
- frequency of entries
- what to submit and in what form
- confidentiality
- examples
- checklists of what they might include.

Guidelines, together with examples, practice and feedback on their practice, usually help students to see what is required.

There follow two examples of ways of structuring a diary. These are drawn from higher education, but they should suggest approaches suitable for students at other stages of education.

Approach 1

Social work trainees are asked to keep a diary to provide examples of particular types of case problems. To prevent the task from becoming unnecessarily onerous, they are advised to record, at most, one incident per day and explain why they considered it significant.

Approach 2

In their first year, students at one university are required to keep a diary of their learning experiences. They are given different questions to consider each week. Some of these (drawn from the first four weeks) are shown below (in the originals, students are given space in which to write their responses).

Keeping a learning diary

Over the next eight weeks, use the sheets and questions that follow to reflect on how you learn and how you can make the most of your learning opportunities.

Week 1
- Have you met any interesting people this week? Who? Why were they interesting?
- What was the most enjoyable experience this week? Why?
- What are you particularly looking forward to in your university course?
- What are your general impressions of life at university so far?

Week 2
- What is the most significant thing you have learned this week (inside or outside your course)?
- Have you used IT to help you achieve anything this week? (For example, research, making contacts, presentation of work.) If so, what?
- Have you been introduced to any new ideas this week? What were they?

Week 3
- Who do you know who is good at asking questions?
- How can you use their techniques to help you question more effectively?

Week 4
- Who or what has influenced the way you have worked this week? How?
- What has given you a sense of achievement this week? Comment on this.
- What was your biggest time-waster this week?
- Which aspects of your course could be improved and how?

Students may later move away from such guidelines and structure the diary more flexibly, but they can help them get started and in the right direction. Students can also be helped by looking at examples of other students' entries (anonymous if necessary), and some examples are given below. These are responses to some of the questions listed above. The quality of the feedback students receive on their diary entries – from tutor and/or peers as appropriate – can help students to focus on detail and develop their capacity to reflect.

I learned new skills on Word 7: bullets, double spacing, grammar check, copy and cut, automatic formatting.

I spend too much time running after people who don't attend meetings. I will in future make them chase after me for information.

Location shooting took up quite a while, finding suitable places and using differing shutter options.

Tom and Arthur are the most influential members of my group. They have drive, determination and get up and go. Both communicate very well and contribute to our discussions. They will listen and evaluate any of my ideas.

The lecturers are friendly and willing; the atmosphere is great; the equipment is first class. But as yet I have not been able to do any digital photography or authoring, due to configuration failure or lack of equipment. The induction was far too disorganized.

The factual area of the course is already of great benefit to me. The terminology used to describe issues of narrative, documentary, etc, are giving my already solid practical knowledge a whole new dimension.

Time has not been especially well spent this week. Apart from being misinformed continually by the school office about my seminar groups, I have had the majority of my still image and digital workshops cancelled. A repeat of this week would kill my enthusiasm.

I've kept on top of my diary. I complete the week's entry and also read the questions for the next couple of weeks, so I am prepared to answer them. By doing it this way, I have been able to give honest answers on a weekly basis, rather than trying to remember what I thought and felt at that time.

LOGS

Logs are less personal than diaries as they are generally a factual record of a learner's activities. A law student might keep a log of court visits, a botanist of plant observations. Here, the purpose is to demonstrate the range of a learner's experience. The law student might be required to observe ten court cases in a minimum of three different categories. The botanist might have to measure plant densities in at least five botanically distinct sites.

A course may well prescribe a format for a log. This serves to teach good observation practice and aids the systematic assessment of the log. In this sense, a log is a form of structured observation that can draw on established methodologies, such as those described by Bowling (1997) or Bell (1993).

If the log is to be used for analysis, then you need to decide in advance the form this will take. This will guide the student in what to record. If there is enough data to permit quantitative analysis, then the standard methods of the subject can be used. Often, though, there will only be enough data to permit qualitative analysis. Miles and Huberman (1994) offer a comprehensive review of methods of analysis of qualitative data, providing more than enough information to meet the needs of any log. What is important, though, is to consider how the methods they suggest will shape the format of the log itself. Failure to consider this before the data is collected may make the log very difficult to analyse.

As with all assessment, if the log itself is to be marked, you need to make the marking criteria explicit. Such criteria will need to specify, as a minimum:

- what to record
- how much detail to record
- how much to record – number and range of items
- over what time period to record
- what format to use
- what analysis the learner is to carry out prior to submission.

JOURNALS

Not all writers distinguish between a diary and a journal, but as the terms are both in use some distinction is presumably intended. Gibbs (1995) suggests that journals lie between diaries and logs:

> They involve reflection, but not usually as private and personal in form as in diaries, and also records of activity or experience, but in a more reflective and analytical way than the record-keeping format of a log.

As with diaries, the more publicly presentable they are, the more journals run the danger of containing what the learner thinks the teacher wants to read rather than what the learner thinks. Equally, journals may be too loose in structure to permit any of the sorts of analysis that might be applied to a log. Like diaries, journals seem better suited to formative and self-assessment than to summative. However, if they are to be assessed, then the observations that we have made about the marking criteria for logs and diaries will also apply in the case of journals.

VIDEO RECORDINGS

Learners can use video to record both what they have seen and what they have done. When recording what they have seen, the video is a form of visual log, but lacks the written log's capacity for structure. (A video could be structured by editing it, but that is expensive and time-consuming.) When used to record what the learner has done, the video provides a medium that permits otherwise transitory events to be assessed. For example, learners might record their steps in producing a play or choreographing a dance or bring back evidence of visits to particular sites or of work-based tasks.

Like the log, video is primarily a recording medium and so is ill suited to reflection or analysis within the medium itself. It is therefore difficult to assess directly, but it can usefully contribute to other forms of assessment. For example, the learner might write a short report, using the video as additional evidence. Where you do wish to assess a video directly, it is best to provide learners with your criteria on a self-assessment form. They can then tell you which bits of the video meet (in their opinion) which criteria, saving you from having to replay the tape repeatedly.

The criteria used to assess a video (or the item to which the video contributes) will determine the type of video that the learners produce. Such criteria are likely to specify:

- what types of event or activity the video is to record
- the number and range of items to show
- any analysis the learner is to carry out after the video is complete.

The same general points apply to audio recording. In some ways audio recording is more flexible than video (for example, editing it is easier), but the lack of the visual element means audio is more limited in its usage.

PORTFOLIOS

Portfolios as a means of recording, collecting and presenting evidence are discussed in Chapter 24.

REPORTS ON THE LEARNER'S OWN WORK

We have discussed reports in Chapters 9 and 17, but here we consider them mainly as devices for collecting evidence.

All the evidence collection methods that we have discussed so far share a common feature: they can be applied to both homogeneous and heterogeneous activities. There is no necessity for the entries in a diary to bear any relation to one another. A log can be used to record essentially different activities. The report, on the other hand, is only used where a coherent account of one activity is required.

Reports are quite demanding on learners, so, before choosing this method, you need to consider whether or not one of the other methods might be more suitable. If the sole purpose is to collect a record of what was done, the log might be preferable. On the other hand, if learners are to analyse what they have done and to draw conclusions, the report is a good format. It is a particularly strong format when the work to be reported on involves some form of investigation with an aim and recommendations. In other words, although we have included reports in this chapter on recording and collecting, reports invariably go beyond these functions.

The more extensive nature of reports is reflected in typical criteria for them, such as:

- appropriate structure used – this might be specified in the criteria or left to the learner's judgement
- topic or problem of the report clearly stated
- appropriate methods of investigation used
- data collected is relevant to the problem
- appropriate conclusions drawn from the data
- appropriate recommendations made.

PROJECTS

Some projects involve the collection of data and so are used in conjunction with some other method for recording it. For example, a project to investigate childcare facilities in a local area might be recorded as a report (see above). Here we will discuss the data collecting aspects of projects within an assessment context (see Chapter 20 for other aspects of projects).

When used for assessment, you need to be clear whether it is the data alone that will be assessed or the process of collecting it as well. (In some cases, the process may be of much greater importance than the data.) Whichever option is chosen will be reflected in the criteria, which, in turn, will help in the decision as to whether or not a project is an appropriate basis for assessment.

Projects that broadly have criteria such as those in the first column of Table 22.1 are devices to assess process and, as such, do not really belong in this chapter. Projects with criteria similar to those in the second column are using the project as a data collection device and, hence, do belong in this chapter.

It is important to decide what is being assessed so that an appropriate method can be chosen. Table 22.2 illustrates the sorts of decisions to be made. First, you decide the focus of the assessment (process or data), then you can consider the appropriateness of various methods. As is often the case, validity is important. Where project process skills are involved, the project is about the only assessment method that can validly assess them.

Table 22.1 *Criteria for different types of project*

Criteria that emphasize process	Criteria that emphasize output
Data collection methods (eg, questionnaires) well designed	Problem well specified
Data collection methods appropriately tested	Appropriate data collected
	Appropriate data display methods used
Data collection carried out to appropriate degree of rigour	Appropriate conclusions reached
Appropriate data analysis methods used	

Table 22.2 *Decision matrix for projects*

	Focus of assessment	
	Process	*Data*
Appropriateness of project	Ideal method with high validity	Can be used, but the high skill levels required may get in the way of the data collection
Appropriateness of other collection methods	No other equally valid method	Consider using a log, report or video

COMPARISON OF METHODS

We have discussed a range of methods of collecting and recording data for assessment. In Table 22.3, we have compared them using a number of key factors.

The second column compares the ability of the methods to cope with heterogeneous data. Diaries, journals and portfolios can cope with such data, the other methods less so. All methods can be used to record both process and outcome, so we have not included these headings in the table.

In the third column, we consider whether or not there is usually a prescribed format. Generally, logs and reports do have a prescribed format, whereas the other methods are more open. This can be an important consideration for assessment as the more open the format, the more difficult it is to match the entries against the criteria.

Other, more specialized aspects of the various methods are given in the fourth column. For example, some methods (such as reports) are well suited to recording conclusions and recommendations.

In the fifth column, we have noted what needs to be added to the basic method listed in the first column in order to create an assessment device. For example, to assess a log, you need an analysis of the log's contents and criteria to assess the material against. Note that the criteria need to be available from the start, to guide the learner in what to record.

Table 22.3 *Comparison of data collection and recording methods*

Method	Able to cope with heterogeneous data?	Prescribed format?	Can also record	Addition required to make into assessment
Diaries	Yes	No	Reflections	Analysis and criteria
Logs	Usually	Usually		Analysis and criteria
Journals	Yes	No	Reflections	Analysis and criteria
Videos	No	No		Criteria
Portfolios	Yes	Sometimes		Criteria
Reports	Partly	Usually	Conclusions and recommendations	Criteria
Projects (as recording devices)	Partly	No	Conclusions and recommendations	Criteria

KEY ACTION POINTS

- Be clear about your reason(s) for choosing a particular recording method.
- Ensure learners are clear about what data they need to record, how they should record it and how much they should record.

- Decide what you are assessing and how.
- Help students as necessary with the capabilities needed to record and analyse data.
- Help students to use recorded data in their assignments.

Chapter 23

Reporting achievement

INTRODUCTION

This chapter answers the question 'What does it all mean?' We have reviewed many ways in which learners can be tested, we have considered ways in which they can record their performance and log their activities, but when it is all done, what does it tell us? In this chapter, we look at how the conclusions that can be drawn can be presented – to a variety of audiences and for a range of uses. Where Chapter 22 considered the recording action taken by students, in this chapter we move to explore the reporting action taken by tutors.

We discussed the differing purposes of assessment in Chapter 2 – assessment for ranking (norm-referenced), assessment against criteria (criterion-referenced) and assessment to aid the students' development (ipsative). These are important for this chapter as they generate differing levels and types of information on which a report might be based. Norm-referencing usually provides the least detailed information on performance. A student's standing in relation to other students is shown, but not how the student has performed against the various criteria (which may also be unstated). This form of assessment is thus limited in the extent to which it is capable of informing future action.

The problem we tackle in this chapter can be illustrated by citing a few typical performance reporting statements.

- Maths: 80 per cent.
- European law: pass.
- Position in class for geography: 16th.
- 'Mary's French grammar is good, but she shows no aptitude for speaking.'
- Degree awarded: Upper Second.

While these are fictitious examples, they are typical of many assessment statements still being made in education today. Yet, a closer study of each one reveals that it tells us nothing about what the person knows or can do. Could the maths student differentiate a quadratic function? Could the law student provide reliable advice to a company thinking of setting up an office in Germany? Could Mary use the subjunctive correctly?

This chapter starts from the assumption that reports on learners' performance need to be more informative than the examples we have just looked at. We cover:

- reporting achievement against criteria (see Chapter 2, where we argue that one of the benefits of criterion-referenced assessment is that it is informative)
- profiles
- portfolios (see also Chapter 24)
- reporting to outside audiences, using the school report as an example.

REPORTING ACHIEVEMENT AGAINST CRITERIA

A good criterion will be specific. For example, the criterion:

Able to conjugate regular verbs in simple sentences in the present tense.

is very specific. The verbs to be conjugated are regular verbs (a clear-cut category). The types of sentences are simple ones (simple in the grammatical sense of the term – that is, with no subordinate clauses). And there is only one tense to consider. If this criterion were felt to be insufficiently precise, then perhaps a list of the regular verbs to be used could be given. However, if we say 'Robert is able to conjugate regular verbs in simple sentences in the present tense' the recipient of this information would have a clear understanding of Robert's performance.

How do we know when we have arrived at a sufficiently clear criterion that we could use in statements of performance? The basic test is to ask 'Is the criterion clear enough to write an assessment item for it?' Our example above on regular verbs passes this test. If we had made the example vaguer ('Knows regular verbs', for example), we could not have written an assessment item. In other words, good practice in criteria and question design provides the basis for good practice in reporting.

Sampling

However, we have skated over one refinement in the reporting. When we say 'Robert is able to conjugate regular verbs in simple sentences in the present tense', do we mean 'on every conceivable occasion' or 'on every occasion that he was tested' or what?

There is no simple answer to this. In trying to formulate an answer, we must note a fundamental feature of assessment, which is that any testing system looks at a minute sample of all the possible performances of a candidate. Suppose Robert were to go and work in France for a year. He might, in that time, utter more than 100,000 simple sentences in the present tense. His assessment might have involved just ten. So, we can eliminate our ever being able to make a statement that refers to performance on all conceivable occasions. This is the concept of sampling (see Chapters 1 and 8 for a fuller discussion of this).

Range

So far, we have examined a criterion that can be tested in well-controlled circumstances. Now consider the criterion:

Able to respond appropriately to irate customers.

Apart from being inherently difficult to test, it is both difficult to predict the range of circumstances that might make customers irate and even more difficult to observe them occurring. In such cases, it makes more sense to think of the skill being demonstrated in a stated range of circumstances, for example, when customers are irate about faulty goods or delays in service. The candidate, though, would not be expected to cope with customers who are irate because the store has caught fire or they have just witnessed an armed till robbery. So, in addition to our not being able to test all occurrences of a performance, neither can we test the full range of circumstances under which a performance might occur. This is the concept of range.

The need for simple criteria

So far, we have considered two short, single-skill criteria. Sometimes a task may involve many skills. For example, the task of questionnaire design might have a criterion such as:

Able to design a questionnaire with appropriate order of questions, appropriate use of open and closed questions, appropriate use of Likert scales, with unambiguous question language, with clear instructions to interviewers.

If the learner can do all these things, then this becomes a usable criterion. However, if the learner can do only some of these things, the criterion becomes harder to use. Generally, a statement of this type would be split up into separate criteria, each tested separately and each capable of being reported on separately, as follows.

Performance report for...
When designing a questionnaire, is able to:
use an appropriate order of questions   ☐
use open and closed questions appropriately   ☐
use Likert scales appropriately   ☐
write unambiguous question language   ☐
write clear instructions for interviewers   ☐

Reporting detail of this type is particularly important when the report has a diagnostic function: what does the learner need to learn next?

The need for integrative criteria

However, a learner may be able to demonstrate all the skills on a list such as the one for questionnaire design skills above, but still have problems putting all the skills together to construct a questionnaire. So, detailed criteria may need to be accompanied by integrative ones, such as:

Able to construct effective questionnaires using the skills listed in...

Summary

To summarize the principles of reporting, then, we have established that behind any reporting method there need to be:

- detailed criteria
- integrative criteria, if appropriate
- a statement about the performance sample
- a statement about the range of circumstances of performance.

Not all of this detail will be found in every reporting method. Sometimes the sample is read implicitly, for example, 'the learner took a 200-hour course and did a 3-hour exam'. Sometimes the range is considered to be obvious, such as 'the learner changed the wheels of three cars in the workshop' – that is, it is not stated that the wheels were not changed on the road or that there were no lorry wheels involved. The level of detail needs to match the use to which the report will be put.

We now go on to consider two reporting formats in common use – profiles and portfolios.

PROFILES

What is a profile?

A profile (also called a record of achievement) is a record of a learner's achievements, either against a prescribed list of items or in a more open format. In contrast to the single grade or mark of much normative assessment, the profile sets out the components of performance separately and gives information on each.

Profiles vary in structure and sometimes include both a formal section (for example, containing a summary of qualifications and assessment results to date) and a more personal section (say, including reflective pieces and action plans). Profiles are not assessment devices as such, but record assessments already made. They can be continually updated and can record achievement from many different assessments.

The uses of profiles

Hitchcock (1990) suggests that profiles improve motivation and communication and help with guidance and diagnosis. More particularly, they can be used:

- on entry to a new phase of education or training, to plan an individual's learning programe
- as a framework for recording results on a particular course
- as a databank for applications – for jobs, courses and so on
- to record summative achievement
- for formative assessment and action planning.

In their simple form, profiles are a useful method of managing individualized learning as the profile shows what has been learnt and what is yet to be learnt.

Example of a simple profile

Profiles can summarize an individual's career to date or be much smaller in scale. The various rating scales illustrated elsewhere in this book (see, for example, those in Chapters 5 and 9) are profiles of performance in specific areas.

In its simplest form, a profile might look like Table 23.1. The skills or knowledge items are listed and, against each, the learner's performance is recorded. Profiles are often the result of self- or peer assessment, but who does the assessing makes no difference to the concept of a profile, so the following discussion applies whatever the source of the assessment.

Table 23.1 *A simple profile*

Skill	Achieved?
Open documents	☐
Save documents	☐
Enter text accurately	☐
Edit text	☐
Search and replace words	☐
Justify text	☐
Embolden text	☐
Change fonts	☐
Create tables	☐
Change table column widths	☐
Put borders around table cells	☐

Not all learners need to learn the same range of material. Profiles are a good way of recognizing this. All you have to do is add a new column 'Needed?' to Table 23.1 and you immediately have a mechanism for both individualizing content and recording achievement.

Other profile formats

Profiles are sometimes extended to provide scales of performance (Gibbs, 1995), such as:

Unsatisfactory/Adequate/Good/Excellent
Not yet encountered/Observed/Undertaken under supervision

A more sophisticated profile could be built around other scales of achievement or experience. For example, you could use Steinaker and Bell's (1979) experiential taxonomy to create a scale such as:

Seen/Participated in/Competent/Internalized/Can teach others

Comparing the format in Table 23.1 with our requirements for a reporting system (detailed criteria, integrative criteria, the performance sample and the range of circumstances), we can see that only the first criterion has been met in Table 23.1.

If we wished to meet all the criteria, then we might elaborate the format, as shown in Table 23.2. In addition to the extra two columns, we have had to add a final, integrative criterion. This example shows that the basic profile format – which is simple enough for any learner to use – can readily be elaborated to provide very detailed assessment information.

Table 23.2 *Elaborated profile reporting format*

Skills	Achieved?	Sample (times)	Range
Open documents	☐	2	One-page documents.
Save documents	☐	5	One-page documents.
Enter text accurately	☐	3	One paragraph of text
Edit text	☐	5	One paragraph of text
Search and replace words	☐	2	Changing one word
Justify text	☐	3	One paragraph of text
Embolden text	☐	2	Single-line headings
Change fonts	☐	3	One paragraph of text
Create tables	☐	2	Two-and three-column tables
Change table column widths	☐	1	Changing within constant total width
Put borders around table cells	☐	1	Borders on all four sides of cells
All the above skills together	☐	1	Three-paragraph A4 documents

However, profiles present students and assessors with challenges:

• they can be time-consuming to operate
• models are evolving and some assessment audiences (such as parents and employers) are still unfamiliar with them
• it takes more time to use the relatively rich information contained in a profile than it does to read a traditional examination result
• to use profiles productively, students need a clear sense of purpose, some ideas on how to use them and reminders to keep them up to date.

PORTFOLIOS

In one sense, portfolios are a form of reporting – 'Here is what I have done'. Most portfolios, though, are bulky, making it hard to form a summary of what has been achieved. Also, the gaps in terms of what has not been achieved are less evident than with, say, profiling. So, in themselves, portfolios are hard to use as reporting devices – they need tools for their summary and interpretation. We discuss some of the options below and other aspects of portfolios in Chapter 24.

Assuming that the portfolio is being assessed against existing criteria, each piece of work will have been matched to one or more criteria. For example, for each item in a portfolio, a report such as that in Table 23.3 might be drawn up where students match the item of work with the criteria. In this case, the learner has completed a market research report, using a range of skills, and has identified what those skills are using the given criteria. Although this format might be satisfactory for reporting a small number of items of work, it would be cumbersome for a large portfolio.

Table 23.3 *Identifying achievements from an item in a portfolio*

Item	Criteria met by item
Report on survey of the market for prepared and unprepared vegetables	Selection of appropriate analytical techniques Analysis of numerical data Presentation of data using charts and diagrams Drawing statistically valid conclusions from data

To overcome this problem, the format of Table 23.3 can be reversed so that the criteria are mapped to the item rather than the other way around. This produces a report like that shown in Table 23.4, which enables us to see that:

- for three criteria, the learner has produced one of the two items needed
- for one criterion the learner has yet to produce an item
- for one criterion the learner has produced both the necessary items.

A particular strength of the format shown in Table 23.4 is that it encourages the learner to identify in any given piece of work all the possible criteria that it meets. With one piece of work at hand (such as the vegetables report) the learner can run down all the criteria (often a long list), asking, 'Does this item show I have met this criterion?' This is an example of the application of the principle of efficiency in assessment – the learner should do the minimum necessary to demonstrate achievement of the criteria. The format also encourages learners to be proactive in considering how they will meet the criteria. It is a format that promotes autonomous learning. The format of Table 23.4 can be modified as needed to fit different reporting needs.

Table 23.4 *Portfolio performance reported against criteria*

Criteria	Items meeting the criteria (minimum two items per criterion)
Selection of appropriate analytical techniques	1. Report on vegetables market 2.
Questionnaire writing	1. 2.
Analysis of numerical data	1. Report on vegetables market 2.
Presentation of data using charts and diagrams	1. Report on vegetables market 2. Presentation on use of leisure time
Drawing statistically valid conclusions from data	1. Report on vegetables market 2.

REPORTING TO OUTSIDE AUDIENCES

Students and tutors are the most important audiences for assessment, especially for formative purposes, as these stakeholders will largely be responsible for any resulting action plan. Other audiences need, however, to be considered, and they are growing in importance. In the final section, we consider how to communicate assessment results to stakeholders external to the educational institution.

There is surprisingly little in the literature on this topic, Lloyd-Jones, *et al.* (1992) being an exception. Yet, reporting results is an important stage that may involve several stakeholders – the students themselves, their parents (if the students are of school age), other teachers and employers.

Lloyd-Jones, *et al.* (1992) point out that reporting can take place in a variety of ways – in writing, orally, non-verbally and implicitly in the organization's structures (such as streaming). On another dimension it can range from formal through informal to subconscious (see the matrix in Lloyd-Jones, *et al.*). In this section, however, we use the term 'reporting' to refer to the periodical and explicit formal communication the educational institution has with those outside the immediate learning environment.

Two models of reporting

Rowntree (1987) distinguishes two roles:

- interacting change-agent (teacher)
- disinterested reporter.

The former is associated with formative assessment, the latter with summative. Rowntree elaborates as follows:

> In other words, the assessor may respond as a teacher, using the knowledge gained to interact with the student in helping him [sic] grow; or he [sic] may respond as a reporter, classifying, labelling, or describing the student for the benefit of others who have an interest in the student.

The assessor, responding as a teacher, looks to the future, to how the student might develop. The reporter, on the other hand, focuses on how the student currently is, making a summative assessment. The reporter tends to pass information down the line without expecting dialogue. The change-agent, however, seeks a response and an involvement in the actions that result.

There may be a tension between the roles, with the assessor having to play both. Such is the case, for example, in the UK's Open University where the predominant role is, however, that of teacher. Tutors are asked to make comments that initiate and maintain a dialogue, the emphasis being on the student's development – that is on the future (see Chapter 6 and Rowntree, 1987).

The school report

We use the school report as an example. The general points apply, however, for external reporting at other stages of education and training.

School reports are issued at the end of an educational phase and are addressed primarily to parents. They are potentially a means for discussion and action planning between the key participants – in this case, teachers/school, students and parents. Communication thus needs to be not one-way (school to parents), nor even two-way (school to parents, parents to school), but three-way, involving the student.

Much traditional reporting was based on norm-referencing. School reports used to include a grade for attainment, a grade for effort and a test result. Additional comments tended to be vague or formulaic – for example, mentioning 'one or two areas of weakness' or the need to 'try harder'.

This method of communication left parents with little option beyond either congratulating the child or (often counter-productively) exhorting them to do better. Thus, the opportunity to take part in joint action planning was missed. Also, the timing of traditional reports – usually just as children put work aside for the holidays – added to the difficulties of sensible planning.

Fortunately, school reporting has now greatly improved, with the increased use of profiling and the more careful integration of reports with action planning. Lloyd-Jones, *et al.* (1992) list the areas on which parents like information:

- what my child has learned
- what you are assessing
- how you are assessing
- what the standards are
- what my child needs to do to improve
- how they can improve
- what performance my child is capable of
- what we as parents can do to help.

They need such information to create a better future. They are looking for a report that helps them to institute change.

CONCLUSION

In reporting, you need to consider the needs of the audiences for information. Reports are best seen as ways of giving feedback, so the points made in Chapter 6 apply here, too.

Rowntree's interacting change-agent model reminds us that students' development requires a partnership between stakeholders. All need to be motivated and engaged, and this has implications for the language and presentation of reports.

Reports also need to be linked to action planning, either by means of the paperwork itself or by a meeting soon after the report, the results of which are formally recorded with statements of who will do what, and when. Action plans then need to be followed up. Some schools use planning diaries as an aid to this, with spaces for comments by parents, students and teachers.

However, even these can easily fall into disuse. The activities of reporting, action planning and follow-up need constant attention. A policy should be designed, fostering participation from all stakeholders and with accompanying guidelines.

You need to think about the timing of reports. As pointed out above, there is little point in sending them out just before a holiday. It would be better to do this just before consultation evenings, providing an agenda for both plenary sessions and individual discussions. You might also time reports just before major changes or decisions, such as the selection of options or a transition (to a new school, to further or higher education or employment). However, time is needed to explore and discuss the reports and to learn fully from them.

Reporting is best seen as an essential part of a teacher's work rather than as something that takes them away from the students. The pay-off of better student performance should more than justify the time taken to produce them. To avoid an onerous workload and maintain quality, a school or college can stagger reports so that not too many have to be completed at any one time. Computers can also be used to make the task easier (see Chapter 13).

KEY ACTION POINTS

- Decide the audience(s) to whom you are reporting the results of assessment.
- Identify what information they need and when they need it.
- Identify the criteria against which to report, together with the sample and range.
- Subdivide complicated, multiple criteria into simpler criteria if necessary.
- Consider the profile and portfolio as means of reporting assessment results.
- Consider how you can involve external stakeholders in the reporting process and in subsequent action.
- Allow sufficient time for reporting.

Chapter 24

Portfolios

INTRODUCTION

We have made various references to portfolios, particularly in Chapters 22 and 23, but they are of growing importance and so are worthy of a chapter to themselves. Here we cover:

- what might be included in a portfolio
- the various uses to which portfolios can be put.

We then look at three of these uses in more detail:

- use within national vocational qualifications
- the more traditional portfolio
- portfolios to demonstrate learning achievement.

We conclude the chapter with a summary of the benefits of using portfolios within assessment.

Portfolios tend to be used in secondary, further and higher education and in training. There is no reason, however, for not also using them with younger students, in a suitably adapted form.

WHAT MIGHT BE INCLUDED IN A PORTFOLIO?

A portfolio is a collection of materials assembled by students to demonstrate achievement. The materials will vary with the age of the student and the curriculum area, but might include:

- completed assignments with feedback from tutors and others

- copies of learning contracts
- notes or drawings
- extracts from diaries, journals, logs
- laboratory or project reports
- charts, posters, maps, diagrams
- designs, paintings, photographs, art works and artefacts
- software
- descriptions/analyses of work placements
- certificates and statements of progress and achievement
- self-assessments.

The contents may be tightly prespecified, collected by students to satisfy evidence requirements, or left entirely to the students' discretion, as with some art portfolios. Students may have completed some of the material as part of their course, while other material may have been generated outside this context – for example, as part of employment or leisure time or voluntary work and not originally intended for assessment. A student in employment might, for example, collect memos, reports, notes on meetings, press releases and financial data for a portfolio as evidence for a management award. They may make reference to other evidence not included in the portfolio, but available if required. This could include material in a form difficult to store in a folder or file, such as video or audiotapes or large art objects.

At one level, students might merely collect evidence of achievement as it occurs and file it in a portfolio (for example, exam certificates or various assignments). Alternatively, the process may be much more explicit and organized, involving students' proactivity regarding:

- drawing up an assessment plan
- deciding what might be appropriate evidence
- seeking out evidence
- analysing the evidence – including cross-referencing to criteria.

This chapter deals with the latter scenario. Merely putting certificates into a folder is better described as filing than constructing a portfolio.

PURPOSES OF A PORTFOLIO

There are two main purposes for a portfolio. First – as is common in art and design and architecture – that of displaying examples of students' work, usually the very best items. More recently, portfolios have been used as collections of evidence to establish that learners have met a set of prescribed performance criteria, such as those incorporated in national standards, published by industry-led bodies in the UK and assessed as National Vocational Qualifications (NVQs) and Scottish National Vocational Qualifications (SNVQs). Here, the assessment methodology lays down very specific standards for how assessment shall be undertaken when using portfolios.

Other purposes include the following.

- To support other assessment tasks. In these cases it would not be sensible or necessary to submit the portfolio in its raw form. We consider this in other parts of the book, where we look at the methods of assessment the portfolio could support (see Chapter 22 and Figure 25.3 in Chapter 25 for an example).
- To support other, non-assessed activity, such as preparation for a job interview.
- To help students reflect on their learning and experience. This leads us to consider the role of the portfolio in the accreditation of prior experience and learning.

In the next three sections, we look in more detail at the portfolio as:

- a means of assessing national vocational qualifications
- the more traditional collection of examples of students' work
- part of the process of accrediting prior experience and learning.

PORTFOLIOS IN THE ASSESSMENT OF NATIONAL VOCATIONAL QUALIFICATIONS

In this approach, the portfolio, in conjunction with the standards, is clearly an assessment device. The purpose and contents of the portfolio are defined by the standards, as Figure 24.1 shows.

From the learner's viewpoint, the published standards define what sorts of items are needed in the portfolio. For example, learners wishing to prove themselves competent as trainers would have to include in their portfolios evidence to substantiate their achievement of the element 'Determine organizational aims and objectives for training and development.' For this one element, a further eight performance criteria are specified (such as, 'all relevant people are consulted...' and 'training and development outcomes required to support the organization are accurately specified'.

So, in the second step in Figure 24.1, candidates must decide what sorts of evidence would demonstrate achievement of this element. In this instance, it might include such items as records of consultative meetings or surveys and examples of training plans.

In the third step, the assessor compares these pieces of evidence against the performance criteria and evidence requirements of the award. In doing this, the assessor must apply stringent criteria to the nature of the evidence. For example, is it valid, current, authentic, consistent and sufficient? (See also Chapter 3, where these terms are discussed).

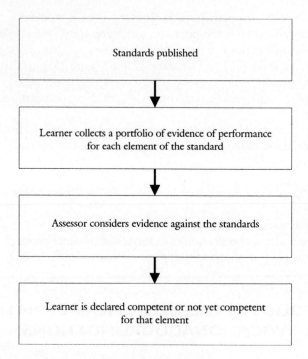

Figure 24.1 *Assessing a portfolio against standards*

We give a fuller account of the assessment process in Chapter 7, in relation to the choices available to students. While in some ways the S/NVQ approach is more limiting than other types of portfolio – the standards are beyond teacher or learner negotiation – many decisions are still left open to the candidate. These include the types of evidence they select, how they structure it and the ways in which they relate it to the standards. As well as the raw evidence, candidates for assessment might also include various forms of analysis and structuring, such as:

- self-assessments
- a description of the contexts in which the evidence was collected
- links between evidence and standards – for example, via a matrix (see Chapter 23)

- reports on periodic reviews of evidence.

These can all play an important part in helping assessors make sense of what would otherwise be merely a collection of raw data.

Helping students prepare a portfolio for national vocational qualifications

Students may be unfamiliar with the purpose of a portfolio. They may thus need help in understanding the rationale behind portfolio assessment.

Students usually also need guidance in how to select relevant evidence and make the most of each item – for example, by showing how it contributes to more than one performance criterion (see Chapter 23). Items need to be clearly titled and signposted as poorly organized portfolios can be very time-consuming to assess.

Simosko and Cook (1996) suggest one possible structure for the portfolio, comprising five components:

- cover – including their name and other relevant student details
- a table of contents
- a narrative statement/personal report/curriculum vitae or other device that links the students' experience to the learning outcomes for which credits or the achievement of performance are claimed, and including information on the context in which the evidence has been produced
- a system for cross-referencing different individual pieces of evidence to the standards, criteria or learning outcomes
- the evidence itself, clearly labelled.

Much becomes clear to students when they see examples of good portfolios. Tutors will need to discuss such matters as:

- the learning or performance criteria students are seeking to meet
- what might constitute acceptable evidence
- how to interpret other criteria, such as currency and authenticity
- how much evidence might be needed or how many items
- ways of structuring a portfolio
- ways of making the assessor's task easier.

It is good practice to timetable formative reviews of the portfolio and to agree actions accordingly.

THE TRADITIONAL PORTFOLIO

Having looked at portfolios for national vocational qualifications, we can now consider the looser definitions that are also still current. Here, 'portfolio' is a word that can be applied to any collection of learners' work, although generally it is used for selections made by each learner themselves. In this sense, a portfolio might contain all of a learner's work, a representative selection or the best so many items. For assessment purposes, the total collection of a learner's work presented as a portfolio is fairly meaningless. In general, learners should be required to think about what they are putting in and why (see the discussion in Chapter 1 of assessment as necessarily involving a sample of a student's performance).

Where such portfolios are being used for summative assessment, the criteria are likely to include:

- what to put in – this might be expressed directly ('include two examples of…') or indirectly, in the sense that the totality of the criteria should guide the learner's selection
- how much to put in
- what criteria will be applied to each item of work (or to items of particular types)
- any criteria that will be applied across the work – such as criteria of breadth or consistency
- any requirement for self-assessment or some form of report on the portfolio.

We mentioned (Chapter 3) that the more assessment can be based on real tasks rather than contrived educational tasks, the more valid it is likely to be. Against this standard, the portfolio has the potential to be a very valid form of assessment. As testimony to this, witness how employers in the art and design world rush to visit end of course shows to inspect portfolios – they know that what they are seeing is proof of talent to come. Few employers show enough faith in exam papers to rush to see them.

PORTFOLIOS TO DEMONSTRATE LEARNING

A portfolio can also be a means for demonstrating a case for entry to, or exemption from, particular courses or units of study. Portfolios can thus facilitate credit transfer.

Here is where we enter a thicket of acronyms. The portfolio could support the accreditation of prior learning (APL). The acronym APAL is perhaps clearer – the accreditation of prior assessed learning (that is, credit for educational programmes successfully completed, often in another institution). This is sometimes also known as APCL – the accreditation of prior certificated learning – or APLA – the accreditation of prior learning achievement. In these cases, the portfolio would contain relevant certificates, the syllabuses and an analysis of how these matched the intended course of study.

Alternatively, the student might be making a claim for learning they have gained from experience, but not necessarily had 'certificated' by an educational institution. This is APEL – the accreditation of prior experiential learning. The student might well be recommended (or required) to compile a portfolio to support such a claim. The student's approach will be similar to that described earlier for NVQs.

Brown, *et al.*, describe APEL as a process involving the transformation of experience 'into a record of "acceptable" knowledge, assessed and accredited. The process of transformation involves self-assessment, reflection and some knowledge of academic contexts'. This represents a major challenge and students generally need support, often from a tutor playing the role of facilitator and adviser. This process can develop the students' capacity to reflect on their learning. As Brown, *et al.* point out, it is best seen as an educative rather than an administrative process (although students may not see it that way, at least initially).

The stages of APEL may include:

- reflecting on experience
- identifying learning
- forming competence statements – the capability the learning has led to
- an action plan – a 'career plan' in its broadest sense
- matching competence statements to the career plan
- assembling the evidence for assessment of the claimed capabilities
- organizing the portfolio
- submitting the portfolio for assessment.

The portfolio is thus more than just a collection of evidence – it is carefully structured and also contains analysis.

BENEFITS OF THE PORTFOLIO

A portfolio approach encourages the use of a wider range of items and experiences than is normal in other forms of assessment. Some of these can be drawn from outside the formal academic environment. Hence, assessment decisions can be based on better information (wider or more detailed) than is often otherwise the case. Using a portfolio, students can also show their development, and capacity to reflect on this and interpret items, for example via a commentary.

The portfolio approach usually gives students freedom to use their own initiative. Within limits that will vary depending on circumstances, students will decide how the portfolio is presented and organized. As with choice generally, however, this can be perceived by some students to be an unwelcome challenge.

The portfolio can also provide information to a number of different stakeholders, such as tutors, other students and employers – for example, on performance during a work placement.

KEY ACTION POINTS

- Ensure clarity over:
  - the type of portfolio your students are to complete
  - the purpose(s) of the portfolio and the benefits to students in completing it
  - what is to be included
  - the structure of the portfolio
  - the criteria against which the portfolio is to be assessed
  - additional material to interpret the contents of the portfolio – such as self-assessments, contents lists, matrices, action plans.
- Schedule regular reviews of progress.

PART SIX

Assessment issues

Chapter 25

Helping learners prepare for assessment

INTRODUCTION

In this chapter, we consider how students can be prepared for assessment. Our treatment here is general as there are sections on preparing for specific types of assessment in the relevant chapters. Much of the material in this chapter is aimed at students in further and higher education, but it can easily be adapted to suit those at other stages of education or training.

Students need to be prepared for a range of possible assessment eventualities. Take just one aspect – the criteria against which their work will be judged. At one end of the spectrum, students may find themselves in situations in which the assessment criteria are fixed and non-negotiable; at the other extreme they may be required to set their own. Most situations will lie between these extremes.

Students should be prepared for the fact that, in some areas of the curriculum, criteria may not be specific. In this case, to avoid being entirely in the dark, they may need to propose criteria to their tutor and get confirmation that these are appropriate.

Particularly at higher levels of study, learning contracts may be used (sometimes called learning agreements). These require the learner to take the initiative in proposing outcomes, criteria and assessment methods, instruments and sources. These details, together with the roles of learner, tutor and other relevant people, may need to be recorded in the contract.

We cannot assume that students will have had prior experience of particular assessment sources, methods or instruments. Some terms may be new to them – for example, 'portfolio'. Other terms may be familiar, but from other contexts, such as 'performance' or 'evidence'. Some may be defined differently by different departments or teachers, such as 'project' or 'presentation'. Hence, we need to ensure that students are clear as to what the language of assessment means in any given context.

As we argued in Chapter 7, students should be encouraged to be proactive. They should not assume that they will be told all they need to know. They should adopt a questioning approach to their assessment, as they do to other aspects of their learning. They should also be encouraged to ask for formative assessment possibilities *en route* to summative ones.

Students need accurate and full information, both on assessment in the course as a whole and for each assignment. We cover these needs in the next two sections of the chapter.

PREPARING FOR ASSESSMENT AT THE LEVEL OF THE COURSE

Students should be given – at the start of their course or programme – as much relevant information as possible about assessment arrangements. At the most general level, this needs to include:

- the purposes assessment serves (see Chapter 1)
- the balance between norm-, criterion- and self-referenced assessment (see Chapter 2)
- the modes of assessment – for example, the balance between formal and informal, formative and summative assessment (see Chapter 4).

They also need to know the:

- expected outcomes of the course and how these are assessed
- sources, instruments and methods used
- number of assessments and the deadline dates for each
- any assessment weighting, and how the overall course grade or mark (or other result) is calculated
- what the grading or marking scheme is – if a general one is in operation
- any requirements as to word limits, referencing of sources and so on
- guidelines on how to answer assignments
- the details of any appeals procedure.

They particularly need to establish the criteria by which their performance will be assessed, if not from formal documents, then by asking their tutor what will lose or gain them marks? Other useful sources of such information include:

- previous assessments, exam papers or assignment questions
- previous students' work, which may be available in the library or department
- previous students.

Each of these sources needs to be interpreted carefully. For example, previous students may not all be reliable in the information they give.

Students should get a copy of any formal description of the assessment – both for the course as a whole and (for use later) for each assignment. Some relevant information may be found in a syllabus. A list of course content on its own is, however, of little use as students need to know what they are supposed to do with the content – memorize it, analyse it, apply it? These things become clear only when the assessment is described.

For school exams, students can often buy useful booklets or multimedia packages containing assessment information, information about the syllabus and test questions. In further and higher education courses, handbooks are sometimes produced that contain not only information about assessment, but other information such as:

- course aims and objectives
- links to employment/other qualifications or courses
- resources required – for example, books, equipment, access to experience.

Figures 25.1, 25.2 and 25.3 give some examples of these. The first extract shown in Figure 25.1 is from the general information on assessment, including a list of the headings under which assessment is made and the proportions of available marks assigned to each of them. The second extract in the figure sets out the assessment requirements for one of the three headings given in the first – 'Managing your own learning'. Figure 25.2 is an extract from official assessment regulations. Students may need help interpreting the inevitably legalistic-type language.

Figure 25.1 *The effective learning programme (ELP) used at the University of Lincolnshire and Humberside*

How are you assessed within ELP?

Each of the two strands of ELP will be assessed. Although you are being assessed for your demonstration of generic (general) learning skills, the skills will be made relevant and related to your subject area.

Assessment for **Managing your own learning** covers seminar and follow-up work and accounts for 40% of the total mark for the unit.

Assessment for **Communication skills** covers writing (30%) and presentation skills (30%). Communication therefore comprises 60% of the total mark for the unit.

Details of the assessment requirements in each area are given in this portfolio, under the headings:

Managing your own learning assessment (page 14)
Writing skills assessment (page 73)
Presentation skills assessment (page 95).

Figure 25.1 *cont.*

Managing your own learning assessment

The assessment for this strand focuses on your participation in seminars, and the work you do to support this. Your tutor will monitor your:

- regular attendance at seminars
- individual contributions to seminar activity

and mark or moderate each of the assessment activities (listed below) that you must evidence in this part of the portfolio.

Use this sheet to monitor your progress towards completing the assessment requirements. When you have collected all the required items, file them with the checklist at the end of the portfolio in the Completed assessment items section (pages 123–130)

Deadline date   Date completed

                                 Reviewing your Learning styles profile (LSP) (pages 43–44)

                                 Action plan for developing your approach to study and your independence in learning (pages 51–52)

                                 Diary comments and responses to diary questions (pages 17–34)

                                 Log of your group presentation skills task (pages 57–62)

                                 Time management plan for the group assignment (pages 63–64)

                                 Reviewing a resource sheet (pages 35–36) for a resource you have found particularly helpful

                                 Evidence of your ability to send and receive e-mail (printouts of one relevant message received and one sent)

                                 On-line IT assessment passes (ie 70% or more) for Word and Windows (results automatically sent to your tutor)

Assessment regulations

The assessment and award of an honours degree is governed by both University and course regulations. Read the following regulations very carefully; they are the official University assessment regulations governing the course. They explain what you need to achieve in order to succeed on this course, and what you must do if you fail to satisfy the examiners or you experience circumstances such as illness which you believe have been detrimental to your performance.

Awards

To obtain an honours degree, students must pass all modules, though, exceptionally, the Board of Examiners may award an Honours Degree to a student who has one failure at the Final Level provided that the student's overall performance throughout the Level merits such an award. In such circumstances, the Board may recommend a lower honours classification than the calculated results indicate.

The pass mark for each unit is 40%; where there is more than one element of assessment in each unit, a minimum of 35% in each element and an overall mean of at least 40% is required for a pass.

Your degree classification will be calculated by the following two methods and your degree will be awarded on the basis of the higher mark:

- the mean score of all units studied
- where seven marks fall into one class, that class shall be recommended, providing the other paper is no more than one class below that indicated by the aforementioned units.

Classification will be based on the following scale

70%	First Class Honours
60–69%	Upper Second Class Honours
50–59%	Lower Second Class Honours
40–49%	Third Class Honours

Re-assessment

Students who fail individual units have the right of one attempt at re-assessment within two years of the initial failure, and in such cases the Board may, at the point of initial failure, place a ceiling on the level of classification to be awarded; the nature of that reassessment will be determined by the Board of Examiners.

Figure 25.2 *Extract from undergraduate degree regulations used at the University of Lincolnshire and Humberside*

PREPARING FOR AN INDIVIDUAL ASSIGNMENT

Some of the points made above are also relevant at the level of an individual assignment. For example, students need to know:

- who will assess the assignment, when and by what methods
- information on length limits, systems of referencing, materials to be used, extent and type of research expected.

Students should also ask if any detailed marking schemes are available. Figure 25.3 is an example of the kind of comprehensive information that needs to be given, in this case, for an assignment on preparing a job application.

---

3 Preparation for job application

This third element involves the identification of a specific job vacancy (or postgraduate qualification) and an analysis of the preparation needed for an application.

The work should be presented as an individual written assignment (750 to 1000 words) supported by a portfolio of relevant material, for example:

- a targeted CV and covering letter
- a general CV and covering letter
- a letter of application
- a completed application form (general or specific)
- preparation for an interview (real or simulated)
- notes following an interview (real or simulated)
- a personal action plan from now to graduation.

You will be assessed principally on the written assignment, while the portfolio should provide appropriate supporting evidence. Your tutor will provide further advice on the appropriate format for your written work.

You should focus on a specific job vacancy (or postgraduate qualification) related to your chosen vocational area and undertake research as if applying for the vacancy. Your assignment should show how your knowledge of the employer's business and of the specific opportunity would be used to construct an appropriate application which relates your strengths and experience to the requirements. You should indicate where your skills and experience need development and how you intend to make progress in these areas. The material in the portfolio will not be specifically marked but a poor level of presentation is likely to be reflected in the mark for this element.

Figure 25.3 *Example of the information required for an individual assignment at the University of Lincolnshire and Humberside*

When preparing for an assignment, students should also be encouraged to review the feedback they received on previous work. This might include advice or information relevant to their current assignment (see Chapter 6).

COMPLETING ASSESSMENTS: PLANNING A TIMETABLE

Managing time is an important part of preparation for assessment. Students need first to have all the relevant information for scheduling to hand. This would include the deadlines, whether or not any extensions are permitted and, if so, in what circumstances (and using what procedures), as well as details of any penalties for late submission.

They then need to plan how to meet these requirements. This should involve thinking through the stages of an assignment. Preparing for a presentation, for example, may include:

- agreeing a title
- identifying an audience
- negotiating criteria
- researching the subject
- making an outline
- checking room layout and equipment
- preparing visual aids
- preparing an accompanying handout
- revising the outline and visuals
- getting feedback from a friend
- making final versions of outlines and visuals
- rehearsing.

For each stage students could:

- note the deadline
- estimate the time needed to complete the task
- allocate a time and date(s) to the task
- monitor progress
- allow some slack time for emergencies.

Students could be encouraged to set SMART goals. These are goals that are:

- specific – that is, in terms of output
- measurable

- appropriate/adequate
- realistic
- time limited.

(For more information on how students might manage the time they spend on assessment, see Lewis, 1994, in the References and further reading section at the end of the book.)

Such planning is even more important if the preparation for assessment runs over a long period of time – as it does, for example, when constructing a portfolio – and/or if students have to use their initiative and make assessment decisions for themselves. Detailed planning is also especially important when different members of a group have to integrate their individual contributions to a project.

KEY ACTION POINTS

- Provide students with information on assessment arrangements for all levels of their course, including each individual assignment.
- Discuss the information with them, ensuring they understand the language of assessment.
- Remind them periodically of the information.
- Help students plan their assessment, for example via learning contracts.
- Help students develop their approaches to time management.

Chapter 26

Marking group work

INTRODUCTION

Assignments requiring students to work in groups have a number of benefits, both academically and more generally in terms of skills development. Group work gives students the opportunity to explore a topic more deeply, prompted by alternative viewpoints and contributions. Many skills can be developed, including those related to research, time and project management, and in the interpersonal domain.

Group assessment can focus on product (an outcome of the group activity) or process (how the group worked) or a mixture of the two. Assessment criteria should, as always, reflect the purposes of the assignment. Sometimes group endeavour is essential if the end is to be achieved – various forms of dramatic and musical productions are obvious examples. A number of different examples of group activity and its assessment are given in other chapters, including Chapters 12, 18, 19 and 20. The material in this chapter is relevant to the assessment of groups at all ages of education, though the terminology will need to be adapted slightly on occasions to reflect particular contexts.

Group work can be a powerful stimulus to learning, but its assessment poses particular challenges. Individuals, not groups, are awarded qualifications, so how can assessment reflect both the performance of the group as a collective and the probably differing degrees of commitment and achievement of the individuals constituting it? Difficulties can include:

- some group members taking it easy while their colleagues do double the work
- the efforts of hard-working and able individuals failing to gain their just reward because they are not matched by others in the group
- the averaging out of differences between students and a narrower spread of marks than if only the individuals had been assessed.

Tutors need to address such issues, even if only because they lead some students to feel that group assessment is profoundly unfair. In this chapter, we consider how the assessment of group activity can also incorporate the assessment of individual members' contributions, especially where the assessor might see only the end product and not the process leading to it.

MARKING THE WORK OF INDIVIDUALS
IN A GROUP

Some would take a simple line on this and say that the solution to the problem is not to accept that there is a problem. In life outside educational courses – at work, in voluntary activity or family life – effort is distributed unevenly. People contribute to differing extents and we have to live with that. So – the argument runs – it is in education. The logical conclusion of this argument is to allot all students the same mark.

This is not an unrespectable argument, and, indeed, if explained clearly in advance it could be said to present a mature group of students with a challenge to which they ought to be able to respond. The greatest difficulty, though, is in getting students to accept the argument and the individuals within the group subsequently to perform at their best.

The other route, and the one on which we concentrate from now on, is to build in an individual mark as well as a group mark, thereby recognizing differing contributions – whether in amount of effort or in performance. There are two main sources of such a mark (or grade) – the tutor and the students. It is not necessarily a case of either/or – both sources of judgement can be combined. However, as we shall see, there comes a point where increasing the complexity becomes unmanageable and unproductive.

The tutor awards the mark

In this section, we assume that first an overall mark or grade has been given to the group. This would seem essential if the activity is a group activity. We go on to look at how individual marks can also be arrived at.

Individual assessment by product

If at all possible, you should assess a product. This requires careful pre-planning. At the beginning of the project, you need to specify the role and contribution of each group member to the product. This can be negotiated by the group, but if you are subsequently to play a part in allocating individual marks, then you should agree the group's decisions.

The outcome of each individual's contribution should thus be specified. This could take a variety of forms – a collection of data, an annotated bibliography, so many minutes of video footage, the construction of a stage set. You then assess the individual contributions.

Individual assessment by process

The purpose of the project might require assessment of the processes used by the group rather than what it produces. Thus, all or part of the group mark and/or the marks of individuals would need to relate to process. In this case, there are a number of possibilities:

- deduce the quality of the process from an analysis of the product
- assess statements of process – for example, the group produces a report on its work, including sections contributed by the individuals, and this can be used as the basis for allotting the individual marks
- look at records taken at the time – such as the minutes of group meetings, logs or diaries
- observe the group working on one or more occasions
- conduct an individual or group viva, including questions about topics such as roles, how the group worked, how critical incidents were handled
- set an exam question on the project – for example, requiring an analysis of the group processes, difficulties met and how these were dealt with, what changes the individual would propose for the next project and so on.

As with all assessment options, each of these has strengths and weaknesses. These are set out briefly in Table 26.1.

The general rule is to deduce process from product. However, there may be several difficulties with this, including the need to be sure of the individual's contribution to that product and that it really is their work. Also, in some cases, there may be no product or the product may not be under the control of the student. For example, what a nurse does to affect a patient's health is only one of a number of variables.

Table 26.1 shows that few of the methods are strong on validity. For example, relying on what an individual said they did is not the same as assessing what they actually did. The one method likely to be most valid (observation) is also the most difficult to implement. Another difficulty could be the generation of unpleasantness between the group members. You could see this possibly emerging, for example, from a group viva.

However, if process really is important, then you must persevere in designing a strategy that assesses it. You could use a combination of the above methods. You will recall that we mentioned in Chapter 3 the value of triangulation, whereby differing sets of evidence, or sources, are considered in reaching a judgement. This indicates a way forward in assessing individuals within a group.

Table 26.1 *Methods for assessing group work*

Method	Strength(s)	Weakness(es)
Deduce process from product	Convenient	May not be valid Difficult to interpret
Use statements about process	Convenient May prompt student reflection	May assess verbal fluency rather than process May be fabricated
Use records of process	Authentic	May be bulky and difficult to interpret
Observe the group	First-hand evidence, valid	Samples may not be typical Observer's presence may influence behaviour
Viva	Searching	May not be valid Difficult to interpret
Exam question	Convenient	May not be valid

The group awards the mark

There is one strong justification for this option if the assessment is to be of process, which is that the group is in the best position to make judgements and has the most information on which to draw. The challenge is to persuade and equip them to use and interpret this knowledge responsibly and intelligently.

Individuals can be assessed globally, for their contribution to the group, or more specifically. For example, they can be assessed on the basis of:

• an agreed role – such as leader, secretary, stage manager, producer
• a particular contribution – such as data collection, interviewing, writing up
• generic group skills – such as time-management, listening, questioning.

The usual way of proceeding is as follows:

• set a mark per student for the task
• decide what proportion of this mark will be for the group performance
• the remaining portion is for allocation to individuals.

This will work whatever the group size, as our example (Table 26.2) shows. In this example, the total mark per student is 60, and 50 per cent of this will be the group mark (all students will get the same mark), with the remaining 50 per cent being available for allocation to individuals within the group.

Table 26.2 *Mark allocations: individual and group assessment*

Group size	Mark per student	Total marks available	Mark available for group (50%)	Mark available for individuals (50%)
5	60	300	150	150
3	60	180	90	90

First, each student is given the group mark. The remaining marks are then allocated to individuals by means of whatever source or combination of sources you decide, for example by means of peers and/or the tutor. If several assessors are involved, the marks for each individual are totalled and averaged. The individual mark is then added to the group mark to give each individual's final total. In the first example, 150 marks can be shared between the five group members. If peer marking is involved, the tutor may need to impose (or, better, agree) ground rules. For example, that:

- the marks cannot be divided evenly
- the mark allocation must be justified by reference to specific criteria set out in advance.

The tutor may also reserve the right to moderate the final mark (taking on the role of external examiner).

CONCLUSION

This chapter considered summative assessment. However, groups will benefit from formative assessment as well. The final assessment – whether it is generated by tutor, peers or some combination of assessment sources – can be discussed at the end of the project, for example in a tutorial (see, too, Figure 12.1 in Chapter 12).

Brown, *et al.* (1997) also describe a system of group control that takes its inspiration from the football field – yellow and red cards. If the group reports that someone is not contributing, that person is given a yellow card and their mark is reduced by a set percentage. If the situation persists, a red card is issued and the student gets no marks. A variation on this is to simply let the group identify members who do not work, with the ultimate sanction of having to complete an alternative individual assignment or lose their right to the group mark. However such sanctions may generate more tension than they are worth. Further advice to consider when setting up groups includes that:

- the optimum size for many groups seems to be about five members (in larger projects, this could be the size you make subgroups)
- thought needs to be given to the basis on which the group forms – randomly, friendship, complementary talents
- student expectations need to be considered, especially those of students who may not have previously encountered group work or whose experiences of it may have been negative
- wherever possible, students should be given choices to make it more likely that they will develop a sense of ownership and responsibility (see Chapter 7).

KEY ACTION POINTS

- Decide whether or not you wish to allocate an individual as well as a group mark.
- If appropriate, negotiate assessment arrangements with the students.
- Ensure students are clear about how the assessment will be conducted, including any weightings, criteria, sources of the assessment.
- Ensure students understand the rationale behind the chosen approach.
- Ensure that all roles and responsibilities in the assessment process are clear.

Chapter 27

Workload

INTRODUCTION

Reviewing the literature on assessment shows that surprisingly little research has been carried out on workload. This applies whether the time is spent by students or by tutors. Brown, *et al.* (1997) comment 'There appear to be no reliable figures on how long it takes to do various assignments or how long it takes to mark them.' This is remarkable, given both the importance of assessment and the resources it consumes.

Assessment workload has become an increasing issue over the past decade. The staff–student ratio (at least in higher education) has changed progressively for the worse and is continuing to deteriorate. There comes a point where assessment practices that are manageable with smaller student groups become unsustainable. Problems multiply – reliability declines, the motivation assessment can bring is reduced, anxiety increases. Feedback to students on their work is particularly likely to suffer. For example, it can result in a lack of detail or follow-up. Then, students may drift and tutors lack information on student progress and, in their ignorance, both may misdirect their efforts. There may be particular problems with assessment in modular schemes.

In such circumstances, tutor teams may need to look again at the overall assessment strategy and how it is implemented. The challenge with declining resources is to at least keep the core aspects of assessment intact – and, if possible, improve them by rearranging assessment so that it is more effective (for example, more valid and reliable), more useful for the student and more manageable for the tutor. The maximum value has to be gained from the use of the time of all concerned.

We focus in this chapter on further and higher education – the stages in education at which there is the greatest scope for individuals to change assessment arrangements. Readers from other parts of the education and training sector may nevertheless find useful ideas that they can adapt to suit their particular context.

WORKLOAD AT THE VARIOUS STAGES OF ASSESSMENT

You should ideally carry out an audit of current assessment arrangements, asking the following questions.

- How is the course currently assessed?
- How frequently are students assessed?
- By whom?
- How long are we spending on each assessment stage?
- How is the time used?

A necessary follow-up question is 'How much time should we be spending on assessment?' Then, a targeted or budgeted time can be used as a standard.

The same information should be available for students, so they know how long they are expected to spend on assessment and can watch how long they actually spend. Little information of either kind exists, although with credit schemes some relevant data is occasionally provided. One guideline in general use in higher education (though we cannot track down the source) is that 1 credit point should occupy 10 hours of notional student learning time. Thus a 30-credit unit will occupy 300 hours, of which a certain number will be 'contact time' and the rest self-directed study.

A further step (not so often taken) is to specify the number of hours students should expect to spend on assessment. About 5–10 per cent of the total is sometimes quoted (that is, 15–30 hours), but an interesting survey carried out at Leeds Metropolitan University found that students were actually spending over a third of their average working week on assessed work (Innis and Shaw, 1997).

This auditing of tutor and student time can be instructive. It can provide some necessary hard data that is often missing. In the light of this, plans can be made to use the resources allocated to assessment more productively.

In the rest of this chapter, we focus on the time spent by tutors (the assessors) in the following five stages:

- designing and preparing for assessment
- giving guidance to students on how to complete assignments
- marking assignments
- giving feedback
- recording and administration.

For each we give some suggestions on how the workload can be kept to a manageable level.

Assessment design

Preparation and design is the stage on which least time is usually spent, yet the time you invest here might offer a greater pay-off than it would for the other stages, especially where the number of students is large.

We have covered planning in the earlier sections of this book and have nothing further to add here.

Redesign can generate better-quality assessment. Methods, sources and instruments are often used unimaginatively and repetitively, based on approaches hallowed by time, but they may no longer be practicable or effective. The introduction of group assessment, for example, can both save tutor time and lead to more effective learning. The process of redesign might involve taking a look at other methods used in different subject areas within the same institution and/or by teachers in other institutions.

As a result of an assessment audit, a team might find that:

- some learning outcomes are being overassessed – and others not assessed or assessed inappropriately
- there are times when assessments are badly scheduled, leading, for example, to student overload
- some outcomes could be assessed more efficiently
- opportunities for formative assessment could be increased.

The first stage should cover both the overall design of the assessment for a course and the preparation of individual assignments. This creates an assessment specification for the course.

Guidance to students

The workload can be reduced if students have full information about assessment. What they need to know is set out in Chapter 25. Clear information will reduce time spent answering student queries, but, more significantly, they are more likely to succeed in their assignments. If assessment is to be efficient, students need detailed criteria and associated guidance on such matters as presentation, length, style, layout of bibliographies, referencing conventions and so on, together with examples of good practice. Assessment is more efficient if all tutors in a department (even across a whole institution) follow the same conventions wherever possible. It is easier both for students (in completing assignments) and tutors (in assessing them) if expectations and requirements are explicit and consistent.

Thus, briefing students carefully on assignments can save time later. The following example of this – a class discussion of an assignment with 120 students – is taken from Gibbs (1992, p17).

Step 1
The course guide clearly specified the assessment task and also stated that it would be discussed in class on a particular date.

Step 2
In the preceding class session the tutor referred students to that part of the course guide and told them she wanted them each to write three queries on how to complete the assignment satisfactorily, and bring their queries to the next class.

Step 3
In the class scheduled for the discussion, the students were asked to form groups of four to six and come up with three queries on the assignment which they wanted the tutor to answer. They were to write the names of the group members and their three queries on a sheet of paper and hand it to their tutor.

Step 4
While sudents were busy working in class on an assigned task the tutor skimmed through the queries and identified those she considered central. She then answered them in a brief presentation and made clear that from then on the students were on their own, though of course they could help each other.

Marking assignments

In this section, we look at two main ways of saving time spent marking:

- reducing the sample of student performance assessed
- choosing sources, methods and instruments of assessment that are less time-intensive.

Reducing the sample
As we pointed out in Chapter 1, assessment can only ever be of a sample of student performance. The size of the sample is always a matter of judgement. You may decide it is possible to reduce the sample by:

- setting shorter tasks – for example, an essay outline instead of the full essay
- setting fewer tasks
- setting assessments less frequently
- some combination of these.

This need not mean that students complete less of the course – several outcomes might, for example, be assessed within one task.

Choosing sources, methods and instruments of assessment carefully
You can save workload by a judicious choice of sources of assessment, methods and instruments.

Some assignments need not be assessed by the tutor – the students themselves may be used as self- or peer assessors. In some cases, students are the best sources anyway, and methods can be used that make this method of assessment logical, such as presentations, posters and objective tests. You can moderate such assessments by sampling. You may need to support students in the early stages by, for example, explaining the rationale and the roles, and ensuring students understand the relevant criteria. (See Chapters 11 and 12 for more on self- and peer assessment.)

Assessment methods as well as sources need scrutiny. It is usually possible to assess any one outcome by a variety of methods. Some consume more tutor time than others. Essays, for example, are time-consuming to mark and additional time may be taken with arrangements to improve reliability, such as meetings and moderation exercises. To aid both student and tutor, assignments might be more tightly structured.

Instruments incorporating the assessment criteria can save time, whether the source is student, peer, or tutor. Pro formas (rating schedules or feedback sheets) can be devised to cover all the assessment methods used within a course – essays, lab reports, posters. They can accompany assignments and can stimulate students to check their own work against the criteria prior to submitting it to someone else for assessment. Students get used to these and they do speed up marking and the interpretation of feedback (examples can be found in Chapters 5 and 9).

Other ways of saving marking time

Where possible, assessment can be undertaken in class. As well as lessening tutor marking time, this has the educational benefit of providing students with speedy feedback. Short, focused assessments can usually easily be handled in class and some assessments have, by their very nature, to be assessed in class, such as tasks requiring group work and individual or team performances in sport, drama or dance.

Double marking can consume time. Sometimes the merits of double marking are, anyway, doubtful. It can contribute little to reliability unless the second marker is truly independent, with no knowledge of the first marker's responses. It may be best, therefore, to limit double marking to problem cases.

Feedback to students

The first point to remember here is that while students do need feedback on their work, this need not always come from the tutor. Other sources – such as themselves and peers – should be used to the full. Senior or postgraduate students, staff in learning resource centres, staff in work placements can also play a part in giving feedback. The tutor's skill lies in orchestrating all the available sources, using each at its point of strength and monitoring the results.

Chapter 12 points out the value of a ladder of assessment, with students first assessing their own work, then getting a peer to give comment, then redrafting before submitting the assignment to the tutor. This gets students to internalize assessment criteria and develop as assessors of their own work, and improves the assignment before it reaches the tutor, thereby making the tutor's job easier and more worth while. Proper support is important. The tutor cannot just leave everyone to it, but should maintain a managing role. This might include ensuring that self-assessment questions and questions for peer groups have accompanying feedback, and leading class feedback sessions, both on the work that has been assessed and the processes of assessment.

You should use automated feedback whenever possible – whether this is fully automated (as, for example, in response to multiple-choice questions) or partially (as, for example, where the tutor draws on a bank of pre-prepared comments covering common eventualities; see Chapter 13). In terms of reducing workload, automation pays off only when student numbers are large, though it may have other educational benefits, such as fuller and faster feedback to students.

When you are the source of feedback, you should consider carefully the basis on which you operate. Overcommenting is as unhelpful as undercommenting – students can handle only so much feedback. Time can be saved and feedback made more helpful by:

- briefing students in advance about which aspects you will concentrate on when giving feedback on a particular assignment
- asking students in advance which aspects they would like feedback about – for example, by asking them to tick items on a checklist
- focusing only on the major areas for improvement in students' work
- if a task has several stages, commenting only on work at the final stage
- using codes to indicate different kinds of feedback, with the codes amplified on a handout – for example, 'A' might mean a referencing error)
- using pro formas as described in the previous section
- giving feedback in class
- using oral instead of written feedback – for example, in class or by audiotape, which the student can keep as a developing record and for revision
- preparing written summary feedback on an assignment for use by the whole group, including, for example, characteristics of the best assignments, areas for improvement, hints for future assignments.

Feedback on an individual's assignment need only be brief if it is enhanced by feedback to the cohort, for example in class or via a handout.

Administration

Assessment needs to be efficiently organized. Defining procedures, publishing these and then keeping to them saves time. Observing assessment deadlines helps both tutor and students manage their time – students in completing assignments and the tutor assessing them. Tutors need to reserve time for assessment in their diaries.

Other aspects of assessment are word length and standards of presentation. Students can, for example, be required to word process their assignments.

Departmental offices, administrators or secretaries can be used to receive and log assignments, record marks and despatch marked assignments and other correspondence.

You need to review assessment procedures periodically and eliminate unnecessarily time-consuming requirements, such as that all work should be double marked. You might also be able to streamline re-sitting arrangements.

CONCLUSION

The number of students on a course will determine where time might best be invested to reduce the workload. For large courses, planning time might subsequently save much time actually undertaking assessment. Thus, activities such as constructing pro formas, setting up peer assessment arrangements and automating assessment – all of which need planning – are particularly worth undertaking if student numbers are large.

Giving students choices of assignments increases time spent on setting tasks, preparing marking schemes and actual assessment. Thus, reducing (or removing) choice might be worth looking at as a way of saving time (although sometimes it will be important to maintain choice; see Chapter 7). Choice in examinations can also lessen validity as students choose their best question and questions can vary in level of difficulty. In addition, marking fewer questions is likely to enhance reliability. Where possible, assignments can also be reused or slightly adapted.

In reducing tutor workload, you should, of course, always consider the learning experience of the student. In this chapter, we have tried to suggest steps that may improve both these aspects of assessment.

KEY ACTION POINTS

- Audit your current assessment activity and the assessment activity of your students.

- In drawing up an action plan based on the audit, consider how you could make the workload manageable by:
  - careful design
  - giving guidance to students
  - modifying your marking arrangements
  - changing the ways in which you give feedback to students
  - changing the ways in which assessment is administered.

Chapter 28

Cheating, fairness and bias

INTRODUCTION

In this chapter, we deal with two ethical aspects of assessment – cheating and fairness. The former relates to student behaviour and the latter to the behaviour of tutors. For both areas, we define the issues and suggest how you might respond. Most of our examples are drawn from higher education, but the general points made also apply to other areas of education and training.

CHEATING

The challenge of cheating

Cheating is a topic that occasionally surfaces in the press, but is rarely discussed in any serious, sustained way within educational institutions. It is of great importance in assessment for obvious reasons. The validity and reliability of results are called into question, and cheating is a classic case of unfairness as the cheating student takes unfair advantage of other students. Cheats do not play the assessment game fairly – they defraud the system, deceive the assessor and trick their peers.

The problem may be greater than we generally suppose or admit. Professor Newstead surveyed 2000 British undergraduates and more than half of the sample admitted to having cheated (reported in *The Sunday Times*, 30 April, 1995):

- 48 per cent falsified data in theses and projects
- 44 per cent made up bogus academic references
- 42 per cent copied verbatim out of books
- 32 per cent hid books in libraries to deny other students access to them

- 16 per cent did other students' work for love or money
- 13 per cent copied from a neighbouring candidate
- 8 per cent used crib sheets
- 6 per cent stole other students' work
- 2 per cent seduced or bribed their tutor
- 1 per cent impersonated another candidate.

A survey of 337 social science students at the University of Wales (reported in *The Times Higher Education Supplement*, 19 December, 1997) revealed that:

- 49.4 per cent admitted plagiarism
- 43.7 per cent said that they had not contributed their fair share to a group project
- 13.8 per cent had obtained answers from a colleague during an exam.

Another report suggested that cheating is on the rise in Australian universities and that fewer than 2 in 100 cheats are ever caught. The following were described:

- a worryingly frequent incidence of medical certificates (students claiming they were unwell during the exam in case they failed so they could, if necessary, sit another exam)
- students going to the lavatory and obviously using that opportunity to consult notes
- a student with a cassette recorder hidden in his jacket pocket, and head-phones under his baseball cap.

The source quoted in the article suggests that cheating ranges from 33 to 75 per cent of all students (*The Times Higher Education Supplement*, 27 September, 1996).

If cheating is increasing, we can speculate on the reasons for it. In higher education, these probably include the greater financial pressure students are under, tougher competition for opportunities after leaving education (students need better grades), reduction in contact time between tutors and students, worsening tutor–student ratios, and a decline in social cohesion. Students were quoted as blaming the setting of too much coursework assessment and the use of 'flawed forms of assessment' in an article entitled 'Prospering cheats on the up' in *The Times Higher Education Supplement* (19 December, 1997).

We have to be careful not to exaggerate the importance of one or two studies, and little research appears to have been carried out on this important topic. However, there certainly seems enough evidence to merit an analysis of how cheating can be minimized, if not eliminated.

Tackling the challenge of cheating

You can reduce cheating in three ways:

- by changing student attitudes
- by detecting cheating
- by preventing cheating.

Changing student attitudes

Some students caught cheating claim they did not think that this was what they were doing. Interpretations of such statements vary according to the context and the assessor's attitude, but, in some cases, it could be that students are genuinely unware of what is and is not acceptable behaviour. There is a difference, for example, between a group discussing an assignment in advance (usually encouraged as a valid form of collaboration) and students copying each other's assignments and passing them off as their own. However, there are many grey areas in between.

In the light of this, tutors might encourage group discussion, both to clarify what might be indeterminate and openly explore attitudes to typical cheating situations and how students think these should be dealt with. The institution's own policies also need to be made clear on, for example, plagiarism.

As well as clarifying the position, group discussion might also create an awareness of the impact of cheating on other students and promote a social obligation not to cheat.

Role-playing is another way of bringing attitudes to the surface and helping students see how their behaviour may affect others. Roles might include the cheating student, a fellow student, tutor, parent, an employer.

You could make the topic vivid to students in a number of ways, including the use of:

- handouts and leaflets
- posters in lecture rooms, workshops and libraries
- slogans on computer screens
- anti-plagiarism leaflets in books borrowed from the library
- reminders when an assessment is set.

Detecting cheating

Identifying some forms of cheating can be difficult and time-consuming, but students expect measures to be in place and operating. They also expect offenders to be punished when cheating is uncovered.

You can prove plagiarism and false referencing only by detective work. Selective checking – especially of suspect students – can be undertaken.

Arrangements to detect cheating in traditional examinations seem to need to be increasingly sophisticated. Papers may, for example, need to be divided into separate sections, with students being allowed to go to the lavatory only after each section. Invigilators need to be aware of the latest electronic devices, such as radio transmitters concealed in pens with cordless earpieces for receiving answers, pagers that allow contact from outside examination rooms, and mobile phones used in lavatories (all methods quoted in the article in *The Times Higher Education Supplement* mentioned above).

Preventing cheating

Given the difficulties of detection, preventing cheating from occurring in the first place is a good investment of time. Three basic principles apply:

- minimize questions where the answers can be memorized or copied from a book
- maximize tests taken in front of a member of staff and check the identity of each student
- where work cannot be carried out in the presence of a member of staff, then build an additional check to catch out the student who has cheated – for example, a viva.

Setting creative assignments that cannot easily be copied and the active provision of guidance, together with the rationale for not cheating, are also important.

Cheating and instrumentalism

We should keep cheating in proportion. It has always gone on and probably still affects only a tiny proportion of assessment results. Generally, good assessment – assessment that is challenging and imaginative – discourages cheating. If students are working on their own projects, for example, they may be less likely to cheat and, if they do, it may be easier to identify. If students are required to memorize vast quantities of data and regurgitate it in an examination, this is both poor assessment practice and more open to deceit.

Kneale (1997) calls attention to a more common phenomenon than cheating, and one that should perhaps concern us more. It is instrumentalism, which is when students do the barest minimum to survive the course. Minimalist behaviour of this kind includes:

- refusal to contribute to classes where no mark is given for it
- selection of 'easy' modules or those without examinations
- lack of attendance
- attendance at only those sessions that are essential to gain the knowledge necessary for assignments.

'Playing the system' in these ways has been lamented by tutors for decades, but it is widely believed to be on the increase. Kneale's book is worth reading for the analysis of responses to a questionnaire sent to staff in a range of universities. As with cheating, some of the problems at least can be overcome by careful and imaginative assessment design.

Finally, 'cheating' should be kept separate from 'valid collaboration'. Teachers will want assessment arrangements to reward those positive aspects of cooperation that are considered so important in situations beyond those of the classroom, such as teamworking, discussion and the sharing of ideas.

FAIRNESS AND BIAS

In Chapter 3, we introduced a number of principles underlying assessment – notably, reliability, validity and practicality. Fairness and lack of bias is another underlying principle.

Fairness in assessment

Your assessment arrangements should not advantage any one student over another. As far as possible, you should try to meet the needs of different students, creating equal assessment opportunities. In setting assignments, for example, you need to consider the needs and interests of older as well as younger students, women as well as men.

Individual needs might arise from factors such as:

* age
* gender
* mode of study – for example, full- or part-time course, distance
* ethnicity
* disability
* sexuality.

Unfairness operates when individual differences – other than those you are properly trying to measure – are ignored. It can also stem from other sources. We have mentioned the 'halo effect' in this book. You will recall that this term is used to descibe instances when a teacher (or group of teachers) forms an overall impression of a student or their work – whether positive or negative – and then makes assessment decisions that are influenced by this view of them. This leads to an assumption that everything that particular student does will be good or bad. In such circumstances, the assessment criteria are not given full weight. Assessors might also assume, for example, that because an assignment is presented well, its content is sound or that good visuals mean that the accompanying text is accurate.

Other forms of unfairness include:

- tutors who are, perhaps unconsciously, influenced in favour of students whose views agree with their own
- tutors who are infuenced by a previous student's work when assessing the next assignment
- tutors wishing, understandably, to encourage a student who is improving, but inflating the mark in the process
- tutors who positively discriminate in favour of a minority student group instead of assessing all students against the same criteria.

Ensuring fairness

Fairness can be made more likely by:

- setting tasks all students can complete, whatever their background
- setting alternative assessments (of the same outcomes) for students who are disadvantaged
- ensuring facilities are available to help students with particular handicaps
- maintaining a variety of assessment methods to give all students an opportunity to excel
- keeping to the assessment criteria and justifying decisions by referring all students to these
- using procedures such as double marking or an appeals process where appropriate.

KEY ACTION POINTS

- Be alert for evidence of cheating in assessment.
- Distinguish cheating from valid collaboration.
- If students are cheating, decide on a strategy to overcome this – for example, aim to:
  - change student attitudes
  - detect and prove cheating
  - prevent cheating.
- Design imaginative assessment to minimize cheating and instrumentalism.
- Review your assessment arrangements for fairness.
- Take action as necessary to promote fair assessment practice.

Chapter 29

Making changes

INTRODUCTION

We begin by summarizing some ways in which assessment seems to be changing, pulling together key themes from earlier chapters in this book. We invite you to consider which of these changes affect you. In a rapidly changing world, it is likely that you will need to modify your existing practice, so we conclude the chapter (and the book) by considering how to develop new assessment methods.

TRENDS IN ASSESSMENT

Table 29.1 is a checklist of ways in which assessment is changing. We show only general tendencies as these will not all be occurring in every part of the curriculum at every stage of education – there will be exceptions to every point. You will need to interpret the list according to your own experience, allowing, for example, for the age of your students and the nature of the curriculum you are responsible for.

Mitchell and Sturton (1993) describe the shift from the 'measurement approach' to an approach based on what one can reasonably infer from evidence (the evidential approach). While the measurement approach stems from psychology and science, the evidential approach is rooted in sociological and legal models. The evidential approach does not claim absolute objectivity, but seeks to draw justifiable conclusions from evidence drawn from a range of different sources. The student often plays a key role in deciding what should be offered as evidence. Portfolios are usually the means for presenting the evidence, and profiles can be used as a reporting device.

Simosko and Cook (1996) suggest that changes such as the above, taken together, make assessment – rather than teaching or even learning – the major purpose of an educational institution. The focus, they argue, has switched from syllabuses, courses and programmes to assessment. Hence, the main role of the professional is no longer that of teacher, but assessor (see their Table 6.1, p126).

Table 29.1 *Shifts in assessment practice*

From	To
Implicit assessment	Explicit assessment
Few stakeholders in assessment	Many stakeholders in assessment
Student as passive/reactive	Student as proactive
Teacher as marker/assessor	Teacher in multifaceted role
Teacher as sole authority	Teacher in negotiation with others
Summative assessment	Coursework
Norm-referenced assessment	Criterion-referenced assessment
Fixed assessment arrangements	Flexible assessment arrangements (eg, flexibility over route, place, time, method)
Limited range of assessment methods	Variety in assessment method
Assessment only in the educational institution	Assessment in multiple locations
Assessment of content knowledge	Assessment of skills/capabilities as well as content
Tutor as audience for students' work	Multiple audiences for students' work (including 'real' audiences)
Assessment of the individual student's performance	Assessment of individual and group performance (eg, via project)
Simple report of assessment results	Complex report of assessment results (eg, profile, portfolio)
Course assessment	Module/unit assessment
Assessment limited to one educational stage	Assessment within the perspective of life-long learning

CHANGING ASSESSMENT PRACTICES

The previous section will, we hope, have stimulated you to consider whether or not your current assessment practice is well adapted to present and likely future requirements. You will probably find you need to make changes.

Changes to assessment can take place at different levels – the individual teacher, course team, department and institution. At any of these, it is possible to make a change. For example, an individual teacher may wish to introduce a new assessment method and may be able to do this without affecting other people. At the other end of the scale, the institution may formulate a mission that requires for its achievement changes in the design and implementation of assessment – for example, to produce more independent learners or achieve better results. Some changes require a concerted effort at more than one level. For example, to achieve a consistent approach to assessment in mathematics would require agreement by individual teachers, course teams and the department.

In the next two sections of this chapter, we look first at deciding what changes are needed, then at how change might be accomplished.

DECIDING ON CHANGES

Whatever the level, it is a good idea to start with an audit of existing practice. Ask the following questions.

- What do we want our students to learn?
- Do we express this adequately in our outcomes?
- Do we assess these outcomes?
- Are we using appropriate criteria?
- Are our methods, instruments and sources appropriate?
- How much time do students and staff spend on assessment?

These and other related matters are covered in the other chapters of this book.

Students should also be involved in the audit. They could be asked to decide which areas to collect data on, select appropriate data collection methods (such as questionnaires and focus groups), collect data and interpret it. Students at one university, for example, were asked:

- to tick from a list of assessment methods the ones they had experienced
- for each method, to rate how valuable they had found it as a learning experience.

They were then asked another 21 questions, covering issues such as:

- information they received on assessment and the timing of this information
- choices about assessment
- self- and peer-assessment
- the amount of effort they put into assessment tasks
- the feedback they received and opportunities to discuss this with their tutors
- the speed with which coursework was returned.

Students' views on such matters are rarely sought. However, they enjoy such participation and their suggestions can be very useful – and not always difficult to accommodate.

You might also consider involving other stakeholders in your audit, such as parents and employers.

IMPLEMENTING CHANGES

Managing change is worth a book in itself and, as this is beyond our remit, here we can offer only one or two practical ideas.

You need first of all to bear in mind that people are likely instinctively to resist any change unless they have themselves been involved in identifying the need for it. Students can be as conservative as teaching staff, hence the need for involvement right from the start. There are various starting points, including the audit suggested above. Others are an analysis of current difficulties or the construction of a vision to achieve. While the choice of starting point is flexible, the end result should always be energy and commitment to change.

You then need to draw up a strategy for change, together with the tactics you are going to use to achieve this. The leader needs to secure the necessary resources – notably time, which is likely to be in short supply. However, much can be achieved in terms of teambuilding and creative output by awaydays with good lunches!

The purposes of the change need to be kept in mind throughout. These may include enhanced student learning, the removal of burdens on staff and the promotion of professionalism. The objectives should not be too complicated or they then run the risk of competing with each other and dissipating effort. The focus should be simple and clear. The benefits should be motivating enough to continue to release energy over what may be a protracted or difficult period of change. It may be a good idea to begin some experimentation early, to show progress and collect data. Change needs to be monitored constantly. Research evidence or contacts from other institutions can also be helpful (and allay fears).

Change is usually best planned and accomplished by teams. The members (and especially the leader) will need high-level interpersonal skills, including being able to listen, question effectively and explain things clearly. Other stakeholders, such as parents and external examiners, should not be forgotten as they often have many good ideas to offer, and their opposition could make things difficult later.

You should give sufficient time for people to become familiar with the change, and you will need to prepare both tutors and students. Support is particularly important during the early days of implementation. The new situation should be evaluated, but should not normally be changed significantly after only one cycle. Usually, though, you will wish to fine-tune arrangements along the lines suggested by the evaluation data.

KEY ACTION POINTS

- Audit your assessment strategy and its implementation.
- Involve your students (and other stakeholders, as appropriate) in the audit.
- Identify changes you need to make and at what level within the organization.
- Gain agreement to the changes and secure the necessary resources.
- Monitor your progress.

Glossary

The number(s) in brackets after a term are the chapter(s) in which it is chiefly discussed. A few items that occur in many places have no particular chapter number assigned to them.

Words in italics are those for which there are entries elsewhere in the Glossary.

Analysis See *Bloom's taxonomy*.

Application See *Bloom's taxonomy*.

Artefact (9) A product that a learner has created, such as a typed letter, a poem or a sculpture.

Assessment (1) Any process that aims to judge the extent of students' learning.

Assignment (4) A complete chunk of *assessment*. An assignment may consist of one or more *tasks*.

Authenticity (3) Refers to evidence that something has been produced by or applies to the candidate.

Behaviour (1) The evidence on which an assessment judgement is based. The outcome of a student's behaviour may be written, oral or practical or in some other form or product; or their behaviour may be directly observed (for example, when giving a presentation of working in a group).

Bloom's taxonomy (8) A method of classifying learning outcomes into six levels of increasing intellectual complexity. The levels are: 1 knowledge (= rote learning); 2 comprehension (= understanding); 3 application; 4 analysis; 5 synthesis; and 6 evaluation.

Competence level (24) A defined standard of performance.

Competent (24) A competent learner is one who has reached a defined standard of performance (*competence level*).

Comprehension See *Bloom's taxonomy*.

Continuous assessment (4) Assessment that takes place at more than one point in a course. See also *final assessment*.

Core skills Capabilities students develop that are of use beyond the specific subject context in which they are first assessed – sometimes called 'transferable' or 'key' skills.

Course (4) A programme of study that is self-contained in the sense of leading to a *summative* assessment. In this sense, module and course (and sometimes unit) are interchangeable.

Criterion (5) Assessment criteria are the rules and measures that are used in order to assess something. Criteria may be explicit and written down or implicit in the way that a tutor marks.

Criterion-referenced assessment (2) Criterion-referenced assessment measures a student's performance against an explicit, previously determined standard (see also *norm-referenced assessment*).

Currency (3) Refers to the need for evidence of performance to be sufficiently recent.

Distractor See *multiple-choice questions*.

Double marking (3) When the same piece of work is marked independently by two people.

Element (24) A subdivision of the behaviour that defines a given *competence level*.

Evaluation (1) The measurement of how the various components of a *course* perform, such as the syllabus, resources and teacher.

Evaluation See *Bloom's taxonomy*.

Evidence (direct/indirect) (1 and 8) Anything that is cited to justify the *assessment* that has been made of a piece of work; what students offer to demonstrate achievement of learning outcomes. Evidence can be 'direct' (such as observation of a student's performance) or 'indirect' (say, a statement from a third party that a student is competent).

Feedback (6) Feedback is any information that a learner receives as a result of an assessment. Feedback may be written or oral, stated or implied. It may be summarized on a feedback sheet or form.

Fill-in-the-blank question (9) A question that presents one or more sentences with a number of missing words that learners have either to supply or select from a jumbled list. The question could also be in the form of a diagram to be labelled.

Final assessment (4) Assessment that takes place only at the end of a course. See also *continuous assessment*.

Formative assessment (4) *Assessment* designed to provide information (*feedback*) to students so they can improve their work.

Halo effect (18) When an assessor's judgement of one criterion is affected by the learner's behaviour on another, such as allowing the neatness of presentation to affect one's assessment of content.

Key See *multiple-choice question*.

Key skills See *core skills*.

Knowledge See *Bloom's taxonomy*.

Learning outcome (3 and 8) A description of the learning that is to be achieved.

Matching question (9) Matching questions present two lists to the learner. Items in one list have to be matched to items in the other list.

Module (4) See *course*.

Multiple-choice question (9) Multiple-choice questions consist of a stem (the initial statement or question), followed by a number of options (various ways in which the stem can be completed or the question answered). One of the options is the correct answer (called the key). The other options, which are incorrect, are called distractors. Sometimes multiple-choice questions have more than one key.

Norm-referenced assessment (2) Norm-referenced assessment measures learner performance against the standard of the group rather than against a pre-determined standard (see also *criterion-referenced assessment*).

Objective question (9) An objective question is one that can be marked without any judgement on the part of the marker.

Option See *multiple-choice question*.

Peer assessment (12) In peer assessment, learners make judgements about one another's work. This requires them to give and/or receive *feedback*.

Peer marking (12) In peer marking, learners allocate marks or grades to the work of their fellow students.

Performance (7) Performance is anything a learner does that can be observed and is regarded as relevant to the assessment criteria. Performance may be oral, written, physical behaviour or the act of creating something.

Performance criteria See *criterion*.

Portfolio (9, 23 and 24) A portfolio is a collection of materials, assembled by a learner to demonstrate achievement.

Poster session (19) An event at which the outcome of students' work is displayed visually, for an audience to comment on and perhaps assess.

Profile (23) A profile (also called a record of achievement) is a record of a learner's achievements either against a prescribed list of items or in a more open format.

Programme (4) A collection of *courses, modules or units*.

Project (9 and 20) A general term, but projects usually have three indicators: a move beyond the immediate educational context from 'the classroom' into 'real life' – projects seek to develop applied learning; student proactivity, for example in choice of topic; an extended time period for setting-up and completion.

Quasi assessment method (9) Methods that are sometimes referred to as assessment methods but are better described as methods of teaching and learning, such as projects and case studies.

Range See *range statement*.

Range statement (8) An indication of the number and variety of situations in which the learner has demonstrated (or should demonstrate) performance.

Record of achievement (11) A folder (usually) containing a record of the learning a student has engaged in and with what outcome. Records of achievement often use forms, with sections for both teachers and learners to complete.

Reliability (3) Reliable assessments are ones where the same marker reaches the same conclusion on different occasions and different markers reach the same conclusion when presented with similar evidence.

Sample (1) A selection from all the possible tasks that a learner could perform. The sample needs to be representative of the learner's achievements and of the learning outcomes.

Self-assessment (11) Assessment where the student is the source – that is, the person who makes judgements on their own learning.

Self-marking (11) Self-marking involves the student awarding themselves a mark, score or grade, usually using a marking scheme provided by the tutor.

Short-answer question (9 and 15) Questions that require the learner to produce answers of, generally, fewer than 50 words and do not require the construction of paragraphs.

Stakeholder (1) Any person or institution having an interest in the outcome of an *assessment*, such as the student, teacher, educational institution, society.

Standards (24) Performance criteria, such as those published by the industry-led bodies in the UK and assessed as National Vocational Qualifications (NVQs) and Scottish National Vocational Qualifications (SNVQs).

Stem See *multiple-choice question*.

Sufficient (1 and 24) Refers to the size of the sample of learning. A sufficient sample covers enough of the syllabus to ensure that the *assessment* is *valid*.

Summative assessment (4) Assessment that counts towards or constitutes a final grade or qualification.

Synthesis See *Bloom's taxonomy*.

Task The smallest component in any given *assignment*, such as one *multiple-choice question* or *short-answer question*.

Test (4 and 16) Tests are assessments that are largely *formative*. They may appear at any point in a course. Feedback from tests is usually designed to help learners identify, and put right, their weaknesses.

Transferable skills (18) See *core skills*.

True/false question (9) A truncated multiple-choice question offering just two options – a statement and its opposite.

Unit (4) A loose term. It is sometimes a subdivision of a *module*; sometimes a collection of modules; sometimes synonymous with module.

Validity (3) A valid *assessment* is one that measures what it claims to measure, and what is important to measure.

References and further reading

The following list may look a little daunting, but please do look up those books that are referred to often during the course of the book as you will find these very informative.

Examples of sources you might find particularly helpful and consider buying or borrowing are the titles by Graham Gibbs and the book for those of you in higher education by Brown, *et al.* (1997). Derek Rowntree (1987) is another thought-provoking treatment of perennial assessment issues and dilemmas. Lloyd-Jones, *et al.* (1992) is one of the few good treatments of assessments in schools (unfortunately it seems to be out of print currently). We have drawn particularly on these books and we acknowledge their contribution to our discussion.

Andresen, L, Nightingale, P, Boud, D, and Magin, D (eds) (1993) *Strategies for Assessing Students*. Birmingham: SEDA Paper 78.

Angelo, T A, and Cross, K P (1993, 2nd edn) *Classroom Assessment Techniques: A handbook for college teachers*. San Francisco: Jossey-Bass.

Armstrong, S, Thompson, G, and Brown, S (1997) *Facing up to Radical Change*. London: Kogan Page.

Ausubel, D P, and Robinson, F G (1971) *School Learning: An introduction to educational psychology*. London: Holt, Rinehart and Winston.

Baker, M (1983) 'The fast feedback system', in *Teaching at a Distance*, 24.

Bell, J (1993, 2nd edn) *Doing your Research Project*. Buckingham: Open University Press.

Bloom, B S (ed.) (1956). *Taxonomy of Educational Objectives: Handbook 1 Cognitive Domain*. London: Longman.

Boud, D (1985) *Studies in Self-assessment: Implications for teachers in higher education*, Occasional Publication No. 26. Kensington, Australia: Tertiary Education Research Centre, University of New South Wales.

Boud, D (1989) 'The role of self-assessment in student grading', *Assessment and Evaluation in Higher Education*, 14 (1) pp20–30.

Boud, D (1995a) *Enhancing Learning Through Self-assessment*. London: Kogan Page.

Boud, D (1995b) 'Assessment and learning: contradictory or complementary?', in Knight, P (ed) *Assessment for Learning in Higher Education*. London: Kogan Page.

Bowling, A (1997) *Research Methods in Health: Investing in health and health services*. Buckingham: Open University Press.

Brailsford, T (1994) 'Examine: a self-assessment system for Windows and Macintosh', *Active Learning*, 1 December.

British Educational Communications and Technology Agency – see under old name of National Council for Educational Technology.

Brown, G, Bull, J, and Pendlebury, M (1997) *Assessing Student Learning in Higher Education*. London: Routledge.

Brown, G, Bull, J and Pendlebury, M (1997). Assessing Student Learning in Higher Education. London: Routledge.

Brown, S, and Knight, P (1994) *Assessing Learners in Higher Education*. London: Kogan Page.

Brown, S, Race, P, and Smith, B (1996) *500 Tips on Assessment*. London: Kogan Page.

Brown, S, Rust, C, and Gibbs, G (1994) *Strategies for Diversifying Assessment in Higher Education*. Oxford: Oxford Centre for Staff Development.

Bull, J (1994) 'Computer-based assessment: some issues for consideration', *Active Learning*, 1 December.

Church, C (1993) 'Quandaries on the quality quest', *The Times Higher Education Supplement*, 16 July, Synthesis Trends Supplement, pvii.

Clarkson, P, and Danner, F (1994) 'Better Testing: A computerized guide to writing objective tests', *Active Learning*, 1 December.

Entwistle, N J (1987, 2nd edn) *Styles of Learning and Teaching*. Chichester: Wiley.

Entwistle, N J (1992, rev. edn) *The Impact of Teaching on Learning Outcomes*. Sheffield CVCP UCoSDA.

Entwistle, N J (1996) 'Motivational factors in students' approach to learning', in Schmeck, R (ed.), *Learning Strategies and Learning Styles*, New York: Plenum Press.

Entwistle, N J, and Percy, K A (1973) 'Critical thinking or conformity: an investigation of the aims and outcomes of higher education', in *Research into Higher Education*, London: SRHE, pp1–37.

Erwin, T D (1997) 'Developing strategies and policies for changing universities', in Armstrong, S, Thompson, G, and Brown, S, *Facing up to Radical Change*, London: Kogan Page, pp64–74.

Erwin, T D, and Knight, P (1995) 'A transatlantic view of assessment and quality in higher education', *Quality in Higher Education*, 1 (2) pp179–88.

Falchikov, N (1995) 'Improving feedback to and from students', in Knight, P, *Assessment For Learning in Higher Education*, London: Kogan Page, pp157–66.

Ford, P, *et al.* (1996) *Managing Change in Higher Education: A learning environment architecture*, Buckingham: Society for Research into Higher Education and Open University Press.

Freeman, R (1983) 'MAIL: from the NEC', *Teaching at a Distance*, 24.

Gagné, R M (1970) *The Conditions of Learning*. London: Holt, Reinhart and Winston.

Gibbs, G (1992) *Developing Teaching: Teaching More Students: 4 Assessing More Students*. London: Polytechnics and Colleges Funding Council.

Gibbs, G (1995) *Assessing Student-centred Courses*. Oxford: Oxford Centre for Staff Development.

Gibbs, G, Habeshaw, S, and Habeshaw, T (1986) *53 Interesting Ways to Assess Your Students*. Bristol: Technical and Educational Services.

Glass, A L, and Holyoak, K J (1986, 2nd ed.) *Cognition*. Maidenhead: McGraw-Hill.

Gronlund, N E (1968) *Constructing Achievement Tests*. Englewood Cliffs, New Jersey: Prentice Hall.

Gronland, N E (1971) Measurement and Evaluation in Teachings. London: Macmillan.

Guildford Educational Services Ltd and Question Mark Computing Ltd. *Better Testing: A computerized guide to writing objective tests*

Habeshaw S, Gibbs G and Habeshaw T (1993) *53 Interesting Ways to Assess Your Students*. Bristol: Technical and Educational Services, Ltd.

Harrow, A (1972) *A Taxonomy for the Psychomotor Domain*. New York: McKay.

Harvey, L, Moon, S, and Geall, V, with Bower, R (1997) *Graduates' Work: Organizational change and students' attributes*. Birmingham: Centre for Research into Quality.

Henderson, P (1993) *How to Succeed in Exams and Assessments*, London: Collins Educational and National Extension College.

HEQC (1994) *Learning From Audit*. London: Higher Education Quality Council.

Hitchcock, B (1990) *Profiles and Profiling: A practical introduction*. London: Longman.

Innis, K, and Shaw, M (1997) 'How do students spend their time?', *Quality Assurance in Education*, 5 (2) pp85–9.

Jeffrey, C (1968) *An Introduction to Plant Taxonomy*. London: J & A Churchill.

Johnston, S (1997) 'Examining the examiners: an analysis of examiners' reports on doctoral theses', *Studies in Higher Education*, 22 (3) pp333–47.

Kahney, H (1986) *Problem Solving: A cognitive approach*. Milton Keynes: Open University Press.

Kneale, P E (1997) 'The rise of the "strategic student": how can we adapt to cope?', in Armstrong, S, Thompson, G, and Brown, S, *Facing up to Radical Change*. London: Kogan Page, pp119–30.

Knight, P (ed.) (1995) *Assessment For Learning in Higher Education*. London: Kogan Page.

Kohn, A (1993) *Punished by Rewards*. Boston, Massachusetts: Houghton Mifflin.

Krathwohl, D R, Bloom, B S, and Masia, B B (1964) *Taxonomy of Educational Objectives*, Handbook II: Affective Domain. New York: David McKay.

Lewis, R (1981) *How to Tutor in an Open Learning Scheme* (self-study version). London: Council for Educational Technology.

Lewis, R (1993) *How to Write Essays*. London: Collins Educational and National Extension College.

Lewis, R (1994) *How to Manage Your Study Time*. London: Collins Educational and National Extension College.

Lloyd-Jones, R, Bray, E, Johnson, G, and Curry, R (1992) *Assessment: From principles to action*. London: Routledge.

Mager, R F (1962) *Preparing Instructional Objectives*. Palo Alto: Fearon Publishers.

Marton, F, and Ramsden, P (1988) 'What does it take to improve learning?', in Ramsden, P (ed.), *Improving Learning: New perspectives*, London: Kogan Page.

Mezirow, J, et al. (1990) *Fostering Critical Reflection in Adulthood: A guide to transformative and emancipatory learning*. San Francisco: Jossey-Bass.

Miles, M B, and Huberman, A M (1994, 2nd ed.) *Qualitative Data Analysis: An expanded sourcebook*. Newbury Park, California: Sage Publications.

Mitchell, L, and Sturton, J (1993) *The Candidate's Role Project*. Research and Development Series, Report No. 12. Sheffield: Employment Department's Methods Strategy Unit.

National Council for Educational Technology (now British Educational Communications and Technology Agency) (1994) *Using IT for Assessment: Directory of software*. Cambridge: National Council for Educational Technology.

National Council for Educational Technology (1996). See http://www.ncet.org.uk/projects/fe/arrfold/keyiss.html

National Extension College (various dates) *NVQ Organizers* (range of titles for various S/NCVQ standards). Cambridge: National Extension College.

Nicol, J (no date) 'Review: Question Mark Designer for Windows, Version 2', *Newsletter 13: Using Computers for Student Assessment.* Centre for Land Use and Environmental Sciences: http://www.clues.abdn.ac.uk:8080/newslets/news13/news13.html

Nuttall, D L (no date) *The Validity of Assessments.* Milton Keynes: Open University Press.

Orsmond, P (1997) 'When teaching interrupts the real work', *The Times Higher Education Supplement*, 3 October, THES Insert, piv.

Peel, A (1994) 'Computer-aided assessment through hypermedia', *Active Learning*, 1 December.

Perraton, H (1995) 'A practical agenda for theorists of distance education', in Lockwood, F (ed.) *Open and Distance Learning Today*, London: Routledge.

Plants, H L, *et al.* (1980) 'A taxonomy of problem-solving activities and its implications for teaching' in Lubkin (ed.) *The Teaching of Elementary Problem-solving in Engineering and Related Fields*, Washington DC: American Society for Engineering Education.

Polya, G (1957) *How to Solve It.* New York: Doubleday Anchor Books.

Race, P (1995) 'The Art of Assessing: 1', *The New Academic* 4 (3) pp3–6.

Rackham, M, and Morgan, T (1977) *Behavioural Analysis in Training.* London: McGraw Hill.

Ramsden, P (1992) *Learning to Teach in Higher Education.* London: Routledge.

Rowntree, D (1987) *Assessing Students: How shall we know them?* London: Kogan Page.

Satterly, D (1981) *Assessment in Schools.* Oxford: Basil Blackwell.

Schön, D A (1991) *The Reflective Practitioner.* Aldershot: Arena.

Simosko, S, and Cook, C (1996, 2nd edn) *Applying APL Principles in Flexible Assessment: A practical guide.* London: Kogan Page.

Stefani, L, and Nicol, D (1997) 'From teacher to facilitator of collaborative enquiry' in Armstrong, S, Thompson, G, and Brown, S, *Facing up to Radical Change*, London: Kogan Page, pp131–140.

Stefani, L A J (1997) 'Reflective learning in higher education: issues and approaches', UCoSDA Briefing Paper 42.

Steinaker, N, and Bell, M (1979) *The Experiential Taxonomy: A new approach to teaching and learning.* New York: Academic Press.

Stephens, D (1994) 'Using computer-assisted assessment: time-saver or sophisticated distraction?', *Active Learning*, 1 December.

The Chambers Dictionary (1993 edition). Edinburgh: Chambers.

The New Shorter Oxford English Dictionary (1993) Oxford: Clarendon Press.

University of Aberdeen. *Efficient and Effective Examination Using Computer-assisted Assessment.* University of Aberdeen. (See http://www.clues.abdn.ac.uk:8080/caa/caaut.html)

University of Aberdeen. *Setting Effective Objective Tests.* University of Aberdeen. (See http://www.clues.abdn.ac.uk:8080/caa/caa.html)

Ward, C (1981) *Preparing and Using Objective Questions.* Cheltenham: Stanley Thornes.

Index

Page numbers in bold refer to glossary entries.